The Second Conference

on

THE CLINICAL DELINEATION OF BIRTH DEFECTS

Part VII
MUSCLE

Held at The Johns Hopkins Hospital,
Baltimore, Md., May 26–31, 1969.
Sponsored by The Johns Hopkins Medical Institutions
and The National Foundation—March of Dimes

Editor

DANIEL BERGSMA, M.D.

Associate Editors

VICTOR A. McKUSICK, M.D.
CHARLES I. SCOTT, JR., M.D.

Assistant Editors

CAMILLE JACKSON
MARJORIE W. LORBER

*Published for The National Foundation—March of Dimes
by The Williams and Wilkins Company, Baltimore*

BIRTH DEFECTS: ORIGINAL ARTICLE SERIES VOL. VII, NO. 2; FEBRUARY 1971

To enhance medical communication in the birth defects field, The National Foundation publishes an *Original Article Series*, a *Reprint Series*, and provides a series of films and related brochures.

Further information can be obtained from:
Daniel Bergsma, M.D.
Vice President for Professional Education and
Director, Professional Education Department
The National Foundation-March of Dimes
1275 Mamaroneck Avenue
White Plains, New York 10605

CONTENTS

G. Milton Shy

Dedication
to
G. Milton Shy (1919–1967)

George Milton Shy died at work on September 25, 1967, a few days before his 48th birthday. The blow had uniquely tragic impact, because only 25 days earlier he had assumed a new position as Professor and Chairman of the Department of Neurology at the College of Physicians and Surgeons, Columbia University. At the peak of his prowess, it could have been predicted confidently that he would have gone on to new achievements.

His influence on research in muscle disease was extraordinary and he had an uncommon talent for the novel. Within a few years he delineated five "new" disorders that are still being unraveled: central core disease, megaconial myopathy, pleoconial myopathy, myotubular myopathy, and nemaline myopathy. His earlier monograph on periodic paralysis serves as a model of thorough investigation, and records the first successful attempt to measure intracellular potentials during an attack. He relished opportunities to upset established notions, and sometimes did it to his own work. Initially skeptical, he became one of the few who made muscle biopsy a fine art, utilizing histochemical and ultrastructural methods. He extended electrophysiologic investigations and he always stimulated metabolic or biochemical approaches. His name has been incorporated into one eponym, the Shy-Drager syndrome, manifest by orthostatic hypotension and signs of basal ganglia disease. He was one of the first to recognize the potential of brain scans and wrote an early monograph on that nonmuscular topic. These achievements are the more remarkable because he learned about electrolyte determinations, isotopes, electrophysiology and morphologic technics while burdened with heavy administrative and teaching responsibilities. He worked with an intensity that is reflected by accomplishment.

His true legacy, however, is the great number of his students. A brilliant lecturer and provocative teacher at the bedside, he stimulated students and associates. With a very personal blend of warmth, humor, wager, sarcasm, innuendo, and plain encouragement, he goaded his staff to defense and rebuttal. The path to laboratory and library was well-trod, students returning with facts rather than opinion. He constantly related clinical observation to anatomy and physiology.

With these talents, he established the Division of Neurology at the new medical school of the University of Colorado in 1951. From 1953 to 1962, he established the first clinical service at the National Institute of Neurological Diseases and Blindness, making it a world center for research and training. From 1962 to 1967, he transformed a languishing department at the University of Pennsylvania. There are now 40 academic neurologists who were trained by Milton Shy at one of these institutions, and at least six of the contributors to this program had the privilege of working with him.

This outstanding career grew from a peripatetic background. Milton Shy was born in Colorado, went to college and medical school in Oregon, and interned at the Royal Victoria Hospital in Montreal. During World War II he was wounded seriously while serving as medical officer with the infantry. After leaving the Army in 1947, he began his neurologic training at the National Hospital, Queen Square, finishing at the Montreal Neurological Institute. This international flavor was sustained throughout his life, and he always reserved a place in his department for distinguished visitors who remained long enough to have a genuine influence. Men like E. A. Carmichael, J. C. Greenfield and F. Buchthal participated in these programs. In return, he encouraged his own students to go abroad.

Milton Shy was a revered physician, investigator, teacher and friend. It is a privilege to dedicate these essays to him.

Lewis P. Rowland

Birth Defects: Original Article Series. Vol. VII, No. 2; February 1971

1

Some Rare Congenital and Metabolic Myopathies

JOHN N. WALTON, T.D., M.D., F.R.C.P.

Four rare forms of inherited myopathy are reviewed. Nemaline myopathy shows certain well-defined clinical characteristics and rodlike structures derived from Z-band protein accumulate within the muscle fibers. Myotubular or centronuclear myopathy presents usually with infantile hypotonia and the majority of the muscle fibers demonstrate central nuclei surrounded by perinuclear halos; developmental arrest may well be followed by perinuclear degeneration. Glycogen storage disease due to acid maltase deficiency is now recognized as an occasional cause of late-onset myopathy. An unusual case of myopathy due to lipid storage in Type I muscle fibers is also described.

Introduction

As our knowledge of the neuromuscular diseases has increased within the last 10 to 15 years, largely as a result of the application of new methods of investigation including quantitative electromyography, serum enzyme studies, histochemistry and electron microscopy, large numbers of what appear to be "new" syndromes or disease entities have been described. Indeed it is rare to find that a year passes without some new syndrome being recognized, with the consequence that classifications of the myopathies require continuing revision and amendment. I propose to comment upon four varieties of myopathy, each of which has been recognized comparatively recently; two of these disorders are at present classified in the category of so-called congenital myopathies; two are of presumed metabolic origin and current evidence suggests that all four are genetically determined.

Congenital Myopathies

This difficult and confusing group has recently been reviewed in detail by Engel,[1] by Walton and Gardner-Medwin[2] and by Dubowitz[3] and I do not propose to consider the matter in detail.

One can summarize the present position by saying first, that in an infant presenting with delay in physical development combined with widespread hypo-

Walton—Professor and Chairman, Department of Neurology, University of Newcastle upon Tyne; Consultant Neurologist, Newcastle General Hospital and Royal Victoria Infirmary, Newcastle upon Tyne, England.

tonia of the skeletal musculature, if one is successful in excluding mental backwardness, malnutrition, disorders of the central nervous system, metabolic disorders and the other multitudinous causes of symptomatic hypotonia,[4] and if the Prader-Willi syndrome of hypotonia, mental retardation and obesity can also be excluded, there exists a small group of patients in whom no cause for the hypotonia is ever discovered even with modern technics of full investigation and, although the children may be late in sitting up and in walking, recovery is eventually complete. This syndrome is uncommon and may well be a disorder of multiple etiology, but in the present state of knowledge it can still reasonably be defined as one of benign congenital or infantile hypotonia. Within the group of infants presenting in this way, however, there are some in whom hypotonia persists and, as the child grows and develops, it is seen that the skeletal muscles are generally weak and atrophic. When spinal muscular atrophy of the Werdnig-Hoffmann type (which arrests in infancy more commonly than is generally realized) has been satisfactorily excluded by electromyography and muscle biopsy, and when the possibility of dystrophia myotonica presenting in infancy with diffuse hypotonia is also ruled out (a process which requires first careful examination of the parents and second electromyographic exclusion of myotonia), the remaining patients fall into the category of the so-called congenital myopathies. While some few of these disorders are progressive, others appear to run a benign and relatively nonprogressive course and there is still considerable uncertainty concerning

Birth Defects: Original Article Series. Vol. VII, No. 2; February 1971

2

BIOGRAPHIC DATA

John N. Walton, born in Rowlands Gill, County Durham, England, received his medical training at the Medical School, Newcastle upon Tyne, which was then a part of the University of Durham, graduating with First Class Honors in 1945. He was resident and subsequently became Medical Registrar at the Royal Victoria Infirmary, Newcastle upon Tyne. He became Research Assistant in the Department of Medicine, University of Newcastle upon Tyne under Professor F. J. Nattrass where he initiated his research on subarachnoid hemorrhage and muscular dystrophy. Professor Walton was a Nuffield Traveling Fellow in Neurology at the Massachusetts General Hospital, Boston in 1953–54 and worked in the Neurological Research Unit at the National Hospital, Queen Square, London in 1954–55.

Professor Walton is at present Professor and Chairman of the Department of Neurology at the University of Newcastle upon Tyne and Consultant Neurologist to the Newcastle General Hospital and Royal Victoria Infirmary there. His principal research interest is in the field of neuromuscular disease. He is Chairman and Secretary of the Research Group on Neuromuscular Diseases of the World Federation of Neurology and Editor-in-Chief of the *Journal of Neurological Sciences*.

their appropriate subdivision. Perhaps most difficult of all is the classification of those patients in whom weakness, wasting and hypotonia are so severe that the child is never capable of standing or walking and may even be sufficiently striking to cause widespread contractures at birth (the syndrome of arthrogryposis multiplex congenita). In many such cases the serum creatine kinase is normal, but electromyographically the evidence indicates that the muscular weakness and wasting is myopathic, and histologic examination of muscle biopsy sections reveals changes indistinguishable from those of muscular dystrophy. These cases continue to be identified by the rather unsatisfactory term of congenital muscular dystrophy, but in the present state of knowledge no more satisfactory designation for these patients is available, though the nature of the disease is obscure. Even more uncertain is the question whether patients less severely disabled and yet presenting with hypotonia and developmental delay in infancy, who demonstrate unquestionable evidence of a non-

specific myopathy on full investigation, should be classified as less severe examples of this syndrome, as Zellweger et al[5] would suggest. Dubowitz[3] feels that these cases should at present be classified as miscellaneous congenital myopathies still awaiting classification and there is justice in this comment. Very probably the disorders previously classified as benign congenital myopathy,[6, 7] congenital universal muscular hypoplasia[8] and benign congenital hypotonia with incomplete recovery[9] belong in this as yet obscure category. Another rare disorder which remains obscure etiologically is that called familial myosclerosis, in which there is a progressive overgrowth of intramuscular connective tissue causing widespread contractures and secondarily impairing the efficiency of the muscle fibers.[10]

It is within the large group of relatively nonprogressive and obscure congenital myopathies that four apparently specific morphologic entities have been identified within recent years, largely on the basis of histologic investigations. In central core disease[11] a high proportion of the muscle fibers contain nonfunctioning central cores. The condition seems relatively benign and nonspecific; this rare disease, usually, it seems, of dominant inheritance (though some reported cases have been sporadic), is still generally regarded as a specific entity. There is now much less certainty about the specificity of the entities described as megaconial and pleoconial myopathy by Shy et al.[12] Giant mitochondria with inclusions have now been observed in electron micrographs of muscle sections obtained from a wide variety of myopathies and a substantial increase in the number of mitochondria present within the muscle cell (what Shy and his colleagues called pleoconial myopathy) seems to be a finding commonly observed in a number of forms of metabolic myopathy[3, 13] which vary considerably in respect to the nature of the primary metabolic defect responsible for the muscular weakness. I wish to comment more specifically upon my personal experience and that of my colleagues in Newcastle with the remaining two forms of specific congenital myopathy which have been identified in recent years, namely nemaline myopathy and myotubular myopathy.

Nemaline Myopathy

We have now had experience with two cases of this syndrome.[14, 15] This condition was first described by Conen et al[16] and by Shy et al.[17] These authors noted that in their respective patients, each of whom showed a clinical picture in early childhood characterized by diffuse hypotonia and nonprogressive muscular weakness, a large proportion of the muscle fibers contained thread- or rodlike bodies lying beneath the sarcolemma. While most reported cases have been sporadic,[14-16, 18-20] Spiro and Kennedy[21] reported the condition occurring in a mother and daughter, a finding suggestive of dominant inheritance, and Hopkins et al,[22] in reviewing a case previously diagnosed by Ford[23] as an example of Krabbe's congenital universal muscular hypoplasia, recognized that the patient was suffering from nemaline myopathy and later discovered that her daughter was also affected. Thus current evidence favors the view that the condition is due to a dominant gene with incomplete penetrance, though this cannot yet be regarded as being certain.

It is important to mention that some doubt has been cast recently upon the specificity of rodlike bodies observed in muscle biopsy sections. Engel[1] in particular has noted that rods may appear in the muscle fibers in cases of the Sjögren syndrome, that they may occur after experimental tenotomy in the cat, and he has seen them in one patient with childhood dermatomyositis treated by chloroquine. These observations and the similar findings of other authors have cast some doubt upon whether nemaline myopathy can be regarded as a specific entity.

However, it must be stressed that the accumulated clinical evidence suggests that this disease is specific, both clinically and pathologically. Most of the reported cases have shown skeletal dysmorphism with kyphoscoliosis, chest deformity, pes cavus, arching of the palate and a long, thin face often with prognathism of the lower jaw.[14] Indeed the descriptions given of many of the reported cases suggest a striking clinical similarity between patients with this disease on the one hand and cases of arachnodactyly (Marfan syndrome) on the other. However, these patients do not show any of the other stigmata of the Marfan syndrome, including dislocation of the lens, cardiac anomalies and excessive excretion of hydroxyproline in the urine.

When one comes to study the pathologic findings, it is plain that nemaline rods may be easily overlooked if sections stained with hemalum and eosin are examined solely with the light microscope. Under phase contrast illumination, the rods may be highly refractile[14] but this is not invariably so, as in our second case, a child aged three years at the time of investigation, the rods were no more clearly apparent in her muscle biopsy section under phase contrast illumination than in ordinary light microscopy. They do, however, stand out in sections stained with trichrome stains (Gomori or picro-Mallory) or phosphotungstic acid hematoxylin (PTAH) (Fig. 1). Recent evidence[14, 15, 19, 20, 24] strongly suggests that the rods are derived from Z-band protein, but their exact chemical composition has not yet been identified, though they show, in high-power electron micrographs, a cross-lattice appearance virtually identical with that of the normal Z-band. Our own observations suggest that the process responsible for rod formation[14, 15] is one of a progressive thickening of

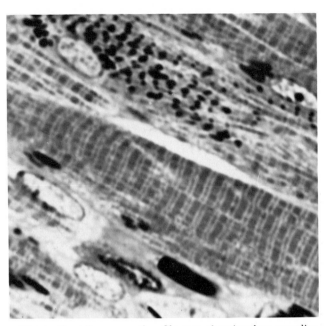

Fig. 1. Nemaline myopathy. Clusters of perinuclear nemaline rods and thickened Z-bands in a biopsy from a case of nemaline myopathy. Araldite embedding, toluidine blue, × 870.

the Z-bands followed by degeneration of contiguous myofilaments (Figs. 2 and 3), so that greatly swollen Z-bands isolated from their myofilaments eventually bud off in the form of rods into the subsarcolemmal space. Recent observations in our second case[15] suggest that this progressive change in the Z-bands seems invariably to begin close to the nuclei. We found that the nuclei themselves often showed unusual appearances in electron micrographs. Many of their nucleoli were extremely prominent and electron dense and on very high power micrographs had a finely granular, almost crystalline structure. In some sections they appeared to be in communication with the nuclear membrane and in the sarcoplasm around the nuclei, usually in the region of rod bodies or thickened Z-bands, moderate numbers of polyribosomes could be seen, a phenomenon suggesting an abortive attempt at regeneration. Alternatively, this finding could indicate that the active-looking nuclei had been elaborating large amounts of ribonucleic acid which had been in turn responsible for the laying down of new protein (possibly nemaline material in the Z-bands) near to the nucleus. This can be no more than speculation at the present time and it is important to recognize that our second patient was only three years old at the time of diagnosis, while our first patient was a mature adolescent. Hence it may be that the histologic and electron microscopic changes in the muscle of patients with nemaline myopathy could vary with the age of the patient (and of the disease process). We believe that precise physiochemical technics like those used by Engel and Gomez[25] and ultimately the use of x-ray crystallography, may prove to be the only sure means of

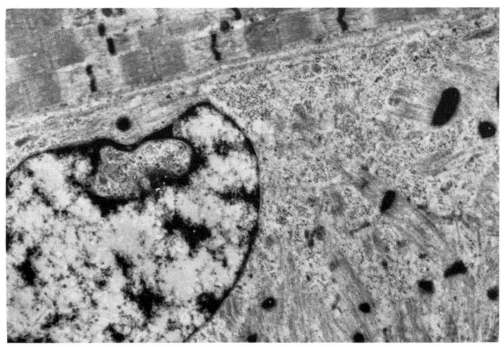

Fig. 2. Nemaline myopathy. Electron micrograph showing perinuclear Z-band expansion and an early stage of "rod" formation. Longitudinal section, × 14,000 (from Fulthorpe *et al*).[15]

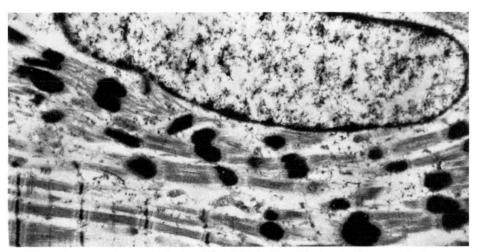

Fig. 3. Nemaline myopathy. Electron micrograph showing Z-band thickening with degeneration of randomly-orientated contiguous myofilaments in a perinuclear situation, × 14,000.

determining the exact nature of nemaline bodies and of elucidating further the nature of this unusual disease process. While it is likely that in disease processes causing degeneration and disintegration of myofibrils, Z-band material indistinguishable from the rods of nemaline myopathy will be found, and thus in a sense the finding lacks specificity. I have no doubt that the clinical and pathologic syndrome I have described must still be regarded as a disease entity in which the Z-band degeneration appears to be the primary process; by contrast, in the other conditions in which small numbers of sporadically occurring nemaline rods have been discovered, this

finding would appear to be a nonspecific epiphenomenon.

Myotubular Myopathy

In 1966 Spiro *et al*[26] described the case of a boy aged 12 who had no family history of neuromuscular disease, but whose motor development was delayed. He was noted to have bilateral ptosis at the age of six months and subsequently developed a divergent squint with partial weakness of all extraocular muscles. He showed slow progressive weakness beginning in the lower limbs, and symmetric wasting and weakness of the limbs and of neck and trunk muscles, involving particularly the distal muscles of the limbs and giving bilateral foot drop. There was also marked facial weakness but no dysphonia or dysphagia. The deep tendon reflexes were absent and the plantar responses flexor. Myotonia could not be detected clinically and an electromyogram showed only scattered fibrillation potentials. The serum creatine kinase was slightly elevated, the serum aldolase normal, and muscle biopsies revealed that 85% of the fibers had one to four central nuclei with perinuclear clear spaces around them. It was noted that this child also had bilateral subdural hematomas evacuated at the age of six months and, from the age of five years, he developed epilepsy and had a diffusely abnormal electroencephalogram, but his intelligence quotient was normal. Spiro et al[26] suggested that this entity should be called myotubular myopathy because the muscle fibers resembled fetal myotubes.

Subsequently Sher et al[27] reported similar pathologic changes in muscle biopsies obtained from two Negro sisters, aged 18 and 16 years respectively, in whom the clinical and pathologic findings were very similar to those observed in the case of Spiro et al.[26] These workers felt that the affected muscle fibers showed many significant differences from fetal myotubes and suggested the descriptive term of familial centronuclear myopathy to identify this syndrome. Since these early reports, approximately 12 cases have now been reported and have been reviewed in detail by Campbell et al.[28] Since this review was submitted for publication, additional cases have been reported by Badurska et al[29] and by Dubowitz.[3]

From these many reports, a relatively consistent clinical picture, varying in severity from case to case, emerges. The overall picture appears to be one of diffuse muscular hypotonia with slender muscles, excessive mobility at joints and an almost constant involvement of the external ocular muscles, giving, as a rule, ptosis or divergent squint associated with marked facial weakness. In the cases already reported, there has been an unusually high incidence of epilepsy and of electroencephalographic abnormality. Plainly the condition is of very variable severity as some of the reported cases are young adults who are alive and comparatively well, while the case described by Engel et al,[30] and one personal case from my department[28] were so profoundly weak and hypotonic as a result of the disease that they died from respiratory infection in early infancy. So far as inheritance is concerned, Sher et al[27] described affected sisters, a finding which would at first sight suggest the possibility of autosomal recessive inheritance, but a muscle biopsy from their mother showed a similar, though less severe, degree of central nucleation of many muscle fibers, and Coleman et al[31] and Munsat[32] found similar abnormalities in muscle obtained from the mother of their single case. Hence

there is some evidence that this condition, too, may be due to autosomal dominant inheritance.

Our own experience now includes investigations in two cases (Figs. 4 and 5), of which one has been fully studied and reported[28] while investigations in the second patient are still in progress.

Our first patient (Fig. 4) was a female child who died at the age of 27 months from an intercurrent pulmonary infection. She was first noted to be severely hypotonic and to have multiple extraocular palsies and facial asymmetry at five months of age. A muscle biopsy taken at 19 months of age showed that 95% of the muscle fibers were abnormally small and that of these more than 85% had centrally placed nuclei with a surrounding sarcoplasm-sparse zone. The remaining 5% of fibers were abnormally large and were of two types. One group resembled so-called Wohlfart B fibers, but the others were larger multinucleated fibers of apparently unique structure. In addition to a definite increase in the absolute number of sarcolemmal nuclei (some fibers contained up to eight or ten per transverse section), these fibers showed that their nuclei were orientated

Fig. 4. Myotubular myopathy. Our first case (on the left) aged 26 months, taken with her normal 13-month-old brother. Note the convergent squint.

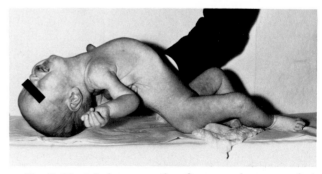

Fig. 5. Myotubular myopathy. Our second case, aged six weeks, demonstrating profound generalized weakness and hypotonia.

in practically all directions and sometimes in a circular pattern such that they delineated an inner circular core of sarcoplasm from an outer and narrower sarcoplasmic area. Many such fibers had a sarcoplasm-free slit with very sharp boundaries which seemed different from the perinuclear sarcoplasm-free halo seen in the smaller fibers. We are as yet unable to explain the significance of this finding.

In autopsy material obtained from our patient, no abnormality was found in the anterior horn cells of the spinal cord and the brain also appeared normal. Electron microscopic studies on the small fibers showed that the perinuclear zone consisted of a focal area of myofibrillar degeneration (Figs. 6, 7 and 8) with myofilamentous debris, mitochondria, myelin figures and empty vesicular structures, some of which were lipid bodies and others resembled so-called lysosomes (Fig. 9). This degenerative process sometimes extended so as to occupy the whole width of the cell with a total loss of sarcomere structure. In our material, the picture was essentially one of a perinuclear degenerative process and we found no evidence of any proliferation of polyribosomes or of the formation of new myofilaments such as one would expect to see in fetal muscle. Hence we agree with Sher *et al*[27] that the term myotubular myopathy would not be an appropriate description for the findings observed in our case, and indeed these pathologic changes could be better identified by the descriptive term pericentronuclear myopathy to indicate that the process around the central nuclei appears to be one of progressive degeneration. We cannot, of course, exclude the possibility that in these

cases there may initially be an arrest of development at the myotube stage, and that subsequently, owing to a lack of the necessary stimulus which is responsible for the subsequent maturation of muscle fibers with peripheral migration of the muscle nuclei, degeneration of the centrally situated myofibrils around the nuclei occurs. Hence the suggestion of Spiro *et al*[26] that this disorder is one of developmental arrest certainly cannot be excluded by our observations, but much more work will be required before the nature of the pathologic process in the muscle fibers in such cases can be elucidated. We certainly have no evidence to support the view put forward by Engel[1] that this process is due to denervation, and Badurska *et al*[29] were unable to support his contention that the abnormal and centrally nucleated fibers were virtually all of histochemical Type I.

Metabolic Myopathies

While myopathy has been recognized to be an important complication of thyreotoxicosis for many years, it is only comparatively recently that attention has been drawn to the various forms of myopathic weakness and wasting which may complicate endocrine disorders as diverse as myxedema, hypopituitarism, Cushing's disease, Addison's disease and metabolic bone disease.[33] Following upon the original description of so-called hypermetabolic myopathy by Luft *et al*,[34] similar cases characterized by muscular weakness and fatigability and associated with an abnormal accumulation of mitochondria within skeletal muscle fibers, and with a

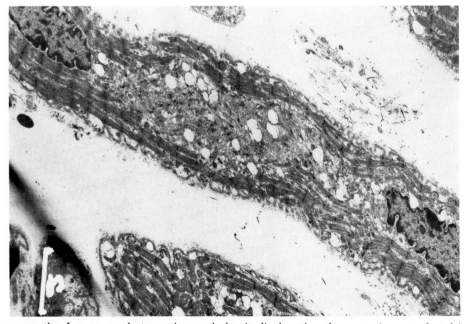

Fig. 6. Myotubular myopathy. Low-power electron micrograph, longitudinal section, demonstrating central nuclei, peripherally-situated myofibrils and central perinuclear myofilamentous debris within a small fiber, × 8,000, scale = 1 μ (from Campbell *et al*).[28]

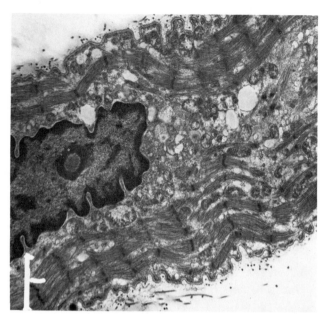

Fig. 7. Myotubular myopathy. A central nucleus with a convoluted nuclear membrane, vacuoles and lipid bodies in the center of the fiber. Note the convoluted appearance of the sarcolemma. Electron micrograph, × 7,060 scale = 1 μ.

"loosely-coupled" state of oxidative phosphorylation, have been described by Wijngaarden et al[13] and others. A recent addition to this group of disorders is the myopathy which has been shown to accompany an increased circulating level of ACTH in patients developing diffuse pigmentation and excessive muscular weakness and fatigability following adrenalectomy for Cushing's disease.[35] Several forms of myopathy complicating acute and chronic alcoholism have also been reported. Yet another obscure myopathy, apparently ameliorated by treatment with estrogens in high doses must now be added.[36]

I wish, however, to concentrate in my comments upon two genetically determined metabolic myopathies, one due to an abnormal degree of glycogen storage in the voluntary muscles, and the second apparently resulting from an abnormal accumulation of lipid. In these comments I do not propose to consider the well-recognized but as yet incompletely elucidated syndromes of periodic paralysis, some of which are accompanied during attacks of weakness by hypokalemia and others by hyperkalemia, while in yet others there is no apparent change in the concentration of serum potassium even at the height of an episode of weakness. The relationship between this group of syndromes on the one hand and myotonia on the other is a subject receiving considerable attention, but one which still remains unclear.

Glycogen Storage Disease

McArdle's disease (myophosphorylase deficiency), first described by McArdle in 1951,[37] a syndrome characterized by muscle pain, cramps and physio-

logic contracture precipitated by exercise, has been shown to be a disorder of abnormal glycogen storage resulting from a deficiency of phosphorylase within skeletal muscle,[38] and a similar syndrome is now recognized to result from phosphofructokinase deficiency.[39] I wish to draw particular attention to the variable clinical manifestations of amylo-1,4-glucosidase (acid maltase) deficiency, a condition often referred to as Pompe's disease or Cori's Type II glycogenosis.

It has been recognized for many years that the classic picture of Pompe's disease is one of diffuse

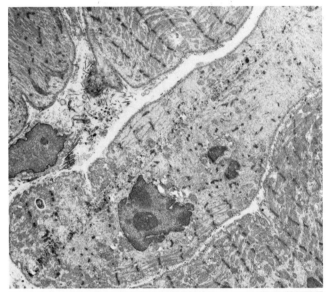

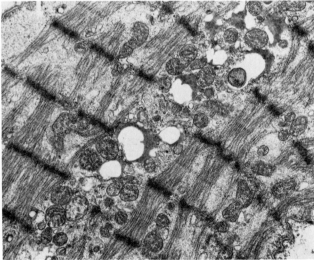

Fig. 8. Myotubular myopathy. Electron micrograph of a small fiber in which almost all myofibrillar structure has been lost; some surviving Z-band material and scanty surviving myofilaments are present, × 6,640.

Fig. 9. Myotubular myopathy. Electron micrograph demonstrating the central accumulation of mitochondria, vacuoles and lipid bodies within a fiber in which there is better preservation of the peripherally-situated myofibrils, × 11,620 (from Campbell et al).[28]

muscular weakness and profound hypotonia observed in infants soon after birth. We have studied two such cases, in both of which the disease ended fatally within the first few months of life. The affected infants were profoundly weak and hypotonic (Fig. 10) and both showed a striking degree of cardiac enlargement (Fig. 11) with markedly abnormal electrocardiograms. In both cases the serum creatine kinase was normal but electromyographic studies revealed evidence of severe myopathy and muscle biopsies showed a very striking degree of vacuolation of virtually all muscle fibers (Figs. 12–14) with an enormous accumulation of glycogen. Death resulted from cardiac failure before the end of the third month of life. The observation that Type II glycogenosis may present with a clinical picture of less severe and profound muscular weakness, first becoming

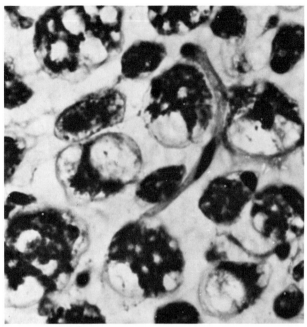

Fig. 12. Quadriceps muscle biopsy, transverse section, from the infant illustrated in Figure 10, demonstrating a gross vacuolar myopathy; formalin-fixed, paraffin-embedded, H and E × 384.

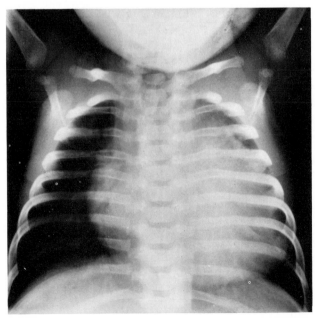

Fig. 10. An infant aged seven weeks with Pompe's glycogenosis. Muscular weakness and hypotonia were profound and there was evidence of cardiac failure; note the liver enlargement.

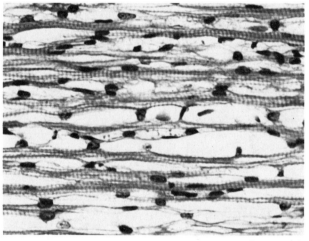

Fig. 13. Longitudinal section of muscle biopsy illustrated in Figure 12. Note the enormous vacuoles from which glycogen has been removed in fixation separating the myofibrils; formalin-fixed, paraffin-embedded, picro-Mallory × 357.

apparent in late childhood, adolescence or adult life[40-44] is more recent. Of the two cases which we have studied, one was a 19-year-old Portuguese undergraduate whose only sib became profoundly weak in the first few months of life and died at the age of four years. Our patient was noted to have diffuse muscular weakness with comparatively little wasting in early childhood. By the age of 14 years she had marked difficulty in climbing stairs and found it impossible to run and was diagnosed as a case of muscular dystrophy. Subsequently her muscular weakness in both arms and legs slowly increased and

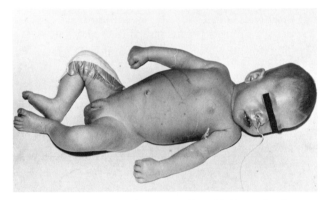

Fig. 11. Chest radiography of the infant illustrated in Figure 10 demonstrating gross cardiomegaly.

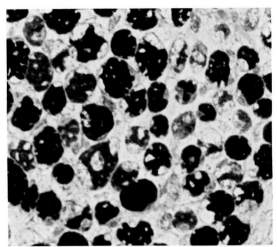

Fig. 14. Muscle biopsy, cryostat section, from the biopsy illustrated in Figure 12; myofibrillar ATPase, × 384.

was more severe in proximal muscles; she had slight dysphagia, but her speech was normal and there was only a mild degree of dyspnea on exertion. The heart was clinically and radiographically normal and the electrocardiogram showed no significant abnormality. Our second patient was a housewife aged 44 years who first noticed weakness of proximal lower limb muscles at about the age of 31 years. Gradually thereafter she began to have difficulty in running and in climbing stairs, and at the time of examination was found to have marked weakness of the glutei, hamstrings, adductors and anterior tibial muscles in the lower limbs, as well as weakness of hip flexion. She had a markedly exaggerated lumbar lordosis and a waddling gait. There was also enlargement of the tongue, but facial muscles were normal, and in the upper limbs weakness was only apparent in the sternocostal portions of the pectoralis major muscles. This patient, too, had been regarded for some years as being a case of muscular dystrophy of the limb-girdle type.

In both of our patients electromyography demonstrated evidence of myopathy in the affected muscles and many pseudomyotonic discharges were provoked by voluntary contraction and by needle movement. The serum creatine kinase was slightly raised in both patients. Muscle biopsy sections demonstrated in each a remarkable vacuolar myopathy (Fig. 15). The muscle fibers contained five times the normal concentration of glycogen, and on electron microscopy the myofibrils were noted to be displaced and distorted by abnormal concentrations of glycogen, some of which lay free in the sarcoplasm but some was concentrated in membrane-bound vacuoles resembling autophagic vacuoles or secondary lysosomes. A few of these vacuoles contained electron-dense material which appeared to be glycolipid. Detailed biochemical studies in these cases demon-

strated that the abnormality of glycogen storage was due to an almost total absence of amylo-1,4-glucosidase (acid maltase). Our own experience, and the similar reports referred to above, clearly indicate that there may be a striking discordance in the clinical presentation of Pompe's glycogenosis even in two different members of the same family (as we presume that the sib of our first patient, dying at the age of four years, was probably affected, though we have no direct proof of this assumption). It is nevertheless clear that this condition may run a much more benign course than has been previously considered to be the case and that this form of glycogen storage is yet another condition to be considered in the differential diagnosis of atypical myopathy developing in childhood or adult life. Our first patient died of cardiac failure shortly after we had investigated her in detail, but our second patient, who is now aged 46 years, is still alive and reasonably well and there has been no significant increase in her muscular weakness while she has remained under our observation.

Lipid Storage Myopathy

We have recently observed a patient suffering from what appears to be yet another new and hitherto undescribed metabolic myopathy, which is presumably genetically determined. A preliminary report on this case has been published by Bradley et al.[45]

The patient, a 25-year-old married woman (Fig. 16) gave a history of difficulty in lifting weights for two years and of difficulty in climbing stairs and in

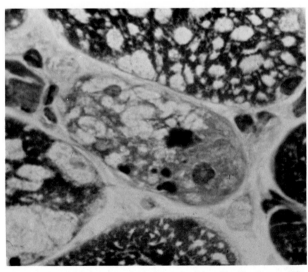

Fig. 15. Quadriceps muscle biopsy, formalin-fixed, paraffin-embedded; transverse section from a female patient aged 19 years with glycogen storage disease due to acid maltase deficiency, demonstrating gross vacuolation of muscle fibers due to glycogen accumulation, H and E × 640.

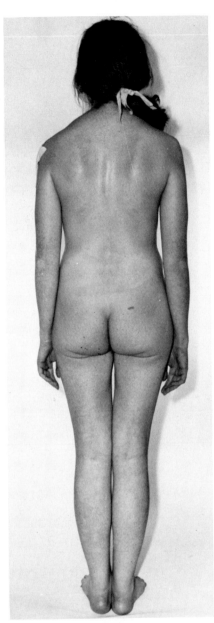

Fig. 16. Lipid storage myopathy in a woman of 25 years. Despite severe muscular weakness and fatigability the bulk of the musculature remains normal.

biopsies were taken from the left deltoid and left quadriceps muscles, and a second deltoid biopsy from this patient was examined after an interval of approximately one year. Examination of paraffin sections from all three biopsies showed scattered foci of nonspecific myopathic degeneration. However, the most impressive change in the second deltoid biopsy was the presence of numbers of vacuolated fibers, some of the vacuoles being subsarcolemmal and others being scattered throughout the fibers (Fig. 17). Careful scrutiny of the initial deltoid and quadriceps biopsies showed scattered small vacuoles which were much less striking than on the second occasion. In frozen sections stained for myosin ATPase and phosphorylase, no striking abnormality other than vacuolation of Type I fibers was observed, but the Sudan black stains (Fig. 18) showed an enormous increase in the amount of lipid in the Type I fibers as compared with control sections. The Type II fibers, by contrast, were normal. Staining with Nile blue sulfate showed that the Type I fibers contained not only abnormal quantities of neutral fat, but also large amounts of free fatty acid. Sections stained with nitro-B.T. revealed increased succinate dehydrogenase activity in the Type I fibers which also appeared to contain unusually large and dense subsarcolemmal mitochondrial aggregates. Examination of sections with the electron microscope revealed that many of the muscle fibers contained large vacuoles adjacent to mitochondria (Fig. 19) and greatly increased numbers of lipid bodies which were similarly situated. Very probably the vacuoles were also lipid bodies whose contents had been eluted during fixation and staining. The ultrastructure of the mitochondria in many of the muscle fibers examined was very poorly defined and in one subsarcolemmal aggregate of mitochondria, a collection of unusual elongated bodies was also seen (Fig. 20). Most of these were arranged in parallel with one another and they appeared to possess a crystalline structure.

We have concluded that the changes described constitute the morbid anatomic expression of a previously undescribed disease entity. The fact that the patient was a child of a consanguineous marriage strongly suggests that the condition is the result of a rare autosomal recessive gene. As we found an excessive concentration of free fatty acids in the muscle fibers and an apparent morphologic abnormality of their mitochondria, it would seem likely that the fundamental defect lies in the pathway of free fatty acid oxidation. Preliminary analysis of the fatty acid content of muscle biopsy specimens in this case suggests that the proportions of the individual fatty acids are normal, but their overall concentration and that of lipid is increased.[46] Further biochemical studies are in progress to determine whether the condition can be attributed to a specific lipase deficiency.

brushing her hair for eight months. There was no family history of muscle disease, but her parents were first cousins. On examination she was found to have weakness of the posterior, and to a lesser extent of the anterior neck muscles, together with diffuse muscular weakness in the limbs involving the proximal muscles including the deltoids, more severely than the distal ones. Electromyographic examination revealed unequivocal evidence of a myopathy in the right biceps and right deltoid, and her serum creatine kinase activity was slightly elevated at 93 IU/l (upper limit of normal 60 IU/l). Initially muscle

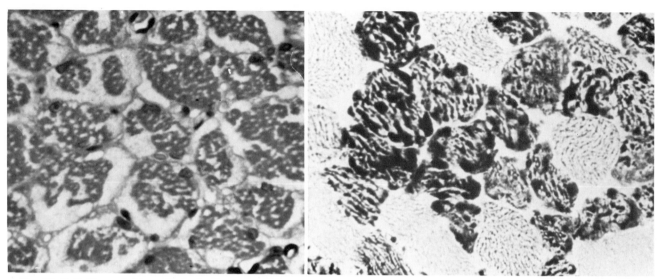

Fig. 17. Deltoid muscle biopsy, formalin-fixed, paraffin-embedded, transverse section from the patient illustrated in Figure 16. There is a marked vacuolar myopathy; subsarcolemmal vacuoles are particularly striking; H and E × 355.

Fig. 18. Lipid storage myopathy, transverse cryostat section from the deltoid biopsy, Sudan black × 355. There is a remarkable accumulation of lipid in the Type I fibers.

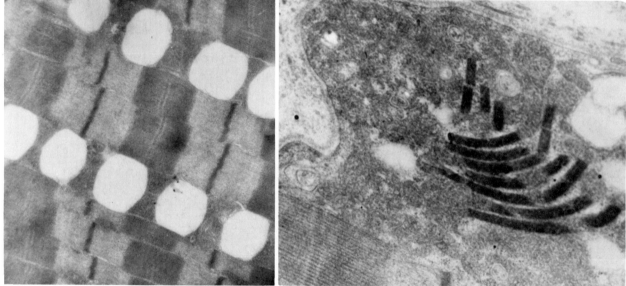

Fig. 19. Lipid storage myopathy; electron micrograph, longitudinal section, × 13,875. Numerous vacuoles are seen between the myofibrils.

Fig. 20. Lipid storage myopathy; electron micrograph showing a subsarcolemmal clump of degenerate mitochondria, some of which also show lamellar inclusions. A group of elongated possibly crystalline, bodies of unknown composition is also seen, 55,500 (from Bradley *et al*).[45]

The patient has been kept under careful continuing clinical observation. Whereas her muscular weakness appeared to increase slowly during the first two years that she was under our surveillance, there is good clinical and other supportive evidence to indicate that she has recently shown slow but spontaneous improvement. A more detailed report of this case will be published in due course when our biochemical investigations have been completed.

Conclusions

As our knowledge of muscle disease has increased and as new methods of investigation have yielded new information, the complexity of differential diagnosis has increased. As yet neither of the obscure congenital myopathies to which I have drawn particular attention, and neither of the metabolic myopathies, is amenable to any form of treatment. There would seem to be a reasonable prospect that as the pathogenesis of these obscure disorders is increasingly elucidated by modern scientific methods of investigation, our hopes of offering an effective treatment for at least some of our patients afflicted by these disorders will increase. At present the clinical science of myology, if such it can be justly called, is passing through a phase of development somewhat comparable to that demonstrated by neurologic medicine in the latter part of the 19th and in the early 20th century. We are now in a phase when many new syndromes and disease entities are being defined and their nature elucidated. There can be little doubt that those conditions which remain obscure and to which I have referred, for instance, under such headings as benign congenital hypotonia, congenital muscular dystrophy and benign congenital myopathy may similarly be clarified in the coming years as our expertise in this field continues to grow and develop. Although in diseases such as progressive muscular dystrophy we continue to sail in seas which are largely uncharted in a pathogenetic sense, knowledge concerning diseases of muscle, and particularly of those which are genetically determined, has widened enormously in the last decade and there can be no doubt that the next decade will see many more new and exciting developments.

Summary

Present knowledge concerning the classification of the group of so-called benign congenital myopathies is reviewed briefly and reasons are given for concluding that although rodlike bodies may be observed in muscle biopsy material obtained from patients with a variety of neuromuscular diseases, the syndrome of nemaline or rod body myopathy may nevertheless be regarded as a circumscribed and well-defined clinical and pathologic entity. Recent observations on cases of so-called myotubular or centronuclear myopathy are also reviewed in the light of personal experience and it is concluded that whereas this condition may represent a condition of developmental arrest of the muscle fibers, there are striking differences between the histologic findings observed in such cases on the one hand and in fetal myotubes on the other. It seems possible that owing to a lack of the necessary stimulus responsible for the maturation of muscle fibers, progressive degeneration of the myofibrils situated around the central nuclei eventually occurs in such cases.

Of the group of metabolic myopathies, attention is particularly drawn to adult myopathy resulting from glycogen storage due to acid maltase (amylo-1,4-glucosidase) deficiency. While this specific biochemical defect usually results in profound muscular weakness and cardiac involvement apparent in early infancy, and few children survive beyond the first few months of life (Pompe's disease), it is now apparent that the condition may give rise to a myopathy superficially resembling limb-girdle muscular dystrophy and first becoming apparent in late childhood or adult life. Finally, a case of myopathy due apparently to abnormal storage of lipid in the Type I muscle fibers, and occurring in a young adult female who was the product of a consanguineous marriage, is described. It is suggested that this disorder may well prove to be the manifestation of a rare autosomal recessive gene.

ACKNOWLEDGMENTS

I am particularly grateful to my colleagues, Drs. P. Hudgson, D. Gardner-Medwin, M. Worsfold, R. J. T. Pennington, M. J. Campbell, W. G. Bradley and J. J. Rebeiz, and to my chief technician, Mr. J. J. Fulthorpe, for permission to include in this paper material reported or in the press in papers of which I was but one coauthor. The work referred to in this report was aided by grants from the Medical Research Council, the Muscular Dystrophy Associations of America, Inc. and the Muscular Dystrophy Group of Great Britain. I also gratefully acknowledge the continuing help and support in secretarial matters of Miss Rosemary Allan. I wish to thank the editors and publishers of *Neurology* (Minneapolis), the *Journal of the Neurological Sciences* and the *Lancet* for permission to reproduce in this paper Figures 2, 6, 9 and 20 which have been published previously.

REFERENCES

1. Engel, W. K.: A critique of congenital myopathies and other disorders. In *Exploratory Concepts in Muscular Dystrophy and Related Disorders*, ed, A. T. Milhorat, Excerpta Medica Foundation, Amsterdam, 1967.
2. Walton, J. N. and Gardner-Medwin, D.: Progressive muscular dystrophy and the myotonic disorders. In *Disorders of Voluntary Muscle*, 2nd Ed., ed, J. N. Walton, Churchill, London, 1969.
3. Dubowitz, V.: *The Floppy Infant. Clinics in Developmental Medicine No. 31.* Spastics International Medical Publications and Heinemann Medical Books, London, 1969.
4. Walton, J. N.: The limp child. *J. Neurol. Neurosurg. Psychiat.* **20**:144, 1957.
5. Zellweger, H.; Afifi, A.; McCormick, W. F. and Mergner, W.: Severe congenital muscular dystrophy. *Amer. J. Dis. Child.* **114**:591, 1967.
6. Turner, J. W. A.: The relationship between amyotonia congenita and congenital myopathy. *Brain* **63**:163, 1940.
7. Turner, J. W. A.: On amyotonia congenita. *Brain* **72**:25, 1949.
8. Krabbe, K. H.: Congenital generalized muscular atrophies. *Acta psychiat.* **33**:94, 1958.
9. Walton, J. N.: Amyotonia congenita—a follow-up study. *Lancet* i:1023, 1956.
10. Walton, J. N. and Gardner-Medwin, D.: Second thoughts on classification of the muscular dystrophies. In *Research in Muscular Dystrophy (Proceedings of 4th Symposium)*. Pitman, London, 1968.
11. Shy, G. M. and Magee, K. R.: A new congenital non-progressive myopathy. *Brain* **79**:610, 1956.
12. Shy, G. M.; Gonatas, N. K. and Perez, M.: Two childhood

myopathies with abnormal mitochondria. I. Megaconial myopathy. II. Pleoconial myopathy. *Brain* **89**:133, 1966.

13. Wijngaarden, G. K. van; Bethlem, J.; Meijer, A. E. F. H.; Hulsmann, W. C. and Feltkamp, C. A.: Skeletal muscle disease with abnormal mitochondria. *Brain* **90**:577, 1967.

14. Hudgson, P.; Gardner-Medwin, D.; Fulthorpe, J. J. and Walton, J. N.: Nemaline myopathy. *Neurology (Minneap.)* **17**:1125, 1967.

15. Fulthorpe, J. J.; Gardner-Medwin, D.; Hudgson, P. and Walton, J. N: Nemaline myopathy: a histological and ultrastructural study of skeletal muscle from a case presenting with infantile hypotonia. *Neurology (Minneap.)*, **19**:735, 1969.

16. Conen, P. E.; Murphy, E. G. and Donohue, W. L.: Light and electron microscopic studies of "myogranules" in a child with hypotonia and muscle weakness. *Canad. med. Ass. J.* **89**:983, 1963.

17. Shy, G. M.; Engel, W. K.; Somers, J. E. and Wando, T.: Nemaline myopathy: a new congenital myopathy. *Brain* **86**:793, 1963.

18. Engel, W. K.; Wanko, T. and Fenichel, G. M.: Nemaline myopathy: a second case. *Arch. Neurol. (Chic.)* **11**:22, 1964.

19. Price, H. M.; Gordon, G. B.; Pearson, C. M.; Munsat, T. L. and Blumberg, J. M.: New evidence for accumulation of excessive Z band material in nemaline myopathy. *Proc. nat. Acad. Sci. (Wash.)* **54**:1398, 1965.

20. Shafiq, S. A.; Dubowitz, V.; Peterson, H. C. and Milhorat, A. T.: Nemaline myopathy: report of a case with histochemical and electron microscopic studies. *Brain* **90**:817, 1967.

21. Spiro, A. J. and Kennedy, C.: Hereditary occurrence of nemaline myopathy. *Trans. Amer. neurol. Ass.* **89**:62, 1964.

22. Hopkins, I. J.; Lindsey, J. R. and Ford, F. R.: Nemaline myopathy: a long-term clinicopathologic study of an affected mother and daughter. *Brain* **89**:299, 1966.

23. Ford, F. R.: Congenital universal muscle hypoplasia (Krabbe). In *Diseases of the Nervous System in Infancy, Childhood and Adolescence*. Charles C Thomas, Springfield, 1960.

24. Gonatas, N. K.; Shy, G. M. and Godfrey, E. H.: Nemaline myopathy: the origin of nemaline structures. *New Engl. J. Med.* **274**:535, 1966.

25. Engel, W. K. and Gomez, M. R.: Nemaline (Z disc) myopathy: observations on the origin, structure and solubility properties of the nemaline structures. *J. Neuropath. exp. Neurol.* **26**: 601, 1967.

26. Spiro, A. J.; Shy, G. M. and Gonatas, N. K.: Myotubular myopathy. *Arch. Neurol. (Chic.)* **14**:1, 1966.

27. Sher, J. H.; Rimalovski, A. B.; Athanassaides, T. J. and Aronson, S. M.: Familial centronuclear myopathy. *Neurology (Minneap.)* **17**:726, 1967.

28. Campbell, M. J.; Rebeiz, J. J. and Walton, J. N.: Myotubular, centronuclear or peri-centronuclear myopathy? *J. neurol. Sci.* **8**:425, 1969.

29. Badurska, B.; Fidzianska, A.; Kamieniecka, Z.; Prot, J. and Strugalska, H.: Myotubular myopathy. *J. neurol. Sci.* **8**:563, 1969.

30. Engel, W. K.; Gold, G. N. and Karpati, G.: Type I fiber hypotrophy and central nuclei. *Arch. Neurol. (Chic.)* **18**:435, 1968.

31. Coleman, R. F.; Munsat, T. L.; Thompson, L. R. and Pearson, C. M.: Histochemical investigation of "myotubular" myopathy. *Lab. Invest.* **16**:647, 1967.

32. Munsat, T. L.: The U.C.L.A. interdepartmental conference on skeletal muscle. Moderator, C. M. Pearson. *Ann. intern. Med.* **67**:643, 1967.

33. Smith, R. and Stern, G. M.: Muscular weakness in osteomalacia and hyperparathyroidism. *J. neurol. Sci.* **8**:511, 1969.

34. Luft, R.; Ikkos, D.; Palmieri, G.; Ernster, L. and Afzelius, B.: A case of severe hypermetabolism of nonthyroid origin with a defect in the maintenance of mitochondrial respiratory control; a correlated clinical, biochemical and morphological study. *J. clin. Invest.* **41**:1776, 1962.

35. Prineas, J.; Hall, R.; Barwick, D. D. and Watson, A. J.: Myopathy associated with pigmentation following adrenalectomy for Cushing's syndrome. *Quart. J. Med.* **37**:63, 1968.

36. Stanton, J. B. and Strong, J. A.: Myopathy remitting in pregnancy and responding to high-dosage oestrogen and progestogen therapy. *Lancet* **ii**:275, 1967.

37. McArdle, B.: Myopathy due to a defect in muscle glycogen breakdown. *Clin. Sci.* **10**:13, 1951.

38. McArdle, B.: Metabolic and endocrine myopathies. In *Disorders of Voluntary Muscle*, 2nd Ed., ed, J. N. Walton, Churchill, London, 1969.

39. Layzer, R. B.; Rowland, L. P. and Ranney, H. M.: Muscle phosphofructokinase deficiency. *Arch. Neurol. (Chic.)* **17**:512, 1967.

40. Courtecuisse, V.; Royer, P.; Habib, R.; Monnier, C. and Demos, J.: Glycogénose musculaire par déficit d'alpha-1,4-glucosidase simulant une dystrophie musculaire progressive. *Arch. franc. Pédiat.* **22**:1153, 1965.

41. Zellweger, H.; Brown, B. I.; McCormick, W. F. and Tu, J. B.: A mild form of muscular glycogenosis in two brothers with -1,4-glucosidase deficiency. *Ann. paediat.* **205**:413, 1965.

42. Smith, H. L.; Amick, L. D. and Sidbury, J. B.: Glycogenosis type II. Report of a case with 4 year survival and associated abnormal glycogen. *Amer. J. Dis. Child.* **111**:475, 1966.

43. Isch, F.; Juif, J. G.; Sacrez, R. and Thiebaut, F.: Glycogénose musculaire à forme myopathique par déficit en maltase acide. *Pédiatrie* **21**:71, 1966.

44. Hudgson, P.; Gardner-Medwin, D.; Worsfold, M.; Pennington, R. J. T. and Walton, J. N.: Adult myopathy from glycogen storage disease due to acid maltase deficiency. *Brain* **91**:435, 1968.

45. Bradley, W. G.; Hudgson, P.; Gardner-Medwin, D. and Walton, J. N.: A new myopathy associated with abnormal lipid metabolism in skeletal muscle. *Lancet* **i**:495, 1969.

46. Owens, G.: Personal communication, 1969.

Genetic Approach to the Nosology of the Muscular Dystrophies

ALAN E. H. EMERY, M.D., D.Sc., Ph.D., F.R.C.P.E.

Phenotypic, biochemical and genetic methods are available for identifying heterogeneity in human disease. Genetic methods include studying the mode of inheritance, tests for allelism and linkage analysis. In the muscular dystrophies, genetic methods have proved particularly valuable in resolving the problem of heterogeneity.

Introduction

Methods available for identifying heterogeneity in human disease may be conveniently summarized as follows:

A. Phenotypic
1. Clinical.
2. Other eg muscle histology and histochemistry.

B. Biochemical
1. Primary.
2. Secondary.

C. Genetic
1. Mode of inheritance.
2. Tests for allelism.
3. Linkage analysis.

Since a primary biochemical defect has not yet been identified in any of the muscular dystrophies, we have therefore to rely on phenotypic and genetic methods to resolve the problems of heterogeneity within this group of diseases. However, secondary biochemical abnormalities may also be useful as exemplified by the serum level of creatine kinase which, among all the dystrophies, only reaches very high levels in boys with the severe Duchenne type of muscular dystrophy. Phenotypic differences, both clinical and morphologic, between the various dystrophies are discussed elsewhere. Here the geneticist's approach to the problem of nosology will be reviewed. Apart from the study of primary biochemical defects genetic methods are the most reliable for identifying heterogeneity.[1]

Mode of Inheritance

To the geneticist, heterogeneity may be considered as being *between* genes (ie different *loci*) or *within*

genes (ie different *alleles* at the same locus). The fact that various clinically distinct forms of dystrophy are inherited differently implies that they are due to genes at different loci. The clinical-genetic correlations within the muscular dystrophies have already been reviewed in detail.[2] However, if one form of dystrophy is clinically similar and inherited in the same manner in two different families this does not necessarily mean that they are both due to the same mutant gene. In fact many so-called "recessive" disorders affected individuals may be heterozygous for

Emery—Professor of Human Genetics, The Medical School, Edinburgh, Scotland.

Birth Defects: Original Article Series. Vol. VII, No. 2; February 1971

two rare alleles (variants) rather than homozygous for the same allele. Examples of this are already known in galactosemia and certain hereditary forms of hemolytic anemia.[3] But when the primary defect is not known and therefore biochemical variants cannot be identified, as in the dystrophies, tests for allelism must be based on either pedigree studies or linkage analysis.

Tests for Allelism

Tests for allelism in human genetics consist of studying the offspring of parents who are phenotypically similar and presumed to be homozygous for the same recessive trait, or the offspring of a parent who is heterozygous for two dominant traits. In the former situation, if the parents are homozygous for

Figs. 1 and 2 published by kind permission of the editor of the Annals of Human Genetics.

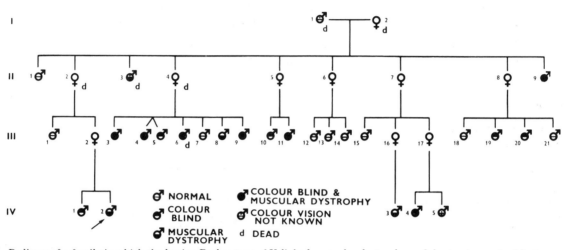

Fig. 1. Pedigree of a family in which the benign Becker type of X-linked muscular dystrophy and deutan type color blindness are segregating (from Emery, Smith and Sanger, 1969).[7]

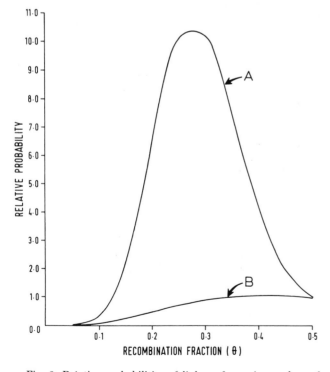

Fig. 2. Relative probabilities of linkage for various values of the recombination fraction for deutan-type color blindness and A) Becker type muscular dystrophy and B) Duchenne type muscular dystrophy (from Emery, Smith and Sanger, 1969).[7]

genes at different loci, then their offspring will be normal. Examples of this are known in recessive albinism, deaf-mutism and amaurosis, but there are no reported instances in the dystrophies. With regard to persons heterozygous for two codominant traits, if the genes are allelic, then individual offspring will inherit either trait but never both or neither. If, however, the genes are not allelic, then individual offspring may inherit both traits or neither trait. This test for allelism has been used in certain of the hemoglobinopathies. Among the dystrophies, however, a "doubly affected" parent has never been described though individuals homozygous for the dominant distal type of muscular dystrophy have been reported in a Swedish isolate.[4]

Linkage Analysis

Because of the relative crudeness of linkage analysis in human pedigrees, such studies can never prove allelism but they can give evidence of nonallelism.

We can either study the recombination between two genetic disorders directly, or indirectly by determining their separate linkage relationships to a common marker trait. Because of the rarity of most hereditary disorders, the former approach has rarely been possible, though recently Schneiderman et al[5] have reported a large family in which Pelger-Huët anomaly (a symptomless abnormality of the white cells with an incidence of about 1 in 5,000) and an autosomal dominant form of dystrophy were segregating. Linkage analysis suggested that the two gene loci are linked with a recombination fraction of 0.29.

The usual procedure in linkage studies is by the indirect method. With regard to the muscular dystrophies none of the dominant or recessive forms have so far been found to be linked to any of the recognized autosomal marker traits. Neither the severe Duchenne nor benign Becker types of X-linked muscular dystrophy are closely linked to the Xg blood group locus. However, though the loci for Duchenne type dystrophy and color blindness are far apart on the X chromosome,[6] there is a suggestion that the loci for Becker type dystrophy and deutan color blindness are within measurable distance, the recombination fraction being 0.28.[7] Thus, the results of linkage studies would suggest that the genes for the Duchenne and Becker types of muscular dystrophy are at two different loci and are therefore not allelic (Figs. 1 and 2).

Conclusions

The geneticist can approach the problem of heterogeneity in a number of ways. However, because of the inherent difficulties in the genetic analysis of human pedigrees and the rarity of many hereditary disorders, this approach has limitations. Nevertheless at the simplest level it is possible to study the mode of inheritance and, where this is the same in two seemingly different disorders, it may be possible to demonstrate nonallelism by linkage studies.

In all such attempts to resolve apparent heterogeneity a word of caution is necessary and the sentiments of Francis Bacon in 1620 are perhaps germane:

"The steady and acute mind can fix its contemplations and dwell and fasten on the subtlest distinctions: the lofty and discursive mind recognizes and puts together the finest and most general resemblances. Both kinds however easily err in excess, by catching the one at gradations the other at shadows."

REFERENCES

1. McKusick, V. A.: On lumpers and splitters, or the nosology of genetic disease. *Perspect. Biol. Med.* **12**:298, 1969.
2. Emery, A. E. H. and Walton, J. N.: The genetics of muscular dystrophy. *Progr. med. Genet.* **5**:116, 1967.
3. Childs, B. and Der Kaloustian, V. M.: Genetic heterogeneity. *New Engl. J. Med.* **279**:1205 and 1267, 1968.
4. Welander, L.: Homozygous appearance of distal myopathy. *Acta genet. (Basel)* **7**:321, 1957.
5. Schneiderman, L. J.; Sampson, W. I.; Schoene, W. C. and Haydon, G. B.: Genetic studies of a family with two unusual autosomal dominant conditions: muscular dystrophy and Pelger-Huët anomaly. *Amer. J. Med.* **46**:380, 1969.
6. Emery, A. E. H.: Genetic linkage between the loci for colour blindness and Duchenne type muscular dystrophy. *J. med. Genet.* **3**:92, 1966.
7. Emery, A. E. H.; Smith, C. A. B. and Sanger, R.: The linkage relations of the loci for benign (Becker type) X-borne muscular dystrophy, colour blindness and the Xg blood groups. *Ann. hum. Genet.* **32**:261, 1969.

Classification of Neuromuscular Disorders

W. KING ENGEL, M.D.

A new type of classification of neuromuscular diseases is presented. It is based on *etiology*; when this is not possible, on *pathogenesis*; if neither is possible, on *distinctive features, biochemical > morphologic > clinical-genetic* ones. The initial categorization designates which *cell type*, lower motor neuron or myofiber, is considered responsible for the major abnormality. This classification is designed to promote understanding of the pathogenesis and etiology of neuromuscular diseases in general and be applicable to a particular patient when the diagnostic studies are completed. It is not arranged as an approach to the initial differential diagnosis of a given patient.

A. Introduction

A classification of diseases provides an orderly arrangement of presumed separate entities. But all disease classifications are somewhat artificial—they represent a guess of systematic errors in Nature's masterplan for normal structure and function. Diagnoses as precise as possible must be the basis of a classification. There must be categories for entities (and patients) not yet precisely defined, ie an "I don't know" group. A "correct" path between excessive grouping and excessive separation of disorders and their variants should be chosen. The question is sometimes asked, why bother to achieve a detailed diagnosis in patients with neuromuscular diseases when so few can be successfully treated? The answer is twofold. First, a number of patients with neuromuscular diseases can be successfully treated, eg inflammatory myopathies with corticosteroids (especially the alternate-day program)[1] or immunosuppressants (such as azathiaprine),[2] hypokalemic periodic paralysis with acetazolamide[3, 4] or potassium, and recurrent neuropathies with corticosteroids.[5, 6] And many of the secondary myopathies are cured by identifying and treating the primary cause. Second, clinical evaluation of any new treatment will be greatly facilitated if based on precisely diagnosed patients, just as the precise diagnostic methods of clinical microbiology developed in the late 1800s greatly facilitated clinical evaluation of the chemotherapeutic agents introduced 50 years later.

Ideally, a disease classification should be based on *etiology;* if not etiology, on *pathogenesis;* if neither is possible, on *distinctive features, biochemical > morphologic > clinical-genetic* ones. With the neuromuscular diseases it seems preferable, intuitively, to have the initial categorization designate which cell type, lower motor neuron or myofiber, is considered responsible for the major abnormality.

The present classification is based on this approach, being designed to promote understanding of the pathogenesis and etiology of neuromuscular diseases in general and be applicable to a particular patient when his diagnostic studies are completed. It is not arranged as an approach to the initial differential diagnosis of a given patient. Muscle diseases (myopathies) can be understood better when compared and contrasted with lower motor neuron disorders (motor neuropathies), hence this combined approach. The principles of this approach to classification are emphasized—details given are exemplary and not necessarily complete. When applying the classification, each patient is categorized by first localizing the major defective cell with diagnostic technics. Then he is advanced in the classification from the general to the specific, as the pathogenesis and etiology are sought, with the hope of arriving at, or setting the stage for finding, a treatment. This approach has the virtue of being a methodical, stepwise progression. Potential disadvantages are that a) a number of diseases affect more than one cell type (which is not a problem if kept in mind) (Figs. 1A and B), and b) in some instances a more direct ap-

Engel—Chief, Medical Neurology Branch, National Institute of Neurological Diseases and Stroke, National Institutes of Health, Bethesda.

Birth Defects: Original Article Series. Vol. VII, No. 2; February 1971

18

W. King Engel, M.D.   19

BIOGRAPHIC DATA

Dr. W. King Engel was born in St. Louis, Missouri. He received a B.A. degree from Johns Hopkins University in 1951 and an M.D. from McGill University Faculty of Medicine in Montreal in 1955. After a rotating internship at the University of Michigan Hospital in Ann Arbor in 1955–1956, he served as Clinical Associate in Clinical Neurology at the National Institute of Neurological Diseases and Blindness in Bethesda, Maryland for a period of one year, followed by two years as Clinical Associate in Experimental Neuropathology. Following this, he spent one year as an Extramural Trainee of the National Institute of Neurological Diseases and Blindness at the National Hospital, Queen Square, London in 1959–1960. In 1960 he returned to the NINDB as Associate Neurologist in Clinical and Experimental Neurology and after one year as Acting Chief, became Chief of the Medical Neurology Branch of the National Institute of Neurological Diseases and Stroke in 1963. He was certified in Neurology by the American Board of Neurology and Psychiatry in 1962. He holds an appointment as Clinical Professor of Neurology at the School of Medicine of George Washington University.

Dr. Engel's particular research interest has been the application of basic research and clinical technics to human neurologic disorders in order to analyze the many facets of each patient's disease. He is a fellow of the American Academy of Neurology and a member of several other neurologic associations. He is the author of many scientific papers in his specialty.

B. Normal Neuron-Myofiber Interactions

A lower motor neuron and the myofibers it innervates together are termed a *motor unit*. Information and concepts concerning myofiber and motor neuron types and their long-term mutual influences are necessary to understand some of the neuromuscular disorders, particularly those in the indeterminate group. Normal human muscle fibers are of two basic histochemical types, I and II, and are rather evenly intermixed heterogeneously in the muscles usually biopsied.[9-11] (There may be two or more subtypes within each major type.) Similar types exist in mammals, more homogeneously in certain muscles, leading to the working hypothesis that in warm-blooded animals Type I fibers are slow twitch fibers characteristic of red muscle and Type II fibers are fast twitch fibers characteristic of white muscle.[11] The term "motor neuron" in this report refers to α-motor neurons and denotes the entire cell, consisting of dendrites, soma, axon, and axonal endings at the neuromuscular junctions. It has not been established for certain whether a given lower motor neuron innervates muscle fibers of both histochemical types (ie a *mixed* motor unit) or whether all of its fibers are of the same histochemical type (ie a *uniform* motor unit). Available evidence suggests that the motor unit is uniform, and that the lower motor neuron determines muscle fiber types.[11] If this is the case, one may postulate Type I and Type II α-motor neurons innervating Type I and II muscle fibers respectively (Fig. 2). Physiologically, Type "S" (slow) and Type "F" (fast) α-motor neurons have been described in warm-blooded animals based on the speed of contraction of the muscle fibers they innervate.[12-14] These may correspond to the postulated Types I and II respectively. As yet the two postulated types of α-motor neurons have not been demonstrated histochemically to be different from each other, even though in the cat both slow and fast α-motor neurons have been distinguished from the other neurons of the anterior horn (interneurons,

proach to the pathogenesis, etiology, and even treatment may be possible without knowing the major cell type affected or certain other classifying details, by use of "multichannel" screening analyses, from shrewd and fortunate guesses and from accidental discoveries. Therefore, simultaneous research on direct approaches must be encouraged even though for classification purposes a stepwise system appears preferable at this time.

In a previous classification[7] we separated neuromuscular disorders into episodic and nonepisodic ones. While that distinction is useful in considering the initial differential diagnosis of a patient,[7,8] it will not be used here.

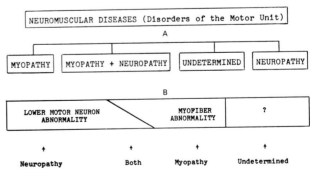

Figs. 1A and B. A. Classification of neuromuscular diseases. B. Diagram demonstrating various degrees of overlap between neuropathy and myopathy.

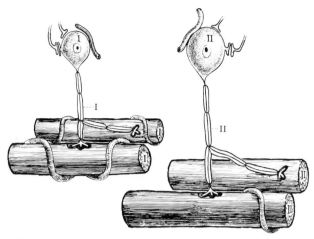

Fig. 2. Diagram indicating uniformity of myofibers within a given motor unit and two different types of motor units.

Renshaw cells, and probably γ-motor neurons). Both types of α-motor neurons have high content of phosphorylase and low succinate dehydrogenase, while the other anterior horn neurons have no detectable phosphorylase and high succinate dehydrogenase.[15-17] (All neurons of the anterior horn are indistinguishable from each other with 14 other histochemical reactions.[15-17])

To hypothesize further, there may well be distinct Type I and Type II schwann cells nurturing the two corresponding different types of motor neurons (Fig. 2). They could react independently or together in the dysschwannian neuropathies. However, histochemically different schwann cells have not yet been identified.

A number of studies suggest that the LMN influences cells in contact with it and in turn is influenced by them. For purposes of analysis, these reciprocal influences have been postulated to be transmitted by hypothetic "factors" (Fig. 3), more fully discussed elsewhere.[18] The LMN contains a number of factors influencing its distal axonal self, its schwann cells, and the myofibers innervated by it. The LMN may be influenced by factors from other neurons ending on its soma and dendrites, and perhaps from glia around the soma, from its schwann cells, and from its myofibers (Fig. 3). The message transmitted by a factor might be encoded as a chemical structure, an electrical property, a pattern of release, or a combination thereof, but since most are only hypothetical, their nature is unknown. Their existence is implied from abnormalities seen in spontaneous human and experimental animal neuromuscular disorders. The source of the LMN factors may be the soma, and possibly they are generated by the abundant synthesizing machinery represented by the ribonucleoprotein of the Nissl substance. For discussion purposes, all these factors are considered as distinct from each other and single, although each

could be multiple or overlapping, and there may be ones additional to those discussed here. The other factors must be functioning fairly well to obtain a suggestion that one is missing. These factors generally relate to long-term function of the LMN, though in some instances to short-term function.

1. *Factor of the LMN related to itself:* An *inhibitory factor* from the proximal LMN is postulated to prevent fasciculations from being generated from the distal axon of the intact motor neuron, while its deficiency would account for the fasciculations in such diseases as amyotrophic lateral sclerosis.

2. *Factors of the LMN related to muscle:* The major *excitatory factor* is generally agreed to be acetylcholine. It is the one chemically defined factor and it determines short-term function. We postulate that in both myasthenia gravis (a disease that is anticholinesterase-responsive and curare-worsened) and the facilitating type of myasthenic syndrome[19, 20] (which is guanidine-responsive and curare-worsened) the neural excitatory factor is relatively deficient, perhaps secondary to partial inadequacy of the soma. In both of these myasthenic

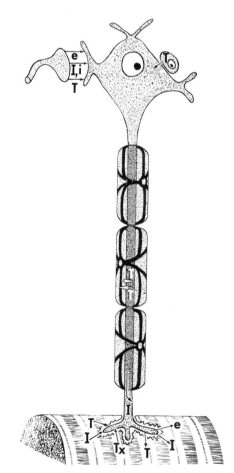

Fig. 3. Diagram illustrating the various "factors," proven or proposed, related to the motor unit.

states, histochemical[21] and clinical evidence of deficiency of the neural trophic factor develops later in the course of disease.

Trophic factor(s) is the hypothetic long-term influence by which the neuron determines myofiber types, controls other aspects of myofiber metabolism and prevents atrophy. Relatively greater impairment of trophic factor than excitatory factor would be expected to cause more myofiber atrophy than weakness, and greater deficiency of trophic factor from one type of α-motor neuron would result in preferential atrophy (or hypotrophy if a congenital disorder) of one myofiber type, ie type atrophy. Type I atrophy is seen in experimental tenotomy[22] and in myotonic dystrophy.[23, 24] Type II atrophy is seen in cachectic atrophy, disuse atrophy, and corticosteroid-induced atrophy[11, 23, 25, 26] wherein the atrophy is judged to be greater than weakness, suggesting selective impairment of the trophic factor, possibly due to insufficiency of the soma. It appears that Type II myofibers are more dependent on the neural trophic factor(s), at least in animals, because in total denervation of adult, or newborn, animals there is preferential atrophy[22, 27, 28] or hypotrophy[29, 30] of Type II myofibers. It is possible that Type II atrophy of cachexia and disuse is caused by mild trophic factor deficiency of all motor neurons, to which the Type II myofibers are more susceptible, or perhaps less likely, a greater impairment of trophic factor release from Type II neurons. In Type II atrophy, excitatory and inhibitory factors and axon conduction velocity seem relatively unimpaired.

Three *inhibitory factors* are postulated. One is the hypothetic influence that prevents innervated myofibers from showing fibrillations, which are characteristic of denervated myofibers. Another hypothetic factor is postulated as preventing normally innervated myofibers from showing myotonia, its absence being postulated to result in myotonia. A third hypothetic inhibitory factor prevents the normally innervated myofiber from accepting more than the one nerve ending. This apparently can be blocked by locally applied botulinum toxin.[31]

When *all neural factors* to the myofibers are removed together, we expect the muscle to show initially more weakness than atrophy, and later atrophy would catch up to equal weakness. This phenomenon is seen in experimental total denervation and seems to occur in ALS and other LMN disorders (motor neuropathies) of humans.

The loci at which neural factors are generated are mostly unknown, though ACh seems to be synthesized at the extreme distal tip of the axon by cholineacetylase. Whether schwann cells contribute any aspect of the LMN factors remains to be studied.

3. Factors of muscle related to the LMN: An *inhibitory factor* is postulated to explain the negative feedback message that stops axonal growth when the motor neuron reaches the muscle fibers it is to innervate. A *taxic factor* seems to attract motor neurons to muscle.

4. Factor of the LMN related to schwann cells: A *trophic factor* is postulated, the absence of which results in degeneration of the myelin segments of schwann cells when wallerian degeneration follows cutting the axon proximally.

5. Factor of the schwann cell related to the LMN: A *trophic factor* seems to be required for normal axon function, because presumed schwann cell abnormalities (dysschwannian neuropathies) result in weakness and denervation atrophy of myofibers. Possibly the trophic influence reaches the axon at nodes of Ranvier where channels of myelin-free schwann cytoplasm rich in oxidative enzymes extend in to touch the axon (Fig. 3).[32-34]

6. Factor of the juxtasomal glia related to the LMN: A *trophic factor* is postulated, analogous to that proposed in the vestibular nucleus by Heydén.[35, 36]

7. Factors of the upper motor neuron, posterior root ganglia, and other afferents related to the LMNs: Short-term *inhibitory* and *excitatory factors* are those unknown transmitter substances acting on the LMN. Spasticity below the level of a spinal cord transection could be explained by loss of an *inhibitor factor*. *Trophic factors* of more long-term influence may also be postulated to play on the LMN from these various afferent neurons.

C. Definitions and Criteria

The present classification deals with human diseases of the lower motor neuron and the skeletal muscle cell (myofiber), for which the general terms *neuropathies* and *myopathies* respectively will be used (Fig. 3). Together they comprise the *neuromuscular diseases*, ie diseases of the motor unit.

A *myopathy* is defined as a disorder of skeletal muscle not secondary to lower motor neuron disease nor manifested as selective myofiber type atrophy. Muscle wasting manifested histochemically as type atrophy is placed in the "undetermined" category. Histologic criteria of a myopathy are not perfect. They include necrosis and phagocytosis of muscle fibers, regenerating muscle fibers, and increase of endomysial connective tissue around individual fibers in a not too severely involved muscle.[25, 37, 38] When these changes represent a "major" aspect of the pathology they are considered indicative of myopathy. The significance of other architectural changes in myofibers is more open to dispute.[22] Certainly not all architectural changes are "myopathic," eg target fibers are clearly indicative of a neuropathy.[39, 40] Abnormalities of myofiber diameter per se are not diagnostic. In terms of histologic and histochemical diagnosis of muscle tissue, the microscopic findings must stand alone. Electromyography (EMG) and serum "muscle enzymes" can be used to formulate the total-patient diagnosis but must not influence the tissue diagnosis. The EMG can provide diagnostic assistance. In diseases considered to be myopathic, typically there is decreased duration and amplitude of motor unit action potentials and an increased number (density) of potentials on maximal and even on minimal contraction. However, certain aspects of the "myopathic" EMG can also be seen in diseases affecting the very terminal portions of the axons randomly within a motor unit, such as recovery from botulism[41, 88] or "neuronitis distalis" (wherein "only terminal ramifications of the neuron are affected")[42] and so its presence in a difficult case cannot be accepted as final proof of a "myopathy." This possibility of a "pseudomyopathic" EMG must be borne in mind when considering interpretation of the "myopathic" EMG seen in central core disease, thyrotoxic "myopathy," corticosteroid-induced atrophy and the early stages of myotonic "dystrophy" (see below).

A *neuropathy* is a disorder of the lower motor neuron and causes neurogenic atrophy of muscle. Histochemically, typical neurogenic atrophy is manifest by small myofibers (of angular cross-sectional contour in minimally affected muscle and rounded contour in severe disease), often excessively dark with DPNH-dehydrogenase, and often with reduced phosphorylase staining. Both Type I and II myofibers are usually affected. Clumps of pyknotic muscle nuclei are present later in the disease. Target fibers[11, 38, 39] and type grouping of muscle fibers[23, 24] are also features of denervation diseases. It is often impossible in paraffin sections to distinguish denervation atrophy from Type I fiber atrophy or Type II fiber atrophy. In most diseases considered to be neuropathic, the EMG records increased duration and amplitude of individual motor unit potentials and decreased number of potentials on maximal contraction.[43] There are also spontaneous fasciculations and fibrillations. Motor nerve conduction velocity is decreased in some neuropathies, as discussed below.

A third category is for diseases in which *both myopathy and neuropathy* are judged to occur (Figs. 1A and B).

The fourth category is *undetermined*, for disorders of the motor unit which are not yet clearly defined as neuropathic or myopathic (Figs. 1A and B).

D. Myopathies

1. *Myopathies associated with and probably secondary to an abnormality outside the myofiber* represent the first category (Fig. 4). In most instances,

the etiology of the myopathy is known. It is not necessarily correct to call a myopathy "secondary" simply because it is part of a generalized disease process because an abnormality, such as an enzyme defect, could be "primary" in several cell types simultaneously.

The subcategories of the "probably secondary myopathies" represent all the basic disease processes: eg endocrine, metabolic, exogenous toxins, neoplastic, infectious and granulomatous, infiltrative, nutritional deficiency, traumatic, vascular (especially ischemic), electrolyte imbalance, immunologic and undetermined. Only a few will be commented upon. The endocrine disorder thyrotoxic "myopathy" shows atrophy but not typical myopathic changes by muscle histochemistry.[38] Serum "muscle enzymes" are not elevated, and distal abnormalities of motor axons have been shown.[242] It is a myopathy only on EMG evidence, which might instead be reflecting a type of subtle panneuropathy or an extremely distal neuropathy as discussed above and below. Focal distant neoplasia is often associated with Type II fiber atrophy (not yet identified as a myopathic phenomenon) and sometimes with polymyositis. Exogenous toxins include chloroquin,[44-46] plasmocid (experimentally),[47] vincristine (experimental animals),[48-50] triorthocresylphosphate (experimentally),[51] and possibly ethanol[52-54] and emetine (experimentally).[55] Curare, which causes a transient muscle weakness, can be considered a myotoxin since its action is attributed to binding to "receptor protein" on the myofiber side of the neuromuscular junction preventing acetylcholine binding and thereby blocking neuromuscular transmission.[56] Infectious and granulomatous conditions include not only the acute and sub-

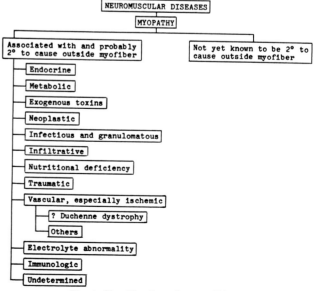

Fig. 4. Classification of myopathies.

acute parasitic (eg cysticercosis,[57]) bacterial, and viral infections, but also the possibility of a subacute or slow virus infection causing some forms of myofiber degeneration is raised by recent electron microscopic findings.[58-60] Two of the possibly viral cases had only minimal or no inflammatory reaction and a considerable number of multivacuolated fibers.[58, 59] Even more difficult to evaluate is another kind of nuclear inclusion in a congenital myopathy.[61] Nutritional deficiency often causes "cachectic atrophy," but since the myopathic versus neuropathic nature of that change is uncertain it is placed in the "undetermined" category. In humans, it is possible that a true vitamin E deficiency myopathy may occur rarely in intestinal malabsorption syndromes,[62] analogous to the well-established vitamin E deficiency myopathy of animals.

Traumatic myopathy includes changes due to gross injury and also slight injury by needle insertion into muscle for electromyographic[63] or injection purposes,[64] or the after-effect of contractures following multiple injections of medication.[65] Since myositis ossificans appears to be an abnormality localized in connective tissue, with any myofiber damage being secondary to the bone formation in muscle and later pressure or immobilization, or both, it is placed in the traumatic category. In myositis ossificans the myofiber changes are nonspecific while formation of bone in the muscle is very characteristic.

The vascular category includes not only the obvious infarctions and ischemias of recognized vascular disease and the anterior tibial syndrome,[66] but also Duchenne muscular dystrophy and "amyloid myopathy" if our two newly proposed ischemia hypotheses prove to be correct. One concerns the ischemia mechanism of small intramuscular blood vessels postulated to explain the typical grouped lesions of necrotic or regenerating fibers in Duchenne dystrophy,[11] based on the striking similarity of both early and late muscle lesions in Duchenne dystrophy to those in arterial-embolized rabbits.[67, 68] Carriers of Duchenne dystrophy, who often can be identified with blood creatine phosphokinase (CPK) assays[69, 70] and histochemistry of the muscle biopsy, facilitated by the recently used alkaline phosphatase technic[71] are also explicable by the ischemia hypothesis.[68] The second hypothesis was stimulated by a 26-year-old patient presenting as "limb-girdle myopathy" of five years' duration, typical clinically, electromyographically, histochemically and with prominently elevated serum "muscle" enzymes; yet the patient was found to have amyloid in the intramuscular blood vessels in two biopsies but not in skin, rectum, or gingiva. No evidence existed for the disorder being a secondary amyloidosis or collagen-vascular disease. An ischemia mechanism was postulated for this case of presumed primary amyloid myopathy.[72] If this conclusion is correct, the patient represents the first documented case, the neuromuscular involvement in other cases of primary amyloidosis being repeatedly shown to be neuropathic (see below). If the polymyositis of collagen-vascular disease is proved to be ischemic, as suggested by Banker and Victor,[73] it too would belong in the secondary vascular category. In ceramide trihexosidase deficiency (Fabry's disease), periodic acid shiff-positive deposits of presumed ceramide trihexosides are abundant in walls of intramuscular arterioles, venules, and capillaries and may account for the muscle pains and lack of endurance typical of this disease.[74]

An abnormal immunologic mechanism is sometimes postulated as the pathogenesis of polymyositis associated with collagen-vascular disease. If correct it would place this disorder in the secondary myopathy category, but since the mechanism remains unproved, it must stay in the "undetermined" category of myopathy. Experimental muscle atrophy,[75] sometimes with necrotic myofibers,[76] has resulted from attempts to produce experimental autoimmune polymyositis, but we are not convinced that the model sought was obtained. Recently an experimental myositis of the diaphragm was produced inadvertently following intraperitoneal injection of thymus extract[77] but it remains to be proved that it did not represent a local reaction to the injected material rather than a generalized phenomenon. Electrolyte imbalance could include the various types of secondary hypokalemic and hyperkalemic periodic paralyses, but review of the classification outlined by Engel[78] and presented here demonstrates that each is caused by abnormality of a specific tissue or exogenous toxin. Thus each is better classified in those categories.

(A) *Secondary hypokalemic periodic paralysis*
1. Thyrotoxic periodic paralysis
2. With urinary potassium wastage
   a. Hypertension, alkaline urine, metabolic alkalosis
      i—Primary aldosteronism (tumor)
      ii—"Congenital" aldosteronism (bilateral cortical hyperplasia)
      iii—Licorice intoxication (secondary aldosteronism)
      iv—Excessive thiazide therapy of hypertension
      v—Excessive mineralocorticoid therapy of Addison's disease
   b. Normotension, alkaline urine, metabolic alkalosis
      i—Hyperplasia of the juxtaglomerular apparatus with hyperaldosteronism
   c. Alkaline urine, metabolic acidosis
      i—Primary renal tubular acidosis

    ii—Fanconi syndrome
  d. Acid urine, metabolic acidosis
    i—Chronic ammonium chloride ingestion
    ii—Recovery phase of diabetic coma
  e. Miscellaneous
    i—Bilateral ureterocolostomies
    ii—Recovery phase of acute renal tubular
       necrosis
 3. With gastrointestinal potassium wastage
  a. Nontropical sprue
  b. Laxative abuse
  c. Pancreatic noninsulin secreting islet cell
     tumor with severe diarrhea
  d. Villous adenoma of the rectum
  e. Any severe or chronic diarrhea, fistula, intu-
     bation, or vomiting
(B) *Secondary hyperkalemic periodic paralysis*
 1. Renal failure—acute or chronic
 2. Adrenal failure

An example of a myopathy tentatively placed in the *"undetermined"* category of probably secondary myopathy is the one, diagnosed by serum enzyme[79] and muscle biopsy histochemical[80] criteria, recently found associated with acute exacerbations of psychosis, especially schizophrenia. The cause of this myopathy is not yet determined but is likely to be secondary and the same as the mechanism which produces the concomitant cerebral (mental) abnormality.

2. For the remaining myopathies, a cause outside the muscle cell has not yet been found, ie they are "not secondary" according to present knowledge. Because of our ignorance they remain idiopathic, but for most this certainly does not prove their cause is "primary" within the muscle cell. There are three major groups of the *myopathies not yet known to be*

secondary to a cause outside the myofiber: a) inflammatory myopathies, b) undetermined (27-Y00), and c) noninflammatory myopathies (Fig. 5).

  a. *Inflammatory myopathies* of this category are identified by polymorphonuclear or mononuclear inflammatory cells around or in blood vessel walls, or less certainly by inflammatory cells among muscle fibers but not in relation to necrotic fibers. (Inflammatory cells, including macrophages, in relation to necrotic fibers are seen in nearly all myopathies and are not indicative of "inflammatory" myopathy.) The diagnosis of inflammatory myopathy is based on quantitative evaluation of the inflammatory cell reactions, since other diseases such as Duchenne muscular dystrophy can have an occasional perivascular cellular reaction.[25, 67, 68] Recently we have been making the diagnosis of "probable myopathy of collagen-vascular disease" in the absence of inflammatory cells if the myofiber changes of atrophy, vacuolation, necrosis and regeneration are in the typical location at the periphery of muscle fascicles (perifascicular atrophy).[25] The inflammatory myopathies associated with the various *collagen-vascular diseases* (Fig. 5) may be secondary (perhaps to larger intramuscular vessel ischemia or an immune abnormality or both) but since that is uncertain they are put in the broad category of "not yet known to be secondary." Individual cases of *unclassified polymyositis* often are found eventually to be a form of collagen-vascular disease, while others remain unclassified or occasionally are related to another cause.

  b. In the *undetermined* category (Fig. 5), the *27-Y00* designation[7] is applied to patients with a definite myopathy, not known to be secondary, not clearly inflammatory, but not further classifiable. Histologically, the patients tend to fall into two

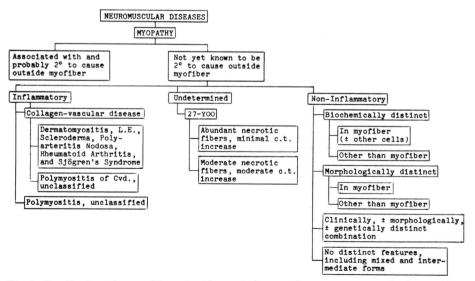

Fig. 5. Classification of myopathies not-yet-known-to-be-secondary to a cause outside the myofiber.

groups, 1) ones with abundant necrotic fibers and minimal connective tissue increase (cases with this characteristic, though not disease-specific, histologic changes have been termed "necrotizing myopathy" by Denny-Brown,[81, 82] some of which may be a form of collagen-vascular disease and some not and 2) others with moderate amounts of both necrotic fibers and connective tissue increase (in these individual patients it is difficult to distinguish between limb-girdle dystrophy and mild inflammatory myopathy, the answer often coming with time).

c. The *noninflammatory myopathies* of the not-yet-known-to-be-secondary category are subdivided into four groups (Fig. 5, Table I): 1) biochemically distinct, 2) morphologically distinct, 3) clinically ± morphologically ± genetically distinct combination and 4) no distinct features. The first two are further subdivided according to whether the distinctive features are in the myofiber or in another cell or fluid. The biochemically distinct ones in which a selective enzyme deficiency of the myofibers has been found are the ones most likely to remain as "primary" diseases of muscle, but conceivably even they could be

secondary to an abnormality of a nonmuscle cell. The others may or may not remain in this category.

1) *Biochemically distinct*, or *specific*, characteristics are defined as occurring only in one disease. Recently we have summarized the general principles of dividing biochemical abnormalities found in neuromuscular diseases regarding their *specificity for disease* into *specific*, *unusual*, and *nonspecific*.[83] Guidelines were also given for cross-indexing each biochemical abnormality according to its presumed *importance to cellular malfunction*, as either *important*, meaning that the defect is responsible directly or indirectly for cellular malfunction, or *unimportant*. Correction of a biochemical abnormality can be of therapeutic significance only if it is "important," regardless of whether it is specific, unusual, or nonspecific. Even when the clinical expression of a biochemical defect(s) is limited to one tissue in the neuromuscular system, such as the LMN or myofiber, it must be determined whether a more fundamental, and possibly more remediable, biochemical lesion might actually be originating in other cells to induce the neuromuscular abnormality. Eventually a "pri-

TABLE I
MYOPATHY, NOT YET KNOWN TO BE 2° TO CAUSE
OUTSIDE MYOFIBER, NONINFLAMMATORY

1) *Biochemically distinct*
   A. In myofiber (± other cells)
      I. Carbohydrate metabolism
         a. Amylophosphorylase deficiency—juvenile; late-onset
         b. Acid maltase deficiency—infantile acute; infantile chronic; adult
         c. Debranching enzyme deficiency
         d. Phosphofructokinase deficiency
         e. Phosphohexosisomerase malfunction
      II. TCA cycle, oxidative phosphorylation
         a. Very loosely coupled mitochondria with marked hypermetabolism
         b. Loosely coupled mitochondria with excess lactate production and normal metabolic rate
      III. Lipid metabolism
         a. Apparent inability to metabolize long-chain fatty acids
      IV. Reaction to electrolyte changes
         a. Glucose-insulin-worsened (acetazolamide-responsive, potassium-responsive) hypokalemic periodic paralysis
         b. Potassium-worsened (glucose-insulin-responsive, sodium-responsive, calcium-responsive) hyperkalemic periodic paralysis-paramyotonia congenita, adynamia episodica hereditaria
      V. Other
         a. Mucopolysaccharide storage disease
   B. In cell (or fluid) other than myofiber
2) *Morphologically-quantitatively distinct*
   A. In myofiber
         a. Rods -rod (nemaline) myopathy—childhood fatal; childhood chronic; late-onset
         b. Segmental loss of cross-striations
         c. Neoplasm (rhabdomyosarcoma)
   B. In cell other than myofiber
3) *Clinically, ± morphologically, ± genetically distinct combination*
         a. Facioscapulohumeral dystrophy
         b. Oculo (± cranio ± somatic) myopathy—with or without other abnormalities
         c. Congenital, morphologically nonspecific myopathy—moderately progressive; very slowly or nonprogressive (proximal limb; paraspinal contracture)
         d. Late distal myopathy
         e. Female sex-limited myopathy
         f. Myotonia congenita
         g. Idiopathic rhabdomyolysis (idiopathic myoglobinuria)
         h. Lipid storage in myofibers and cerebral neurons
4) *No distinct features (including mixed and intermediate forms)*
         a. Limb-girdle dystrophy—a "wastebasket," including cases of "female pseudohypertrophic dystrophy"

mary myopathy" will come to mean a proved inherited abnormality of the myofiber, presumably of the DNA, or RNA or any other subcellular component that may have independent inheritance. At the present time we are far from making this firm designation in any myopathy.

Myopathies with biochemically distinct abnormalities in myofibers are listed in Table I. Abnormalities in *carbohydrate metabolism* include a) juvenile[84-86] and late-onset[87, 88] amylophosphorylase deficiency; b) infantile acute,[89, 90] infantile chronic[91-93] and adult[94, 95] acid maltase deficiency; c) debranching enzyme deficiency (limit dextrinosis)[96-99]; d) phosphofructokinase deficiency[100, 101] and e) phosphohexosisomerase malfunction.[102] The recent demonstration of quantitatively and histochemically normal phosphorylase in the skeletal muscle of presumed carriers (the two parents of three affected sibs) of juvenile phosphorylase deficiency seems to exclude that method of carrier detection in the disease.[103] In *oxidative phosphorylation* defects there are a) very loosely coupled mitochondria with marked hypermetabolism[104] and b) loosely coupled mitochondria with excess lactate production and normal metabolic rate[11, 105] (eventually this may turn out to be only biochemically special and not perfectly distinct). Earlier described Swedish cases with excess lactate production, exercise-induced muscle pain, and myoglobinuria may also be in this group.[106] In *lipid metabolism* defects there seems to be one, the apparent inability to utilize long-chain fatty acids.[107] In ganglioside storage disease (Tay-Sach's disease), β-N-acetygalactosaminidase deficiency was detectable in skeletal muscle homogenates,[108] but we could not detect any accompanying muscle abnormality clinically or histochemically.[74] Regarding abnormal reactions of the myofibers to *electrolyte changes*, there are two basic types: a) glucose-insulin worsened (acetazolamide-responsive[3, 4] and potassium-responsive) hypokalemic periodic paralysis (thyrotoxic periodic paralysis is also glucose-insulin-worsened and potassium-benefited, but because it is secondary it is classified under the secondary myopathies), and b) the potassium-worsened (glucose-insulin-responsive, sodium-responsive, calcium-responsive) "hyperkalemic" periodic paralysis (encompassing adynamia episodica hereditaria and paramyotonia congenita[109-112] (Table I). What has been described as "normokalemic" periodic paralysis[113] may be a form of potassium-worsened hyperkalemic periodic paralysis. Myotonia congenita does not have weakness produced by potassium or glucose-insulin and so is not in this general category. In another group is the *mucopolysaccharide* storage disease of skeletal muscle and heart; the underlying enzymatic defect is not yet known but the stored substance has been characterized chemically as a peculiar heteropolysaccharide-protein complex or a

glycoprotein.[114, 115] It accumulates mainly in Type II myofibers. As yet there are no myopathies with a recognized biochemically distinct defect of *amino acid or protein metabolism*, but very likely some will be found.

Biochemically distinct abnormalities in a cell (or fluid) other than the myofiber, which might ordinarily be placed here occur in two multisystem diseases: a) IgG hypercatabolism[116, 117] of myotonic dystrophy, a disease which also has a special defect of hyperinsulinism without hypoglycemia[118, 119]; and b) IgA hyposynthesis of ataxia-telangiectasia, a disease which also has a special defect of hyperinsulinism without hypoglycemia, poor lymphocyte transformation response, and other immunologic abnormalities.[120-122] However, we consider that evidence is more in favor of myotonic dystrophy being a motor neuropathy than a myopathy (see dysneuronal neuropathy). Ataxia-telangiectasia is judged histochemically[38] to have an independent myopathic component in addition to a neuropathy. In a classification of myopathies, ataxia-telangiectasia would be in this biochemically distinct group (if its myopathy is not secondary), but in the present total neuromuscular classification it must be put in the combined "myopathy and neuropathy" group.

Examples of biochemical features nondistinct but unusual are: a) in myofiber—glycogen excess quantitatively; b) in cell (or fluid) other than myofiber—no blood lactate rise with exercise.[83] Examples of ones nondistinct and not even unusual are: a) in myofiber—reduced LDH-5[241]; b) in cell or fluid other than myofiber—increased serum CPK or SGOT.[83] These are all *false classifying features*.

2) The *morphologic element* in the classification (Fig. 5, Table I) provides a way of subdividing biochemically nondistinct patients. It is hoped that morphologic changes will provide insight into biochemical abnormalities. The morphologic element allows comparison of changes in a given subcellular organelle of one patient or disease with another and with experimental animal models. As in the biochemical element of this classification, numerous *disease controls* must be the basis upon which a change is considered "distinct" or "specific." Cautions regarding interpretation of morphologic changes as specific have been previously expressed.[123, 124] Often a morphologic change itself is not specific but is distinct in identifying a disease when present in "abundance" and is the major change, eg rods of rod myopathy.[124] The "morphologically distinct" term thus has a quantative aspect to it. Whether a morphologic change be specific, unusual, or nonspecific, one must not immediately conclude that it is necessarily primary or even a step in the pathogenesis.

Morphologically-quantitatively distinct features in myofibers are: a) rods, in rod (nemaline) myopathy with infantile fatal,[125] childhood fatal,[74] childhood chronic,[10, 126-132] and late-onset[133, 134] forms; b) segmental loss of cross-striations[25] and c) neoplastic changes of muscle cells (rhabdomyosarcoma), which are currently placed here though probably they will be found eventually to be secondary to exogenous carcinogens (eg virus, chemical, radiation). If central core disease is a myopathy it belongs here, but because it seems more likely to be caused by abnormal motor innervation,[10, 11, 123] we have classified it with the not-yet-known-to-be-secondary neuropathies. Numerous subsarcolemmal blebs and numerous single (or 2–3) vacuoles in centers of myofibers are features virtually distinctive of amylophosphorylase deficiency and hypokalemic periodic paralysis respectively, but each is better classified as biochemically distinct.

A *morphologically-quantitatively distinct feature in a cell other than the myofiber* is the acanthocyte. Acanthocytes occur in patients who lack β-lipoprotein (Bassen-Kornzweig disease[135]) and ones with normal plasma lipoproteins.[136-138] However, the former may have neuropathy,[135] while the latter usually have both myopathy and neuropathy and thus are classified in that dual category.

Morphologic features not distinct, but either unusual or nonspecific are *"false classifying features."* Examples of *unusual morphologic features* are a) "ragged red fibers"[25, 139] typically but not exclusively seen in oculo (± craniosomatic) myopathy and b) multiple vacuoles per fiber not in association with collagen-vascular disease are seen in occasional nonfamilial, moderately progressive myopathies of children and adults[58, 59, 74]; whether they indicate viral etiology[58, 59] is yet to be proved. Morphologic features within muscle fibers that are themselves *not qualitatively specific* regarding disease are rods,[123] cytoplasmic bodies,[10, 140] tubular aggregates,[11, 141, 142] large mitochondria with crystalline inclusions,[58, 143, 145] groups of mitochondria,[123, 143] honeycomb proliferation of T-tubules,[74, 124, 146-148] target fibers,[10, 39, 40] targetoid fibers,[10, 40] "moth-eaten" fibers by DPNH dehydrogenase reaction,[74] preferential loss of Z-band,[47] smearing of Z-band,[40, 55, 124] small fibers with single central nuclei on a given cross-section,[123] lakes of glycogen, vacuoles with lipoid/myelin figures ("spheromembranous degeneration"), myofibrillar rings (ring fibers) with or without sarcoplasmic masses, and neutral lipid droplets.

3) Some myopathies, not known to be secondary, lack distinct biochemical and morphologic features but have a *clinically, ± morphologically, ± genetically distinct combination* of features (Fig. 5, Table I). Myopathies of this category are listed in the table. A few will be commented upon. It is often difficult to use a genetic pattern as a classifying feature of individual cases because of problems with incomplete penetrance and the small size of human families.

The X-linked pseudohypertrophic dystrophy of Duchenne would be placed here if our opinion that it is secondary to small-vessel ischemia (see above) is not correct.[11, 67] In facioscapulohumeral (FSH) dystrophy, the biopsy typically has, in addition to rare necrotic and regenerating fibers, occasional small angular fibers excessively dark with the DPNH-dehydrogenase reaction that look like ones in denervation atrophy.[25] Whether the latter indicate a neuropathic element is uncertain. Cases alleged to be scapuloperoneal syndrome are often difficult to distinguish, if indeed they are different, from FSH dystrophy. Each case clinically identified as oculo (± cranio-somatic) neuromuscular disease (or fragment thereof) must be carefully studied to determine if it is myopathic, neurogenic, both, or indeterminate—it cannot be diagnosed as ocular "myopathy" on clinical evidence alone. Several myopathic forms of the oculo (± cranio-somatic) syndrome have been noted, eg a) with "ragged red" fibers in clinically normal limb muscles,[25, 139] b) with salt craving,[143] c) with salt craving, magnesium deficiency, juxtaglomerular hyperplasia, and central nervous system disease[149] and d) with retinal pigmentary degeneration, "cardiomyopathy," and sometimes with small stature (Kearn syndrome).[150] The elevated spinal fluid protein and occasional small, angular, DPNH-dehydrogenase-dark myofibers in biopsies of these patients raise the possibility of a concomitant LMN abnormality, but the evidence is not yet strong enough for them to be placed in the combined "Myopathy and Neuropathy" category. Congenital, morphologically nonspecific myopathies are of two general types: a) moderately progressive, and b) very slowly or nonprogressive.[123] The latter have some forms causing proximal limb weakness,[123] and others causing major contractures of paraspinal muscles.[151] Female sex-limited myopathy[152] and late distal myopathy[153] appear to be clinically-genetically distinct conditions. Myotonia congenita is in the clinically distinct category, the diagnosis being made after exclusion of other myotonic disorders, such as paramyotonia congenita (by ionic loading tests; see biochemically distinct myopathies) and myotonic dystrophy.[117] Idiopathic rhabdomyolysis (idiopathic myoglobinuria), after known causes are ruled out,[154] is a distinct clinical syndrome, but even among the currently idiopathic group several different causes probably will be found. Lipid storage in myofibers and cerebral neurons appears to be a clinically-morphologically distinct disorder.[25] In the clinically distinct syndrome of ophthalmoplegia-ataxia-parkinsonism-neuropathy-myopathy,[74, 155] myopathy and denervation are mixed and so the disorder is classified in the combined category.

4) Finally there are the *noninflammatory not-yet-known-to-be-secondary myopathies* with *no distinct features* (Fig. 5, Table I). So-called limb-girdle dystrophy is in this category, since that diagnosis is made by exclusion and serves as a "wastebasket." It includes most if not all cases that have been called female pseudohypertrophic dystrophy.

It may be mentioned that the word "dystrophy" was used in earlier times to denote noninflammatory diseases of muscle and applied to both hereditary ones, such as Duchenne dystrophy and myotonic dystrophy, and acquired ones, such as vitamin E deficient dystrophy of animals. Lack of a precise definition or usage of the word has led to its gradual abandonment except where retained in the names of four major hereditary conditions (Duchenne, FSH, myotonic, and limb-girdle dystrophies) for historic reasons only. "Myopathy" is now the general term used for diseases of muscle.

E. Neuropathies

1. The first category indicates those *neuropathies* clearly *associated with and probably secondary to abnormalities outside the neuron* itself (Fig. 6). They are divided into *dysschwannian* and *dysneuronal* ("*axonal degeneration*") neuropathies. The terms "dysschwannian" and "dysneuronal" only emphasize the major pathology; the distinction is useful but somewhat artificial because in certain disease states both types of involvement are seen histologically[156, 157] (Fig. 7).

a. *Dysschwannian neuropathies* are currently attributed to disorders of schwann cells, consequent to which neuron function is impaired. *Segmental demyelination* of peripheral nerves is their pathognomonic feature, initially without axonal disintegration. Dysschwannian neuropathies, in contrast to dysneuronal neuropathies, cause greater slowing of motor nerve conduction velocity than the degree of clinical muscle weakness would suggest. In a given patient, such electrical findings might be considered tentative evidence of a dysschwannian disorder if nerve histologic studies are not available. That segmental demyelination could be the result of axonal dysfunction due to loss of an essential axon-to-schwann-cell factor, and not vice versa as generally assumed, is a theoretic possibility which, if true, would necessitate rearrangement of this aspect of the classification. How schwann cell malfunction results in muscle atrophy is not known. Four possibilities are: a) it results in loss of schwann-cell-to-axon trophic factor which causes mild but progressive axon degeneration that is initially reversible; b) it simply impairs axonal conduction which diminishes release of neural trophic factor to muscle along with excitatory factor without initially or necessarily causing complete axonal death; c) impairment of axonal conduction results in sufficient muscle disuse to produce disuse atrophy (this mechanism is un-

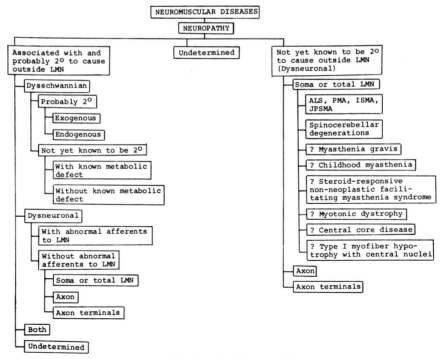

Fig. 6. Classification of neuropathies.

NEUROPATHIES

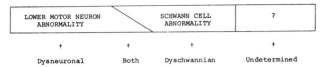

Fig. 7. Diagram demonstrating various degrees of overlap between dysneuronal and dysschwannian neuropathies.

likely since Type II atrophy is not typically seen in dysschwannian neuropathies) or d) the abnormal schwann cell releases a "toxin" that impairs neuronal function. The first mechanism is the most likely. Later or sooner after schwann cell malfunction, the axon dies.

The *dysschwannian neuropathies* are subdivided into 1) ones in which the schwann cell involvement is associated with and probably secondary to a cause outside the schwann cell and 2) ones not yet known to be secondary (Fig. 6).

1) *Probably secondary dysschwannian neuropathies* are then subdivided into a) *exogenous* ones, such as toxic (eg diphtheria,[158-163] buckthorn neuropathy[164]) and dysimmune (eg experimental allergic neuropathy[165, 166]) and b) *endogenous*, ie *endometabolic* (eg hyperphytanicacidemia or Refsum's disease on the basis of electron microscopic and motor conduction studies)[167] (Fig. 6). Experimentally and clinically, lead toxicity usually causes a dysschwannian degeneration.[168-170] Some might like to divide endogenous ones into those with prominent "hypertrophy" (schwann cell and collagen proliferations) and those without, but that is probably a false classifying factor.

2) Of the *dysschwannian neuropathies not yet known to be secondary*, some are associated with a *known metabolic defect within the schwann cell* (± other cells) (eg metachromatic leukodystrophy)[171, 172] and some are *not* (eg certain hypertrophic forms of peroneal muscular atrophy (Charcot-Marie-Tooth) syndrome,[157, 173] hypertrophic interstitial neuropathy of Dejerine and Sottas,[157, 174] acute idiopathic polyneuropathy with elevated spinal fluid protein (Landry-Guillain-Barré syndrome),[175] and idiopathic chronic or relapsing sensorimotor polyneuropathy with elevated CSF protein[157, 176]) (Fig. 6). Schwann cell neoplasms are also in this not-yet-known-to-be-secondary dysschwannian category now, though eventually they may be found to be secondary to exogenous viral, chemical or radiation carcinogens.

b. The *probably secondary dysneuronal neuropathies* are divided into two groups (Fig. 6). 1) Ones with *abnormal afferents to the lower motor neuron* represent a theoretical category; it seems probable that sufficient deafferentation could impair trophic or excitatory function or both of the LMN.

2) The *probably secondary, dysneuronal neuropathies without known abnormal afferents to the LMN* also have a presumed cause outside the lower motor neuron (Fig. 6). That cause operates on the LMN other than through schwann cells. The characteristic LMN pathology is axonal degeneration usually accompanied by wallerian degeneration (not segmental demyelination), and there is no or only very little slowing of motor nerve conduction time until weakness is rather severe.[177, 178] These neuropathies can be divided somewhat artificially (Fig. 6) into disorders of: a) *soma (cell body) or total LMN*, b) *axon* eg deficiency—thiamine[179]; exogenous toxin—arsenic,[157] triorthocresylphosphate,[180] isonicotinic acid hydrazide,[181, 182] acrylamide,[183] vincristine,[184] ethanol,[157] organophosphorus,[185] organomercury,[185] nitrofurantoin[186]; endometabolic—porphyria[187] which is possibly due to an "endotoxin"; *etc.* and c) *axon terminal*, eg botulinum toxin which blocks ACh release,[188] and hemicolinum which blocks ACh formation.[189, 190] (Parenthetically and without inferring the site of action, it may be mentioned that some antibiotics such as cholistin, neomycin, streptomycin, kanamycin and polymyxin also block neuromuscular transmission.[191]) In the *cell body or total LMN* category belong infection by poliomyelitis virus and possibly cases of ALS secondary to a distant neoplasm[192] or toxin (eg organic mercurials[193, 194]). Also belonging there would be the facilitating myasthenic syndrome (Lambert-Eaton-Rooke) accompanying a distant neoplasm[19, 195] if it is a soma or total LMD disorder (as the present author suspects), and myasthenia gravis if it is found to be secondary and a disorder of the soma or total LMN (see below). If "thyrotoxic myopathy" is actually a motor neuropathy, as suggested above on the basis of no absolute "myopathic" findings, then on the basis of normal nerve conduction velocities it is likely to be a dysneuronal neuropathy affecting distal axons (perhaps caused by a soma or total LMN abnormality). Morphologic abnormalities of distal axons have been demonstrated in "thyrotoxic myopathy."[242] This pathogenesis would be similar to our conception of myasthenia gravis and be in accord with the demonstrated worsening of myasthenia gravis by administered thyroid hormone.[243] It would also be in accord with the occasional case of "fasciculating thyrotoxic myopathy" observed by others. Since we are uncertain about most of these neuropathies, a separate category for "undetermined" is omitted. Actually, total LMN cannot be distinguished from selective damage of the soma—if there were a condition with selective somal damage, the axonal remainder of the neuron would in turn be affected too. In fact, all three anatomic distinctions may be invalid in some instances, since each could be a manifestation of metabolic abnormality in the soma, as autoradi-

ographic evidence suggests for acrylamide neuropathy which has prominent axonal damage.[196] Additional ways to classify the axonal degeneration neuropathies have been suggested.[156, 185]

c. Some probably secondary neuropathies have both segmental degeneration and wallerian degeneration in significant degrees, suggesting a *combined pathogenesis of dysschwannian and dysneuronal types respectively* (Fig. 7).

d. A final category of the probably *secondary neuropathies* is *undetermined*, for those unclassified diseases and individual cases (Fig. 6). These may be divided into toxic, deficiency, endometabolic, etc. For example, the few cases of α-lipoprotein deficiency (Tangier disease)[197, 198] are placed here since their neuropathy had not been well-analyzed histologically, although their normal nerve conduction velocities suggest they belong in the dysneuronal group.[197] So too some of the neuropathies with distant neoplasm have been thought to be axonal degeneration.[156]

2. In the second major category are neuropathies in which a cause outside the lower motor neuron has not yet been found (Fig. 6). They are, according to present knowledge, *neuropathies not yet known to be secondary*, ie they are *idiopathic*, but at least some might eventually be found secondary to causes outside the neuron. They are "dysneuronal" and, like the dysneuronal secondary neuropathies, show wallerian degeneration and essentially unimpaired motor nerve conduction times early in the disease.

A less important and possibly artificial distinction is division of the idiopathic neuropathies into three categories, depending on what is currently thought to be the major site in the LMN of the physiologic or morphologic defect, or both, viz *soma or total LMN*, *axon*, and *axon terminals* (Fig. 6). Since all are of uncertain cytopathologic locus, a separate category for "undetermined" is omitted.

Examples of idiopathic motor neuropathies seeming to be an *abnormality of the soma or total LMN* are: a) the so-called motor neuron diseases, such as amyotrophic lateral sclerosis (ALS), progressive muscular atrophy (PMA), infantile spinal muscular atrophy (ISMA),* and juvenile proximal spinal muscular atrophy (JPSMA) (ISMA and JPSMA may be two manifestations of one disease[199]), b) possibly the motor neuropathy we see by muscle biopsy histochemistry in virtually every patient with various types of spinocerebellar degeneration (axonal degeneration having been demonstrated in the Friedreich's ataxia subgroup[157]); and c) possibly myasthenia gravis. Myasthenia gravis belongs here if our concept,[18, 24, 200, 201] based on clinical, EMG and

muscle biopsy findings is correct that the disease is not just a neuromuscular junction disease but actually is caused by a soma or total lower motor neuron abnormality which is manifested at the neuromuscular junction as a decrease of excitatory factor and, to a lesser extent, of trophic factor. If the postulated LMN disorder of myasthenia gravis is in turn found to be secondary to an immunologic, thymic or metabolic abnormality, it will be moved to the "secondary" category. This hypothesis indicates that pathogenic abnormalities, such as collections of abnormal antibodies or lymphocytes, should be sought at the LMN soma in the spinal cord. One possible way to subclassify cases of myasthenia gravis would be according to response to various therapeutic agents, eg pyridostigmin, prednisone or ACTH. Two other disorders possibly belonging in the soma-or-total-LMN category are the childhood myasthenic syndrome responsive to long-term (three years) ACTH[204] followed by alternate-day prednisone,[74] as well as the steroid-responsive nonneoplastic facilitating myasthenic syndrome.[20]

In myotonic dystrophy, it is our opinion that available evidence is more suggestive of a motor neuropathy than a myopathy. Since there is no evidence that it is secondary to malfunction of schwann cells or other cells, it is placed in this dysneuronal category. It is possible that axon terminals are abnormal randomly in a motor unit, perhaps due to a mild LMN soma abnormality. Evidence favoring neuropathy is: a) no elevation of serum "muscle" enzymes; b) early histologic and histochemical changes of atrophy (usually Type I atrophy but sometimes mixed atrophy or Type II atrophy) with few or no necrotic or regenerating fibers and no increased endomysial connective tissue[205]; c) late histologic changes of atrophy with many pyknotic nuclear clumps and only a few necrotic fibers, resembling late denervation atrophy[205]; d) with methylene blue vital staining, early and significant abnormality of motor axon terminals on myofibers resembling those seen in neuropathic[206, 207] disease; e) elevated cerebrospinal fluid protein in some cases[208] (although this could be related to the brain degeneration seen in those cases). The EMG is "myopathic," but perhaps it is actually "pseudomyopathic"[211] due to a patchy axon terminal abnormality within motor units or "shrinkage" of entire units. Myotonia, an intrinsic phenomenon of muscle fibers firing repetitively when irritated, we postulate as possibly resulting from partial loss of neural control, ie loss of neural "inhibitory factor."

Central core disease has been postulated to be due to an abnormality of motor innervation, mainly because of the morphologic and histochemical similarity between central cores and target fibers, which are indicative of denervation[10, 11, 23, 39, 40, 123] and preference of both for Type I myofibers.[10, 11, 123]

---

* It has been speculated, on the basis of morphologic studies, that LMN involvment in ISMA may be secondary to glial abnormality of the anterior roots.[202] A familial form of arthrogryposis multiplex congenita attributed to spinal anterior root fibrosis may be of relevance.[203]

Although the EMG is "myopathic,"[132, 212] it might actually be "pseudomyopathic" on a neural basis.

"Type I fiber hypotrophy with central nuclei" seemed to be a distinct entity in two patients and was postulated to be due to defective neural influence.[11, 29, 30] A subsequently born sib of the first case[29] has recently been found to have the same condition (Dr. Karl Meyers, personal communication). A third case had the same condition.[213] Other cases with myofiber hypotrophy and central nuclei not so purely limited to Type I fibers[214-217, 233] are more difficult to name and classify, but perhaps they should be considered impure forms of somewhat similar pathogenesis. Other cases with single central nuclei (at a given cross-sectional level) in many fibers are even more difficult to classify[218] because of the lack of specificity of this finding.[67, 219]

Some of the idiopathic dysneuronal familial and nonfamilial "peripheral neuropathies," such as the neuronal type of peroneal muscular atrophy (Charcot-Marie-Tooth disease), relapsing degeneration of dorsal root ganglion cells, and progressive asymmetric degeneration of dorsal root ganglion cells,[157] are attributed to "axonal dysfunction." This cytopathologic localization may have to be changed if axonal malfunction is found eventually to be secondary to abnormal metabolism of the LMN soma as mentioned above.

Because the *axon terminal* has been implicated by some investigators as the site of abnormality in myasthenia gravis,[190, 220] that disease might be thought to fit into the classification as a currently idiopathic, dysneuronal neuropathy localized to the axon terminal. However, since we think myasthenia gravis is more likely a soma or total LMN disorder, it is tentatively so classified as noted above, as are other idiopathic myasthenic syndromes.

3. *Undetermined types of neuropathy.* The congenital oculocranial-somatic neuropathy (atypical Moebius syndrome) with pituitary hypogonadism may be placed here.[221]

The major process causing spasms in the syndrome of diphenylhydantoin-responsive continuous muscle spasms with myokymia, myotonia and hyperhydrosis[227-232] seems to be an abnormality of peripheral nerve.[228, 230, 232] Although one of our patients had present both neuropathy and active myopathy by histochemistry, neuropathy by EMG, and significantly elevated serum "muscle" enzymes, the myopathic changes were tentatively considered to have been caused by the severe muscle spasms because the elevated "muscle enzymes" and basal metabolic rate returned to normal when the muscle spasms were successfully treated with diphenylhydantoin.

Primary familial amyloidosis typically has a sensory-motor neuropathy with a more severe sensory component. It has mainly axonal degeneration.[222]

Whether the neuropathy results from a metabolic defect in the neuron or outside it or from pressure or ischemia caused by amyloid deposits in the nerves or vasonervorum is not yet established. Many cases called "hereditary sensory radiculoneuropathy"[223] are actually shown to contain significant amyloid deposits in nerves and dorsal root ganglia when carefully studied and thus are more correctly classified as primary familial amyloidosis. Possibly there is a true hereditary sensory radiculoneuropathy remaining after amyloidosis has been excluded.

Ceramide trihexosidase deficiency (Fabry's disease) is associated with a neuropathy, more subjective than objective and virtually entirely sensory.[74, 224, 225]

F. Myopathy and Neuropathy

Some patients with neuromuscular disease have definite histochemical evidence in the muscle biopsy of both a *neurogenic and a myopathic process* (Figs. 1A and B). Deciding between a double or single diagnosis can be difficult in a given case. It is arbitrary to state how many necrotic and regenerating fibers to allow in the biopsy of a neuropathy before adding myopathy to the diagnosis, or how many atrophic, angular fibers excessively dark with the DPNH dehydrogenase reaction to allow in a myopathy before adding the diagnosis of neuropathy. The same problems arise when interpreting EMG and serum enzyme findings prior to integrating them with histochemical results, as well as when attempting a synthesis of all studies of a patient.

Three conditions previously thought to have myopathy and neuropathy together require reconsideration and more cautious interpretation. First, although peroneal muscular atrophy (Charcot-Marie-Tooth disease) at one time was singled out as having both,[226] we now find that any chronic neuropathy with moderate to severe involvement of muscle may have occasional necrotic and regenerating fibers.[24, 37, 38] Second, the atrophic fibers in polymyositis of collagen-vascular disease are not necessarily indicative of an additional neuropathic process —they could be, but we do not know their actual significance. Occasional fibrillations by EMG are not a conclusive argument that the atrophic fibers of that area are denervated. Third, a distant neoplasm has been thought often to be associated with both neuropathy and myopathy in a given patient. Certainly either myopathy, especially polymyositis, or neuropathy can be associated with a distant neoplasm, but we are not convinced that all three occur together. In paraffin sections, additional denervation cannot be diagnosed until it has been distinguished by histochemistry of fresh-frozen sections from Type II atrophy, common in neoplasia. And additional myopathy cannot be diagnosed if there has been recent minor trauma to the site by EMG needles[63] or external force[64] prior to muscle biopsy, a factor to be considered in all chronic neuropathies, actually in all patients.

We have diagnosed both myopathy and neuropathy occurring in a given patient with these diseases: ataxia-telangiectasia, eight cases[74]; acanthocytosis with normal lipoproteins, four cases, two families[74, 136]; and the ophthalmoplegia-ataxia-parkinsonism-neuropathy-myopathy syndrome,[155] three cases.[74]

G. Neuromuscular Diseases, Undetermined Type

Some neuromuscular disorders which cannot yet be definitively categorized as neuropathic or myopathic remain "undetermined" (Figs. 1A and B and 8). These are subdivided into ones with 1) selective myofiber type involvement, 2) characteristic but not necessarily diagnostic clinical and muscle biopsy findings and 3) noncharacteristic, nondiagnostic muscle biopsy but typical clinical or EMG abnormalities or both.

1. Categories of undetermined type of neuromuscular diseases having selective myofiber type involvement are shown in Figure 8. (The total concept of selective vs nonselective muscle fiber involvement in all neuromuscular diseases is detailed elsewhere[11]). Type I myofibers are selectively involved in central core disease[10, 11, 123] and in Type I fiber hypotrophy with central nuclei.[11, 29, 30] Since each disease has been postulated to be due to

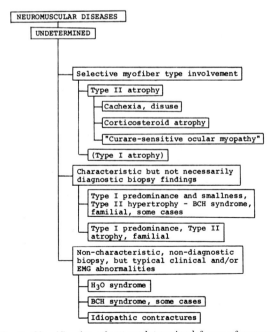

Fig. 8. Classification of yet undetermined forms of neuromuscular diseases.

an abnormality of motor innervation, they are both placed tentatively in the not-yet-known-to-be-secondary neuropathy category (see above).

Preferential atrophy of Type II myofibers (Type II atrophy) is the histochemical manifestation of cachectic and disuse atrophy, corticosteroid-induced atrophy, and is also seen in many myasthenia gravis patients, as well as in some other disorders.[11, 18, 23, 24, 196, 200] We think it is likely to be a reflection of LMN abnormality (see above). The corticosteroid-induced Type II atrophy of humans[11, 196] is associated with a "myopathic" EMG, but possibly that could be a "pseudomyopathic" EMG caused by subtle neurogenic trophic deficiency (see above) resulting in quantitatively smaller motor units more easily recruited during voluntary effort. Preferential atrophy of Type II fibers is seen in animals following acute total denervation.[22, 26, 28] "Curare-sensitive ocular neuromuscular disease" (we reject the original author's designation of "myopathy" and are concerned about the criteria for curare sensitivity) is placed here because of the uncertain nature of its pathogenesis[234, 235]; biopsies of the limb muscles show only Type II atrophy.[123]

The Type I fiber atrophy category does not have any clinical disorders in it at this time. Type I atrophy is often seen in myotonic dystrophy[23, 24, 140] but that disorder seems better as a possible dysneuronal neuropathy. Type I atrophy following tenotomy is an experimental condition.[22]

2. *Characteristic but not necessarily diagnostic biopsy findings* are seen in some cases of the benign congenital hypotonia (BCH) syndrome,[236] in the form of Type I fiber predominance and slight smallness, Type II fiber hypertrophy.[74, 123] Type I predominance with Type II "atrophy" (? hypotrophy) has been seen in four members of one family and two of another.[74] In the latter it accompanied a form of virtually nonprogressive chronic distal weakness, neuropathic by EMG.

3. The category with *noncharacteristic, nondiagnostic biopsy but typical clinical or EMG abnormalities or both* includes the H_3O syndrome (hypotonia, hypomentia, hypogonadism, obesity syndrome),[7, 123, 237, 238] wherein usually the muscle biopsy is normal histochemically. Whether hypotonia of this syndrome is secondary to a CNS disorder is not known. Some cases of the BCH syndrome have slight Type II fiber smallness. Idiopathic contractures of children, often congenital, have been reported in the hamstring[239] and quadriceps[240] muscles. This grouping must be considered tentative pending establishment of the cause of the contractures. Both neurogenic (eg infantile spinal muscular atrophy) and myopathic diseases can cause contractures. Injections of medication into the quadriceps of

infants must be remembered as one cause of contracture.[65] If the contractures affect several joints, the phenomenon is termed "arthrogryposis multiplex congenita," which also can be neurogenic or myopathic and is not a single disease entity.

H. Conclusion

A classification is not a fixed arrangement of diseases to be viewed simply as a thing to be memorized. Rather, it must be dynamic and considered a tentative pattern of grouping based on information currently available. It should be subjected to constant testing—each item in it must be challenged as to its placement and whether additional information can advance or change its location.

REFERENCES

1. DeVivo, D. C. and Engel, W. K.: Alternate-day glucocorticoid treatment of polymyositis. Unpublished observations.
2. McFarlin, D. E. and Griggs, R. C.: Treatment of inflammatory myopathies with azathioprine. *Trans. Amer. neurol. Ass.* **93**:244, 1968.
3. Resnick, J. S.; Engel, W. K.; Griggs, R. C. and Stam, A.: Acetazolamide prophylaxis in hypokalemic periodic paralysis. *New Engl. J. Med.* **278**:582, 1968.
4. Griggs, R. C.; Engel, W. K. and Resnick, J. S.: Acetazolamide therapy in hypokalemic periodic paralysis: Prevention of attacks and improvement of persistent weakness. *Ann. intern. Med.*, in press.
5. Austin, J. H.: Recurrent polyneuropathies and their corticosteroid treatment. *Brain* **81**:157, 1958.
6. DeVivo, D. C. and Engel, W. K.: Remarkable recovery of a steroid-responsive recurrent polyneuropathy. *J. Neurol. Neurosurg. Psychiat.* **33**:62, 1970.
7. Engel, W. K.: A clinical approach to the myopathies, in a symposium *Review of Current Concepts of Myopathies*, Vol. 39, ed. W. K. Engel. *Clinical Orthopaedics and Related Research*, Chap. 2, Philadelphia, 6, 1965.
8. Resnick, J. S.: Episodic muscle weakness, in a symposium *Review of Current Concepts of Myopathies*, Vol. 39, ed. W. K. Engel. *Clinical Orthopaedics and Related Research*, Chap. 5, Philadelphia, 63, 1965.
9. Dubowitz, V. and Pearse, A. G. E.: A comparative histochemical study of oxidative enzyme and phosphorylase activity in skeletal muscle. *Histochemie* **2**:105, 1960.
10. Engel, W. K.: The essentiality of histo- and cytochemical studies of skeletal muscle in the investigation of neuromuscular disease. *Neurology* **12**:778, 1962.
11. Engel, W. K.: Selective and non-selective susceptibility of muscle fiber types—A new approach to human neuromuscular disease. *Arch. Neurol.* **22**:97, 1970.
12. McPhedran, A. M.; Wuerker, R. B. and Henneman, E.: Properties of motor units in a homogenous red muscle (soleus) of the cat. *J. Neurophysiol.* **28**:71, 1965.
13. Wuerker, R. B.; McPhedran, A. M. and Henneman, E.: Properties of motor units in a heterogenous pale muscle (M. gastrocnemius) of the cat. *J. Neurophysiol.* **28**:85, 1965.
14. Burke, R. E.: Motor unit types of cat triceps surae muscle. *J. Physiol.* **193**:141, 1967.
15. Campa, J. F. and Engel, W. K.: Histochemistry of motor neurons and interneurons in the cat lumbar spinal cord. *Neurology* **20**:559, 1970.
16. Campa, J. F. and Engel, W. K.: Histochemical differentiation of motor neurons and interneurons in the anterior horn of the cat spinal cord. *Nature* **225**:748, 1970.
17. Campa, J. F. and Engel, W. K.: Histochemical classification of anterior horn neurons. *Neurology* **20**:386, 1970.
18. Engel, W. K.: Motor neuron disease, in *The Cellular and Molecular Basis of Neurologic Disease*, eds. G. M. Shy; E. S. Goldensohn and S. H. Appel. To be published.
19. Lambert E. H.; Eaton, L. M. and Rooke, E. D.: Defect of neuromuscular conduction associated with malignant neoplasms. *Amer. J. Physiol.* **187**:612, 1956.
20. Vroom, F. Q. and Engel, W. K.: Nonneoplastic steroid responsive Lambert-Eaton myasthenic syndrome. *Neurology* **19**:281, 1969.
21. Engel, W. K. and McFarlin, D. E.: Skeletal muscle pathology in myasthenia gravis—histochemical findings. *Ann. N. Y. Acad. Sci.* **135**:68, 1966.
22. Engel, W. K.; Brooke, M. H. and Nelson, P. G.: Histochemical studies of dennervated or tenotomized cat muscle. Illustrating difficulties in relating experimental animal conditions to human neuromuscular disease. *Ann. N. Y. Acad. Sci.* **138**:160, 1966.
23. Engel, W. K.: Histochemistry of neuromuscular disease—Significance of muscle fiber types. "Neuromuscular Diseases," in *Proceedings of the VIII International Congress of Neurology*, Excerpta Medica, vol. II, Amsterdam, 67, 1965.
24. Engel, W. K. and Brooke, M. H.: Muscle biopsy as a clinical diagnostic aid, in *Neurological Diagnostic Techniques*, ed. W. S. Fields. Charles C Thomas, Springfield, 90, 1966.
25. Engel, W. K.: Muscle biopsies in neuromuscular diseases. *Pediat. Clin. N. Amer.* **14**:963, 1967.
26. Pleasure, D. E.; Walsh, G. O. and Engel, W. K.: Atrophy of skeletal muscle in patients with Cushing's syndrome. *Arch. Neurol.* **22**:118, 1970.
27. Bajusz, E.: "Red" skeletal muscle fibers: relative independence of neural control. *Science* **145**:938, 1964.
28. Hogenhuis, L. A. H. and Engel, W. K.: Histochemistry and cytochemistry of experimentally denervated guinea pig muscle. I. *Acta Anat. (Basel)* **60**:39, 1965.
29. Engel, W. K.; Gold, G. N. and Karpati, G.: Type I fiber hypotrophy and central nuclei—A rare congenital muscle abnormality with a possible experimental mode. *Arch. Neurol.* **18**:435, 1968.
30. Engel, W. K. and Karpati, G.: Impaired skeletal muscle maturation following neonatal neurectomy. *Develop. Biol.* **17**:713, 1968.
31. Hofman, W. W.; Thesleff, S. and Zelena, J.: Innervation of botulinum poisoned skeletal muscles by accessory nerves. *J. Physiol.* **171**:27p, 1964.
32. Morgan-Hughes, J. A. and Engel, W. K.: Histochemical patterns in single peripheral nerve fibers. *Arch. Neurol.* **19**:613, 1968.
33. Morgan-Hughes, J. A. and Engel, W. K.: Structural and histochemical patterns in single peripheral nerve fibers. *Arch. Neurol.* **8**:438, 1963.
34. Williams, P. L. and Landon, D. N.: Paranodal apparatus of peripheral myelinated nerve fibers of mammals. *Nature* **198**:670, 1963.
35. Heyden, H.: RNA in brain cells, in *The Neurosciences*, eds. G. C. Quarton; T. Melnechuk and F. O. Schmitt. Rockefeller University Press, New York, 248, 1967.
36. Heyden, H.: Biochemical changes accompanying learning, in *The Neurosciences*, eds. G. C. Quarton; T. Melnechuk and F. O. Schmitt. Rockefeller University Press, New York, 765, 1967.
37. Engel, W. K.: Diseases of the neuromuscular junction and muscle, in *Neurohistochemistry*, ed. C. Adams. Elsevier Publishing Co., Amsterdam, 622, 1966.
38. Engel, W. K.: Muscle biopsy, in a symposium *Review of Current Concepts of Myopathies*, vol. 39, ed. W. R. Engel. *Clinical Orthopaedics and Related Research*, chap. 7, Philadelphia, 80, 1965.
39. Engel, W. K.: Muscle target fibers—a newly recognized sign of denervation. *Nature* **191**:389, 1961.
40. Resnick, J. S. and Engel, W. K.: Target fibers—structural and cytochemical characteristics and their relationship to neurogenic muscle disease and fiber types, in *Exploratory Concepts in Muscle Dystrophy and Related Disorders*, ed. A. T. Milhorat. Excerpta Medica Foundation, New York, 255, 1967.
41. Tyler, H. R.: Physiological observations in human botulism. *Arch. Neurol.* **9**:661, 1963.
42. Hausmanowej-Petrusewicz, I.; Jedrzejowska, H.; Kamieniecka, Z.; Niebrój-Dobosz, I.; Strugalska, M.; Rafalowska, J. and Fidziańska, A.: *Atlas Chorob Miesni (Atlas of Muscle Diseases)*. Polish Medical Publishers, Warsaw, 46, 1968.
43. Buchthal, F.: *An Introduction to Electromyography*. Scandinavian University Books, Oslo, 1957.
44. Whisnant, J. P.; Espinosa, R. E.; Kierland, R. R. and Lambert, E. H.: Chloroquine neuromyopathy. *Proc. Mayo Clin.* **38**:501, 1963.
45. Garcin, R.; Rondot, P. and Fardeau, M.: Note on the evolu-

tion of muscular lesions observed during a prolonged treatment by chloroquine after discontinuation of the drug. *Rev. neurol.* **118:**649, 1965.

46. Smith, B. and O'Grady, F.: Experimental chloroquine myopathy. *J. Neurol. Neurosurg. Psychiat.* **29:**255, 1966.
47. Price, H. M.; Pease, D. C. and Pearson, C. M.: Selective actin filament and Z-band degeneration induced by plasmocid. An electromicroscopic study. *Lab. Invest.* **11:**549, 1962.
48. Anderson, P. J.; Song, S. K. and Slotwiner, P.: The fine structure of spheromembranous degeneration of skeletal muscle induced by vincristine. *J. Neuropath. exp. Neurol.* **26:**15, 1967.
49. Slotwiner, P.; Song, S. K. and Anderson, P. J.: Spheromembranous degeneration of muscle induced by vincristine. *Arch. Neurol.* **15:**172, 1966.
50. Karpati, G.; Carpenter, S.; Clarke, J. T. R. and Wolfe, L. S.: Experimental vincristine myopathy (abstract). *J. Neuropath. exp. Neurol.* (in press).
51. Prineas, J.: Triorthocresyl phosphate myopathy. *Arch. Neurol.* **21:**150, 1969.
52. Ekbom, K.; Hed, R.; Kirstein, L. and Astrom, K. E.: Muscular affections in chronic alcoholism. *Arch. Neurol.* **10:**449, 1964.
53. Hed, C.; Lundmark, C.; Fahlgren, H. and Orell, S.: Acute muscular syndrome in chronic alcoholism. *Acta med. Scand.* **171:**585, 1962.
54. Perkoff, G. T.; Hardy, P. and Velez-Garcia, E.: Reversible acute innocular syndrome in chronic alcoholism. *New Engl. J. Med.* **274:**1277, 1966.
55. Engel, A. G.: Pathological reactions of the Z disk, in *Exploratory Concepts in Muscular Dystrophy and Related Disorders*, ed. A. T. Milhorat. Excerpta Medica Foundation, New York, 398, 1967.
56. Goodman, L. S. and Gilman, A.: *The Pharmacological Basis of Therapeutics.* The Macmillan Company, New York, 600, 1965.
57. Jacob, J. C. and Mathew, N. J.: Pseudohypertrophic myopathy in cysticercosis. *Neurology* **18:**767, 1968.
58. Chou, S. M.: Myxovirus-like structures in a case of human chronic polymyositis. *Science* **158:**1453, 1967.
59. Carpenter, S.; Karpati, G. and Wolfe, L. S.: Virus-like filaments and phospholipid accumulations in a case of chronic myopathy. *J. Neuropath. exp. Neurol.*, in press.
60. Chou, S. M. and Gutmann, L.: Picornavirus-like crystals in subacute polymyositis. *Neurology* **20:**205, 1970.
61. Jenis, E. H.; Linquist, R. R. and Lister, R. C.: New congenital myopathy with crystalline intranuclear inclusions. *Arch. Neurol.* **20:**281, 1969.
62. Blanc, W. A.; Reid, J. D. and Andersen, D. H.: Avitaminosis E in cystic fibrosis of the pancreas. A morphologic study of gastrointestinal and striated muscle. *Pediatrics* **22:**494, 1958.
63. Engel, W. K.: Focal myopathic changes produced by electromyographic and hypodermic needles ("needle myopathy"). *Arch. Neurol.* **16:**509, 1967.
64. Hathaway, P. W.; Dahl, D. S. and Engel, W. K.: Myopathic changes produced by local trauma. *Arch. Neurol.* **21:**355, 1969.
65. Norman, M. G.; Temple, A. R. and Murphy, J. V.: Infantile quadriceps contracture after intramuscular injections. *New Engl. J. Med.* **282:**964, 1970.
66. Mumenthaler, M.; Baasch, E. and Ulrich, J.: The tibialis anterior syndrome. Paralysis of the extensor muscles of the foot due to vascular causes. *Schweiz. Arch. Neurol. Psychiat.* **86:**137, 1960.
67. Hathaway, P. W.; Engel, W. K. and Zellweger, H.: Experimental myopathy after microarterial embolization. *Arch. Neurol.* **22:**365, 1970.
68. Engel, W. K.: Duchenne muscular dystrophy: A histologically based ischemia hypothesis compared with experimental ischemia myopathy, in *The Pathology of Muscle Disorders*, ed. C. F. Pearson. To be published.
69. Emery, A. E. H.: The use of serum creatine kinase for detecting carriers of Duchenne muscular dystrophy, in *Exploratory Concepts in Muscular Dystrophy and Related Disorders*, ed. A. T. Milhorat. Excerpta Medica Foundation, New York, 90, 1967.
70. Richterich, R.; Rosin, S.; Aebi, U. and Rossi, E.: Progressive

muscular dystrophy. V. The identification of the carrier state in the Duchenne type by serum creatine kinase determination. *Amer. J. hum. Genet.* **15:**133, 1963.
71. Engel, W. K. and Cunningham, G. G.: Alkaline phosphatase-positive abnormal muscle fibers of humans. *J. Histochem. Cytochem.* **18:**55, 1970.
72. Engel, W. K. and Hathaway, P. W.: Proximal myopathy with amyloid intramuscular blood vessels. To be published.
73. Banker, B. Q. and Victor, M.: Dermatomyositis (systemic angiopathy) of childhood. *Medicine* **45:**261, 1966.
74. Engel, W. K.: Unpublished observations.
75. Tal, C. and Liban, E.: Experimental production of muscular dystrophy-like lesions in rabbits and guinea-pigs by an autoimmune process. *Brit. J. exp. Path.* **43:**525, 1962.
76. Dawkins, R. L.: Experimental myositis associated with hypersensitivity to muscle. *J. Path. Bact.* **90:**619, 1965.
77. Goldstein, G.: The thymus and neuromuscular function. *Lancet* ii:119, 1968.
78. Engel, A. G.: Lecture at the American Academy of Neurology Spinal Courses, Chicago, May 1968. Unpublished.
79. Meltzer, H.: Creatine kinase and aldolase in serum: abnormality common to acute psychoses. *Science* **159:**1368, 1968.
80. Engel, W. K. and Meltzer, H.: Histochemical abnormalities of skeletal muscle in patients with acute psychoses. *Science* **168:**273, 1970.
81. Denny-Brown, D.: The nature of polymyositis and related muscular disease. *Trans. Coll. Phycns Philad.* **28:**14, 1960.
82. Adams, R. D.; Denny-Brown, D. and Pearson, C. M.: *Diseases of Muscle: A Study in Pathology.* Paul B. Hoeber, New York, 1962.
83. Engel, W. K. and Hatcher, M. A.: Evaluating significance of biochemical abnormalities in inherited neuromuscular disorders, in *Progress in Neuro-Genetics*, eds. A. Barbeau and J. R. Brunette. Excerpta Medica Foundation, Amsterdam, 17, 1969.
84. McArdle, B.: Myopathy due to a defect in muscle glycogen breakdown. *Clin. Sci.* **10:**13, 1951.
85. Pearson, C. M.; Rimer, D. G. and Mommaerts, W. F. H. M.: A metabolic myopathy due to absence of muscle phosphorylase. *Amer. J. Med.* **30:**502, 1961.
86. Schmid, R. and Mahler, R.: Chronic progressive myopathy with myoglobinuria: Demonstration of a glycogenolytic defect in the muscle. *J. clin. Invest.* **38:**2044, 1959.
87. Engel, W. K.; Eyerman, E. J. and Williams, H. E.: Late-onset type of skeletal muscle phosphorylase deficiency: A new familial variety with completely and partially affected subjects. *New Engl. J. Med.* **268:**135, 1963.
88. Peterson, I. and Broman, A. M.: EMG findings in a case of botulism. *Nord. Med.* **65:**259, 1961.
89. Hers, H. G.: Alpha-glucosidase deficiency in generalized glycogen storage disease (Pompe's disease). *Biochem. J.* **86:**11, 1963.
90. Hers, H. G.; Verhue, W. and Mathieu, M.: The mechanism of action of amylo-1,6-glucosidase, in *Control of Glycogen Metabolism*, eds. W. J. Whelan and M. P. Cameron. Ciba Foundation Symposium, J. & A. Churchill, Ltd., London, 165, 1964.
91. Zellweger, H.; Brown, B. I.; McCormick, W. F. and Tu, J. B.: A mild form of muscular glycogenosis in two brothers with alpha-1,4-glucosidase deficiency. *Ann. paediat. (Basel)* **205:**413, 1965.
92. Smith, H.; Amick, L. and Sidbury, J. B., Jr.: Glycogenosis Type II. Report of a case with 4 year survival and associated abnormal glycogen. *Amer. J. Dis. Child.* **111:**475, 1966.
93. Swaiman, K. F.; Kennedy, W. R. and Sauls, H. S.: Late infantile acid maltase deficiency. *Arch. Neurol.* **18:**642, 1968.
94. Engel, A. G. and Dale, A. J. D.: Autophagic glycogenosis of late onset with mitochondrial abnormalities: light and electron-microscopic observations. *Mayo Clinic Proc.* **43:**233, 1968.
95. Engel, A. G.; Seybold, M. E.; Lambert, E. H. and Gomez, M. R.: Acid maltase deficiency: Comparison of infantile, childhood, and adult types. *Neurology* **20:**382, 1970.
96. Sidbury, J. B., Jr.: The genetics of the glycogenoses affecting muscle, in *Exploratory Concepts in Muscular Dystrophy and Related Disorders*, ed. A. T. Milhorat. Excerpta Medica Foundation, New York, 83, 1967.
97. Cori, G. T.: Glycogen structure and enzyme deficiencies in glycogen storage disease. *Harvey Lect.* **48:**145, 1953.

98. Illingworth, B. and Brown, D. H.: Glycogen storage diseases, Types III, IV, and VI, in *Control of Glycogen Metabolism*, eds. W. J. Whelan and M. P. Cameron. Ciba Foundation Symposium, J. & A. Churchill, Ltd., London, 336, 1964.

99. Larner, J.: Glycogen storage disease, type V, in *Control of Glycogen Metabolism*, eds. W. J. Whelan and M. P. Cameron. Ciba Foundation Symposium, J. & A. Churchill, Ltd., London, 371, 1964.

100. Tarui, S.; Okuno, G.; Ikura, Y.; Tamaka, T.; Suda, M. and Nishikawa, M.: Phosphofructokinase deficiency in skeletal muscle. A new type of glycogenosis. *Biochem. biophys. Res. Commun.* 19:517, 1965.

101. Layzer, R. B.; Rowland, L. P. and Ranney, H. M.: Muscle phosphofructokinase deficiency. *Arch. Neurol.* 17:512, 1967.

102. Satoyoshi, E. and Kowa, H.: A myopathy due to glycolytic abnormality. *Arch. Neurol.* 17:248, 1967.

103. Hatcher, M. A.; Engel, W. K. and Derrer, E. C.: Unpublished observations.

104. Luft, R.; Ikkos, D.; Palmieri, G.; Ernster, L. and Afzelius, B.: A case of severe hypermetabolism of nonthyroid origin with defect in the maintenance of mitochondrial respiratory control: A correlated clinical, biochemical and morphological study. *J. clin. Invest.* 41:1776, 1962.

105. Van Wijngaarden, G. K.; Bethlem, J.; Meijer, A. E. F. H.; Hulsman, W. C. and Feltkamp, C. A.: Skeletal muscle disease with abnormal mitochondria. *Brain* 90:577, 1967.

106. Larsson, L. E.; Linderholm, H.; Müller, R.; Ringvist, T. and Sörnäs, R.: Hereditary metabolic myopathy with paroxysmal myoglobinuria due to abnormal glycolysis. *J. Neurol. Neurosurg. Psychiat.* 27:361, 1964.

107. Engel, W. K.; Vick, N. A.; Glueck, C. J. and Levy, R. I.: A skeletal muscle disorder associated with intermittent symptoms and a possible defect of lipid metabolism. *New Engl. J. Med.* 282:697, 1970.

108. Kolodny, E. H. and Brady, R. O.: Further studies on the elucidation of the enzymatic defect in Tay-Sachs disease. *Neurology* 20:388, 1970.

109. Gamstorp, I.: Adynamia episodica hereditaria and myotonia. *Acta Neurol. Scand.* 39:41, 1963.

110. Eulenburg, A.: A familial form of congenital paramyotonia followed through 6 generations. *Neurol. Cbl.* 5:265, 1886.

111. Drager, G. A.; Hammill, J. F. and Shy, G. M.: Paramyotonia congenita. *Arch. Neurol. Psychiat.* (Chic.) 80:1, 1958.

112. Engel, W. K.; Resnick, J. S. and Griggs, R. C.: Conference on hypokalemic periodic paralysis. To be published.

113. Poskanzer, D. C. and Kerr, D. N. S.: A third type of periodic paralysis with normokalemia and favorable response to sodium chloride. *Amer. J. Med.* 31:328, 1961.

114. Holmes, J. M.; Houghton, C. R. and Woolf, A. L.: A myopathy presenting in adult life with features suggestive of glycogen storage disease. *J. Neurol. Neurosurg. Psychiat.* 23:302, 1960.

115. Karpati, G.; Carpenter, S.; Wolfe, L. S. and Sherwin, A.: A peculiar polysaccharide accumulation in muscle in a case of cardioskeletal myopathy. *Neurology* 19:553, 1969.

116. Wochner, R. D.; Drews, G. A.; Strober, W. and Waldmann, T. A.: Accelerated breakdown of immunoglobulin G (IgG) in myotonic dystrophy. *J. clin. Invest.* 45:321, 1966.

117. Engel, W. K.; McFarlin, D. E.; Drews, G. and Wochner, R. D.: Protein abnormalities in neuromuscular disease. *J. Amer. med. Ass.* 195:754 and 837, 1966.

118. Huff, T. A.; Horton, E. S. and Lebovitz, H. E.: Abnormal insulin secretion in myotonic dystrophy. *New Engl. J. Med.* 277:837, 1967.

119. Gordon, P.; Griggs, R. C.; Nissley, S. P.; Roth, J. and Engel, W. K.: Studies of plasma insulin in myotonic dystrophy. *J. clin. Endocr.* 29:684, 1969.

120. McFarlin, D. E.; Strober, W.; Wochner, R. D. and Waldmann, T. A.: Immunoglobulin A production in ataxia telangiectasia. *Science* 150:1175, 1965.

121. McFarlin, D. E. and Oppenheim, J. J.: Impaired lymphocyte transformation in ataxia-telangiectasia in part due to a plasma inhibitory factor. *J. Immunol.* 103:1212, 1969.

122. McFarlin, D. E.; Strober, W.; Barlow, M. H. and Waldmann, T. A.: Immunological abnormalities in ataxia-telangiectasia. *Ass. Res. nerv. Dis. Proc.* (in Press).

123. Engel, W. K: A critique of congenital myopathies and other disorders, in *Exploratory Concepts in Muscular Dystrophy and Related Disorders*, ed. A. T. Milhorat. Excerpta Medica Foundation, New York, 27, 1967.

124. Fardeau, M.: Ultrastructural lesions observed in progressive muscular dystrophies: Critical study of their specificity, in *International Congress on Muscle Diseases*, eds. N. Canal and G. Scarlato. Excerpta Medica Foundation, Amsterdam, 9, 1969.

125. Shafiq, S. A.; Dubowitz, V.; Peterson, H. C. and Milhorat, A. T.: Nemaline myopathy: Report of a fatal case with histochemical and electron microscopic studies. *Brain* 90:817, 1967.

126. Conen, P. E.; Murphy, E. G. and Donohue, W. L.: Light and electron microscopic studies of myogranules in a child with hypotonia and muscle weakness. *Canad. med. Ass. J.* 89:983, 1963.

127. Shy, G. M.; Engel, W. K.; Somers, J. E. and Wanko, T.: Nemaline myopathy—A new congenital myopathy. *Brain* 86:793, 1963.

128. Engel, W. K.; Wanko, T. and Fenichel, G. M.: Nemaline myopathy, a second case. *Arch. Neurol.* 11:22, 1964.

129. Price, H. M.; Gordon, G. B.; Pearson, C. M.; Munsat, T. L. and Blumberg, J. M.: New evidence for excessive accumulation of Z-band material in nemaline myopathy. *Proc. nat. Acad. Sci.* (*Wash.*) 54:1398, 1965.

130. Engel, A. G. and Gomez, M. R.: Nemaline (Z-disk) myopathy: Observations on the origin, structure, and solubility properties of the nemaline structures. *J. Neuropath. exp. Neurol.* 26:601, 1967.

131. MacDonald, R. D. and Engel, A. G.: Structure and composition of nemaline rods: Evidence that they represent replicating Z-disk. *Neurology* 20:413, 1970.

132. Hausmanowej-Petrusewicz, I. *et al: Atlas Chorób Mięsni* (*Atlas of Muscle Diseases*), addendum Polish Medical Publishers, Warsaw, 1968.

133. Engel, W. K. and Resnick, J. S.: Late-onset rod myopathy —A newly recognized acquired and progressive disease. *Neurology* 16:308, 1966.

134. Engel, A. G.: Late-onset rod myopathy (a new syndrome?): light and electron microscopic observations in two cases. *Mayo Clin. Proc.* 41:713, 1966.

135. Schwartz, J. F.; Rowland, L. P.; Eder, H.; Marks, P. A.; Osserman, E. F.; Hirschberg, E. and Anderson, H.: Bassen-Kornzweig syndrome: Deficiency of serum β-lipoprotein. *Arch. Neurol.* 8:438, 1963.

136. Engel, W. K.: A discussion of an adult form of acanthocytosis by E. M. R. Critchley, D. B. Clark, and A. Wikler. *Trans. Amer. Neurol. Ass.* 92:135, 1967.

137. Critchley, E. M.; Clark, D. B. and Wikler, A.: An adult form of acanthocytosis. *Trans. Amer. neurol. Ass.* 92:132, 1967.

138. Engel, W. K. and Vick, N. A.: Unpublished observations.

139. Olson, W. H.; Engel, W. K. and Einaugler, R. B.: Morphologic changes of peripheral muscle in progressive disabilities of ocular motility. *J. Neuropath. exp. Neurol.* 29:150, 1970.

140. Engel, W. K. and Brooke, M. H.: Histochemistry of the myotonic disorders, in *Progressive Muskeldystrophie, Myotonie, Myasthenie*, ed. E. Kuhn. Springer-Verlag, Heidelberg, 203, 1966.

141. Engel, W. K.: Mitochondrial aggregates in muscle disease. *J. Histochem. Cytochem.* 12:46, 1964.

142. Engel, W. K.; Bishop, D. W. and Cunningham, G. G.: Tubular aggregates in Type II muscle fibers: Ultrastructural and histochemical. *J. Ultrastruct. Res.* 31:507, 1970.

143. Shy, G. M.; Gonatas, N. K. and Perez, M.: Two childhood myopathies with abnormal mitochondria. I. Megaconial myopathy. II. Pleconial myopathy. *Brain* 89:133, 1966.

144. Price, H. M.; Gordon, G. B.; Munsat, T. L. and Pearson, C. F.: Myopathy with atypical mitochondria in Type I skeletal muscle fibers. *J. Neuropath. exp. Neurol.* 26:475, 1967.

145. Zintz. R.: Dystrophishe Veränderungen in äusseren Augenmuskeln und Schultermuskeln bei der sog. Progressiven Graefeschen Ophthalmoplegie, in *Progressive Muskeldystrophie, Myotonie, Myasthenie*, ed. E. Kuhn. Springer-Verlag, Berlin, 109, 1966.

146. Engel, A. G. and MacDonald, R. D.: Ultrastructural reactions in muscle disease and their light microscopic correlates, in *Proceedings of the International Congress on Muscle Diseases*, eds. N. Canal and G. Scarlato. Excerpta Medica Foundation, Amsterdam, 8, 1969.

147. Margreth, A.: Personal communication, May 19, 1969.

148. Schotland, D. L.: An electron microscopic investigation of myotonic dystrophy. *J. Neuropath. exp. Neurol.* 29:241, 1970.

149. Pleasure, D. E. and Engel, W. K.: Unpublished observations.
150. Kearns, T. P.: External ophthalmoplegia, pigmentary degeneration of the retina and cardiomyopathy: a newly recognized syndrome. *Trans. Amer. ophthal. Soc.* **63**:559, 1966.
151. Dubowitz, V.: Some unusual neuromuscular disorders, in *International Congress on Muscle Diseases*, eds. N. Canal and G. Scarlato. Excerpta Medica Foundation, Amsterdam, 23, 1969.
152. Henson, T. E.; Muller, J. and DeMyer, W. E.: Hereditary myopathy limited to females. *Arch. Neurol.* **17**:238, 1967.
153. Welander, L.: Myopathia distalis tarda hereditaria. (Thesis). *Acta med. scand. Suppl. 265*, Stockholm, 1951.
154. Rowland, L. P.; Fahn, S.; Hirschberg, E. and Harter, D. H.: Myoglobinuria. *Arch Neurol.* **20**:537, 1964.
155. Stephens, J.; Hoover, M. L. and Denst, J.: On familial ataxia, neural amyotrophy, and their association with progressive external ophthalmoplegia. *Brain* **81**:556, 1958.
156. Woolf, A. L.: "Dying Back" of neuron in primary axonal degeneration, in *Motor Neuron Diseases*, eds. F. H. Norris, Jr. and L. T. Kurland. Grune and Stratton, Inc., New York, 386, 1968.
157. Dyck, P. J.; Gutrecht, J. A.; Karnes, W. E. and Dale, A. J. D.: Histologic and teased-fiber measurements of sural nerve in disorders of lower motor and primary sensory neurons. *Mayo Clin. Proc.* **43**:81, 1968.
158. McDonald, W. I.: The effects of experimental demyelination on conduction in peripheral nerve: A histochemical and electrophysiological study. I. Clinical and histological observations. *Brain* **86**:481, 1963.
159. McDonald, W. I.: The effects of experimental demyelination on conduction in peripheral nerve: A histologic and electrophysiological study. II. Electrophysiological observations. *Brain* **86**:501, 1963.
160. Webster, H.; Spiro, D.; Waksman, B. and Adams, R. D.: Phase and electron microscopic studies of experimental demyelination. II. Schwann cell changes in guinea pig sciatic nerves during experimental diphtheritic neuritis. *J. Neuropath. exp. Neurol.* **20**:5, 1961.
161. Thomas, P. K. and Lasalles, R. G.: The pathology of diabetic neuropathy. *Quart. J. Med.* **35**:489, 1966.
162. Cavanagh, J. B. and Jacobs, J. M.: Some quantitative aspects of diphtheritic neuropathy. *Brit. J. exp. Path.* **45**:309, 1964.
163. Morgan-Hughes, J. A.: Changes in motor nerve conduction velocity in diphtheritic polyneuritis. *Riv. Pat. nerv. ment.* **86**:253, 1965.
164. Calderon-Gonzalez, R. and Rizzi-Hernandez, H.: Buckthorn polyneuropathy. *New Engl. J. Med.* **277**:69, 1967.
165. Waksman, B. H. and Adams, R. D.: Allergic neuritis. *J. exp. Med.* **102**:213, 1955.
166. Cragg, B. G. and Thomas, P. K.: Changes in nerve conduction in experimental allergic neuritis. *J. Neurol. Neurosurg. Psychiat.* **27**:106, 1964.
167. Fardeau, M. and Engel, W. K.: Ultrastructural study of a peripheral nerve biopsy in Refsum's disease. *J. Neuropath. exp. Neurol.* **28**:278, 1969.
168. Gamboult, A.: Contribution a l'étude anatomique de la névrite parenchymateus subaique et chronique—Névrite segmentaire per-axile. *Arch. Neurol.* (*Paris*) **I**:11, 1880–1881.
169. Fullerton, P. M.: Chronic peripheral neuropathy produced by lead poisoning in guinea pigs. *J. Neuropath. exp. Neurol.* **25**:214, 1966.
170. Lawport, P. W. and Schochet, S. S.: Demyelination and remyelination in lead neuropathy. *J. Neuropath. exp. Neurol.* **27**:527, 1968.
171. Webster, H. D.: Schwann cell alterations in metachromatic leukodystrophy, preliminary phase and electron-microscopic observations. *J. Neuropath. exp. Neurol.* **21**:534, 1962.
172. Dayan, A. D.: Peripheral neuropathy of metachromatic leucodystrophy: Observations on segmental demyelination and remyelination and the ultracellular distribution of sulphatide. *J. Neurol. Neurosurg. Psychiat.* **30**:311, 1967.
173. Dyck, P. J. and Lambert, E. H.: Lower motor and primary sensory neuron diseases with peroneal muscular atrophy. I. Neurologic genetic and electrophysiologic findings in hereditary polyneuropathies. *Arch. Neurol.* **18**:603, 1968.
174. Dyck, P. J. and Gomez, M. R.: Segmental demyelination in Déjérine-Sottas disease: Light, phase-contrast and electron microscopic studies. *Mayo Clin. Proc.* **43**:280, 1968.

175. Wisniewski, H.; Terry, R. D.; Whitaker, J. N.; Cook, S. D. and Dowling, P. C.: Landry-Guillain-Barré syndrome. *Arch. Neurol.* **21**:269, 1969.
176. Thomas, P. K.; Lascelles, R. G.; Hallpike, J. F. and Hewer, R. L.: Recurrent and chronic relapsing Guillain-Barré polyneuritis. *Brain* **92**:589, 1969.
177. Lambert, E. H.: Electromyography in amyotrophic lateral sclerosis, in *Motor Neuron Diseases*, eds. F. H. Norris, Jr. and L. T. Kurland. Grune and Stratton, Inc., New York, 135, 1968.
178. Dyck, P. J. and Lambert, E. H.: Lower motor and primary sensory neuron diseases with peroneal muscular atrophy. II. Neurologic genetic and electrophysiologic findings in various neuronal degenerations. *Arch. Neurol.* **18**:619, 1968.
179. Swank, R. L.: Avian thiamin deficiency. A correlation of the pathology and clinical behavior. *J. exp. Med.* **71**:683, 1940.
180. Cavanagh, J. B.: Peripheral nerve changes in orthocresyl phosphate poisoning in the cat. *J. Path. Bact.* **87**:365, 1964.
181. Cavanagh, J. B.: On the pattern change in peripheral nerves produced by isoniazid intoxication in rats. *J. Neurol. Neurosurg. Psychiat.* **30**:26, 1967.
182. Schlaepfer, W. W. and Hager, H.: Ultrastructural studies of INH-induced neuropathy in rats. I. Early axonal changes. *Amer. J. Path.* **45**:423, 1963.
183. Fullerton, P. M. and Barnes, J. M.: Peripheral neuropathy in rats produced by acrylamide. *Brit. J. industr. Med.* **33**:210, 1966.
184. Gottschalk, P. G.; Dyck, P. J. and Kiely, J. M.: Vinca alkaloid neuropathy: Nerve biopsy studies in rats and in man. *Neurology* **18**:875, 1968.
185. Cavanagh, J. B.: Organo-phosphorus neurotoxicity and the "Dying Back" process, in *Motor Neuron Diseases*, eds. F. H. Norris, Jr. and L. T. Kurland. Grune and Stratton, Inc., New York, 292, 1968.
186. Cavanagh, J. B.: The significance of the "Dying Back" process in experimental and human neurological disease. *Int. Rev. exp. Pathol.* **3**:219, 1964.
187. Cavanagh, J. B. and Ridley, A. R.: The nature of the neuropathy complicating acute intermittant porphyuria. *Lancet* **ii**:1023, 1967.
188. Brooks, V. B.: An intracellular study of the action on repetitive nerve volleys and of botulinum toxin on miniature end-plate potentials. *J. Physiol.* **134**:264, 1956.
189. Hofmann, W. W.: The pharmacology of the hemicoliniums. *Ann. N. Y. Acad. Sci.* **135**:276, 1966.
190. Desmedt, J. E.: Presynaptic mechanisms in myasthenia gravis. *Ann. N. Y. Acad. Sci.* **135**:209, 1966.
191. Gold, G. N. and Richardson, A. P.: An unusual case of neuromuscular blockade seen with therapeutic blood levels of colistin methane-sulfonate (Coly-Mycin). *Amer. J. Med.* **41**:316, 1966.
192. Norris, F. H. and Engel, W. K.: Carcinomatous amyotrophic lateral sclerosis, in *The Remote Effects of Cancer on the Nervous System*, eds. L. Brain and F. Norris. Grune and Stratton, New York, 24, 1965.
193. Brown, I. A.: Chronic mercurialism; cause of clinical syndrome of amyotrophic lateral sclerosis. *Arch. Neurol. Psychiat.* (*Chic.*) **72**:674, 1954.
194. Kantarjian, A. A.: A syndrome clinically resembling amyotrophic lateral sclerosis following chronic mercurialism. *Neurology* **11**:639, 1961.
195. Elmqvist, D. and Lambert, E. H.: Detailed analysis of neuromuscular transmission in a patient with the myasthenic syndrome sometimes associated with bronchogenic carcinoma. *Mayo Clin. Proc.* **43**:689, 1968.
196. Pleasure, D. E.; Walsh, G. O. and Engel, W. K.: Atrophy of skeletal muscle in patients with Cushing's syndrome. *Arch. Neurol.* **22**:118, 1970.
197. Engel, W. K.; Dorman, J.; Levy, R. I. and Fredrickson, D. S.: Neuropathy in Tangier disease-α-lipoprotein deficiency manifesting as familial recurrent neuropathy and intestinal lipid storage. *Arch. Neurol.* **17**:1, 1967.
198. Kocen, R. S.; Lloyd, J. K.; Lascelles, P. T.; Fosbrooke, A. S. and Williams, D.: Familial α-lipoprotein deficiency (Tangier disease) with neurological abnormalities. *Lancet* **ii**:1341, 1967.
199. Hogenhuis, L. A. H. and Engel, W. K.: Early onset chronic motor neuropathies. Clinical and muscle histochemical studies in "Neuromuscular Disease," *Proc. of the VIII International Congress of Neurology* (*Vienna*)**I**:67, 1965.

200. Engel, W. K. and McFarlin, D. E.: Skeletal muscle pathology in myasthenia gravis—histochemical findings. *Ann. N. Y. Acad. Sci.* **135**:68, 1966.
201. Brody, I. A. and Engel, W. K.: Denervation of muscle in myasthenia gravis. *Arch. Neurol.* 11:350, 1964.
202. Chou, S. M. and Fakadej, A. V.: Ultrastructure of chromatolytic motorneurons in a case of Werdnig-Hoffman disease. *Neurology* 20:381, 1970.
203. Pena, C. E.; Miller, F.; Budzilovich, G. N. and Feigin, I.: Arthrogryposis multiplex congenita: Report of two cases of radicular type with familial incidence. *Neurology* 18:926, 1968.
204. Griggs, R. C.; McFarlin, D. E. and Engel, W. K.: Severe occult juvenile myasthenia gravis responsive to long-term corticosteroid therapy. *Trans. Amer. neurol. Ass.* 93:216, 1968.
205. Engel, W. K. and Brooke, M. H.: Histochemistry of the myotonic disorders, in *Progressive Muskeldystrophie, Myotonie, Myasthenie*, ed. E. Kuhn. Springer-Verlag, New York, 203, 1966.
206. Coers, C. and Woolf, A. L.: *The Innervation of Muscle.* Oxford University Press, London, 1959.
207. MacDermot, V.: The histology of the neuromuscular junction in dystrophica myotonica. *Brain* 84:75, 1961.
208. Refsum, S.; Engesest, A. and Lönnum, A.: Pneumonencephalographic changes in dystrophia myotonica. *Acta psychiat. scand.* 34:98, 1959.
209. Refsum, S.; Lonnum, A.; Sjaastad, O. and Engeset, A.: Dystrophia myotonica. Repeated pneumoencephalographic studies in ten patients. *Neurology* 17:345, 1967.
210. Rosman, N. P. and Rebeiz, J. J.: The cerebral defect and myopathy in myotonic dystrophy. *Neurology* 17:1106, 1967.
211. Engel, W. K.: A discussion of congenital myopathy with target fibers by D. L. Schotland. *Trans. Amer. Neurol. Ass.* 93:109, 1967.
212. Warmolts, J. R. and Engel, W. K.: A critique of the "myopathic" electromyogram. *Trans. Amer. neurol. Ass.* (in press).
213. Badurska, B.; Fidziańska, A.; Kamieniecka, Z.; Prot, J. and Strugalska, H.: Myotubular myopathy. *J. Neurol. Sci.* 8:563, 1969.
214. Bethlem, J.; VanWijngaarden, G. K.; Meijer, A. E. F. H. and Hülsmann, W. C.: Neuromuscular disease with type I fiber atrophy, central nuclei, and myotube-like structures. *Neurology* 19:705, 1969.
215. VanWijngaarden, G. K.; Fleury, P.; Bethlem, J. and Meijer, A. E. F. H.: Familial "myotubular" myopathy. *Neurology* 19:901, 1969.
216. Coleman, R. F.; Thompson, L. R.; Niehuis, A. W.; Munsat, T. L. and Pearson, C. M.: Histochemical investigation of "myotubular" myopathy. *Arch. Path.* 86:365, 1968.
217. Munsat, T. L.; Thompson, L. R. and Colman, R. F.: Centronuclear ("myotubular") myopathy. *Arch. Neurol.* 20:120, 1969.
218. Sher, J. H.; Rimalovski, A. B.; Athanassiades, T. J. and Arsonson, S. M.: Familial centronuclear myopathy: A clinical and pathological study. *Neurology* 17:727, 1967.
219. Resnick, M. and Engel, W. K.: Ultrastructural and histochemical correlation of experimental muscle regeneration. *J. Neurol. Sci.* (in press).
220. Thesleff, S.: Acetylcholine utilization in myasthenia gravis. *Ann. N. Y. Acad. Sci.* **135**:195, 1966.
221. Olson, W. H.; Bardin, C. W.; Walsh, G. O. and Engel, W. K.: Moebius syndrome: Motor neuron involvement and hypogonadotrophic hypogonadism. *Neurology*, in press.
222. Dyck, P. J. and Lambert, E. H.: Dissociated sensation in amyloidosis. *Arch. Neurol.* **20**:490, 1969.
223. Denny-Brown, D.: Hereditary sensory radicular neuropathy. *J. Neurol. Neurosurg. Psychiat.* 14:237, 1951.
224. Sweeley, C. C. and Klionsky, B.: Glyco-lipidosis: Fabry's disease, in *The Metabolic Basis of Inherited Disease*, eds. J. B. Stanbury, J. B. Wyngaarden and D. S. Fredrickson. McGraw-Hill, New York, 618, 1960.
225. Kocen, R. S. and Thomas, P. K.: Peripheral nerve involvement in Fabry's disease. *Arch. Neurol.* 22:81, 1970.
226. Haase, G. R. and Shy, G. M.: Pathological changes in muscle biopsies from patients with peroneal muscular atrophy. *Brain* 83:631, 1960.
227. Isaacs, H.: Syndrome of continuous muscle fiber activity. *J. Neurol. Neurosurg. Psychiat.* 24:319, 1961.
228. Isaacs, H.: Continuous muscle fiber activity in an Indian male with additional evidence of terminal motor fiber activity. *J. Neurol. Neurosurg. Psychiat.* 30:126, 1967.
229. Gamstorp, I. and Wohlfart, G.: A syndrome characterized by myokymia, myotonia, muscular wasting and increased perspiration. *Acta psychiat. scand.* 34:181, 1959.
230. Mertens, H. G.: Das Neuromyotonie-Syndrom, in *Progressive Muskeldystrophie Myotonie Myasthenie*, ed. E. Kuhn. Springer-Verlag, Berlin-Heidelberg, 295, 1966.
231. Greenhouse, A. H.; Bicknell, J. M.; Pesch, R. N. and Seelinger, D. F.: Myotonia, myokymia, hyperhidrosis, and wasting muscle. *Neurology* 17:263, 1967.
232. Wallis, W. E.; Plum, F. and Van Posnak, A.: Generalized muscular stiffness, fasciculations, and myokymia of peripheral nerve origin. *Arch. Neurol.* 22:430, 1970.
233. Spiro, A. J.; Shy, G. M. and Gonatas, N. K.: Myotubular myopathy. Persistence of fetal muscle in an adolescent boy. *Arch. Neurol.* 14:1, 1966.
234. Ross, R. T.: Ocular myopathy sensitive to curare. *Brain* 86:67, 1963.
235. Ross, R. T.: The effect of decamethonium on curare sensitivity ocular myopathy. *Neurology* 14:684, 1964.
236. Walton, J. N.: Amyotonia congenita: Follow-up study. *Lancet* i:1023, 1956.
237. Prader, A. A.; Labhart, A. and Willi, H.: Ein Syndróm von Adipositas, Kleinwuchs, Kryptorchismus und Oligophrenie nach myatonieartigem Zustand im Neugeborenenalter. *Schweiz. med. Wschr.* 86:1260, 1956.
238. Zellweger, H. U.; Smith, J. W. and Cusminsky, M.: Muscular hypotonia in infancy; diagnosis and differentiation. *Rev. Canad. Biol.* 21:599, 1962.
239. Petajan, J. H.; Momberger, G. L.; Aase, J. et al: Arthrogryposis syndrome (Kuskokwim disease) in the Eskimo. *J. Amer. med. Ass.* 209:1481, 1969.
240. Dubowitz, V.: "Pseudo" muscular dystrophy. Research in muscular dystrophy. *Proceedings of the Third Symposium.* J. B. Lippincott Co., Philadelphia, 57, 1965.
241. Brody, I. A.: The significance of lactate dehydrogenase isozymes in abnormal human skeletal muscle. *Neurology* 14:1091, 1964.
242. Woolf, A. L.: Pathological anatomy of the intramuscular nerve endings, in *Disorders of Voluntary Muscle*, ed. J. N. Walton, Little, Brown and Co., Boston, 203, 1969.
243. Engel, A. G.: Thyroid function and myasthenia gravis. *Arch. Neurol.* 4:663, 1961.

Biochemical Approaches to the Study of Muscle Disease*

J. B. PETER, M.D., Ph.D.

Several current approaches to the biochemistry of dystrophic muscle are reviewed with emphasis on the possible merits and limitations of each method. General difficulties in the study of diseased muscle apply more or less to each of the approaches. Data on dystrophic muscle obtained by technics developed for the study of normal muscle must be carefully assessed before reliable conclusions can be drawn.

Introduction

This paper will review some of the biochemical approaches of various investigators to the study of muscle diseases, especially dystrophy. The difficulties inherent in each of these approaches, which overlap considerably, will be emphasized. Particular attention will be paid to the muscular dystrophies because these are the most common diseases of muscle and have also been the most refractory to meaningful biochemical endeavors.

Biochemical Approaches

Table I outlines, in a probably incomplete and hopefully not offensive form, some common biochemical approaches to muscle disease. Indiscriminate assay of one or more enzymes is too often the approach of investigators with no particular interest in dystrophy who, at the urging of an interested clinician, will occasionally assay dystrophic muscle for the content and character of enzymes or isoenzymes of particular interest to themselves and too often of no apparent relevance to the problem of muscular dystrophy. On the other hand there may be much value in general surveys of the content of a variety of enzymes in dystrophic muscle by single research groups with sufficient resources or by cooperative studies of a number of laboratories using a well-defined protocol. Currently efforts are underway to organize such a cooperative group for the systematic examination of the enzymes of dystrophic muscle. A few studies have suggested some biochemical differences of muscle from Duchenne compared to adult dystrophy and also differences between

Peter—Associate Professor of Medicine, Department of Medicine, UCLA School of Medicine, Los Angeles.
* Supported in part by NIH grants HD02584, NS07587 and GM15759.

BIOGRAPHIC DATA

Dr. J. B. Peter was born in Omaha, Nebraska and educated at Creighton University, Saint Louis University School of Medicine and the University of Minnesota where he received B.S., M.D. and Ph.D. (biochemistry) degrees respectively. He is Associate Professor of Medicine at UCLA. His clinical and research interests center on neuromuscular and rheumatic diseases.

muscles of children with Duchenne dystrophy depending on the presence or absence of hypertrophy (formerly called pseudohypertrophy) of the calves.[1] As yet these studies provide no insight into the etiology or pathogenesis of dystrophy. Their significance is also dubious because similar changes have been reported in muscle from patients with Kugelberg-Welander disease,[2] a denervating process.

Approach No. II (Table I) should soon define as many defects of glycolysis or deficiencies of glycolytic or glycogenolytic enzymes in rare muscle diseases as are currently known for rare hemolytic anemias. This approach is worthy of further effort but seems unlikely to define an absolute deficiency of any glycolytic enzyme in Duchenne muscular dystrophy because rates of lactate production by such muscle are only moderately decreased when corrected to a reasonable reference base (cf below and references[3-5]). More recently a number of investiga-

Birth Defects: Original Article Series. Vol. VII, No. 2; February 1971

38

tors have begun detailed studies of nucleic acid metabolism and amino acid incorporation by dystrophic tissue.[6, 7] This approach is complicated by the spectrum of degeneration and regeneration in dystrophic muscle and by the infiltration of diseased tissue by mononuclear cells. Changes which have been reported[6] have not yet been shown to be pathognomonic of a dystrophic or myopathic process as opposed to a denervating disease.[7]

Long-suffering investigators have repeatedly attempted to grow in culture recognizable muscle from children with Duchenne dystrophy but to date these efforts have generally met the usual impasse which confronts those who try to culture mature muscle. Time lapse photography of recognizable muscle cultures from children with dystrophy has shown some suggestive differences, but the technics of culture of mature human skeletal muscle are not yet reliable.[8, 9] On the other hand, human fetal muscle can be readily grown in culture. Technics to detect Duchenne dystrophy *in utero* might allow culture of the dystrophic muscle at the time of spontaneous or therapeutic abortion. Much work is needed in this area.

Recently many tissue culture devotees (IV, Table I) have abandoned attempts to grow recognizable muscle in culture from biopsies of mature skeletal muscle and have been satisfied to grow fibroblasts in the hope that these less differentiated cells will also show the fundamental abnormalities which result in one or another type of muscle disease. There is much to recommend this approach as it has been extremely fruitful in defining enzyme deficiencies in a wide variety of heritable diseases. Nevertheless the devotees of this approach must recognize that if the fundamental defects in the muscular dystrophies involve components which are peculiar to differentiated cells (eg the contractile proteins of regulatory proteins of muscle) their efforts with fibroblasts are unlikely to be fruitful. On the other hand, the intellectual impairment of children with Duchenne dystrophy[11] might indicate that the fundamental abnormality is not restricted to muscle and might be detectable in fibroblasts. The merit of this approach is also supported by recent description of differences in the acid mucopolysaccharide content of cultured fibroblasts from the skin of patients with myotonic dystrophy,[10] a disease with abnormalities in several organ systems.

Investigators who fractionate skeletal muscle and study its components individually (V, Table I) recognize that this approach has been very fruitful in modern biochemistry. Study of individual reactions in tissue slices or homogenates is for these investigators too fraught with difficulty in interpretation of the results obtained in such complex systems. They must recognize however that muscle works by integrating its components into a working unit; it is pos-

TABLE I
BIOCHEMICAL APPROACHES TO THE STUDY OF MUSCULAR DYSTROPHY

I. Assay of a wide variety of enzymes.
II. Thorough study of important metabolic pathways in muscle (eg glycolysis).
III. Tissue culture of recognizable skeletal muscle.
IV. Tissue culture of fibroblasts from dystrophic patients.
V. Fractionate muscle and study its subcellular components individually.
VI. Other approaches.

sible that failure of such integration is the basis of one or more of the dystrophies. Unfortunately those who would divide and conquer have as yet no guidelines for design of experiments to define such failures of integration. Nevertheless, reliable technics are now available for fractionation of small samples of muscle into their subcellular components.[12, 23] This approach needs more devotees, because the number of subcellular systems worthy of careful examination is quite large. The incisiveness of this approach is illustrated by our recent studies of skeletal muscle mitochondria isolated from patients with Duchenne dystrophy. These clearly show that oxidative phosphorylation of the isolated mitochondria is entirely normal except when the disease is very far advanced.[25, 26] This contrasts with the conclusions of other investigators who made a most questionable extrapolation from findings with homogenates of dystrophic muscle and concluded that mitochondria were abnormal in Duchenne dystrophy.[27] In addition our recent studies show that oxidative phosphorylation with palmitoyl-L-carnitine as substrate is normal in skeletal muscle mitochondria in Duchenne dystrophy,[26] in contrast to predictions of several investigators studying this question in animal models of dystrophy by indirect technics.[28, 29]

Of necessity this outline of the biochemical approaches to muscle disease is incomplete. New approaches are badly needed.

General Problems in Biochemical Studies of Diseased Muscle

Table II lists a few of the most difficult problems of the investigator studying diseased muscle. Much of the early work on dystrophic muscle from humans and lower animals is relatively worthless because the activities of various enzymes or the concentrations of other components were referred to wet weight of the tissue. When dystrophy is advanced a significant portion of the wet weight of a "muscle" biopsy may be composed of adipose and connective tissue. The use of wet-weight tissue as a reference base under these circumstances is unreasonable and typically will result in values lower than normal, unless adi-

TABLE II

PROBLEMS IN BIOCHEMICAL STUDIES OF DISEASED MUSCLE

Abnormalities in Grossly Abnormal Tissue—the problem of a proper reference base

Abnormalities Common to Clinically and Genetically Distinct Diseases—the problem of the "fetal" state

The Aristotelian Approach: changes which occur early may be of causal or pathogenic significance—the problem of comparing technics of different accuracy, precision and sensitivity.

---

pose or connective tissue contains more of the substance than does normal muscle. This difficulty is in part circumvented by using noncollagenous nitrogen or noncollagenous protein nitrogen content of the tissue as the reference. With this correction activities or concentrations which were low when referred to wet-weight tissue will often fall within the normal range. No other reference base has found wide acceptance, but other independent references should be considered. For example, enzyme activities and metabolite concentrations might better be compared with the concentration or activity of something peculiar to muscle, eg myosin or actomyosin content or ATPase activity. There are, however, technical difficulties here if a sizable biopsy is required for determination of the reference base itself. Using actomyosin as a reference base we have recently demonstrated significant decreases in the troponin content of muscle in Duchenne dystrophy but not in a variety of other muscle or neuromuscular diseases.[13] The decreased content of troponin might explain the slowed contraction of Duchenne dystrophic muscle.

The choice of a reference base should be less crucial now that estimation of serum enzymes allows detection of Duchenne dystrophy in very early or even preclinical form, as well as detection of female carriers of the Duchenne dystrophic trait. The efforts of investigators studying the biochemistry of dystrophic muscle must be combined with those of clinicians who determine the serum enzymes as one basis for determining the genetic counseling to be given parents, female relatives and sisters of boys with Duchenne dystrophy. With such collaboration, biopsies from patients in the early stages of their disease should be possible. Our experience with hundreds of muscle biopsies at UCLA proves that two grams of quadriceps or gastrocnemius may be routinely removed from patients four to seven years old. There is essentially no risk of accelerating the patient's weakness if the biopsy is done by an experienced surgeon and if postoperative ambulation is delayed no more than 24 hours after the surgery. I wish to stress the lack of postbiopsy complications as it has been the dread of accelerating the weakness which has made

many investigators hesitate to biopsy early in Duchenne dystrophy. As emphasized below interpretation of the significance of any biochemical change in a biopsy of muscle with far-advanced dystrophy or any other muscle or neuromuscular disease is difficult at best, and in the presence of multiple biochemical changes the significance of any one abnormality cannot be assessed.

The investigator studying Duchenne muscular dystrophy (DMD) is also beset by the problem of the "fetal" state. "Fetal" state refers to the fact that among other abnormalities the pattern of isoenzymes in dystrophic muscle often resembles that of fetal rather than mature muscle.[14] The possible relevance of such a change in isoenzymes to the pathogenesis of DMD is not clear since similar changes are also found in denervated muscle.[14, 15] Nevertheless, despite the nonspecificity of the change the important question which may be relevant to the pathogenesis of DMD is whether the change in isoenzyme pattern in DMD is due to disappearance of certain isoenzymes characteristic of mature muscle with consequent reversion to a fetal pattern or whether the fetal pattern manifests a previous failure of dystrophic fibers to mature normally and receive their full complement of isoenzymes. Histochemical studies in early DMD indicate that such muscle does mature normally to the extent that at least two different types of fibers may be recognized by standard histochemical technics. This does not rule out the possibility that in one or more forms of human dystrophy there is a failure of maturation in certain components of muscle as has already been demonstrated for the inherited muscular dystrophy of chickens.[16]

A final problem in biochemical studies of diseased tissue is one which may result from an improper extrapolation from Aristotelian logic. This problem has its roots in the proper notion that those biochemical changes which occur first are more likely to be of causal or pathogenetic significance than those which are detectable only in far-advanced disease. Here there is no argument. The problem arises in trying to ascertain which changes occur first, because the technics employed to detect changes in muscle vary widely in their sensitivity, accuracy and precision. In addition, the diligence and care with which a given technic is applied may result in a smaller range of normal and hence an increased opportunity of detecting nonspecific deviations of diseased tissue from the normal. It should be obvious that detection of a given abnormality early in the course of muscular dystrophy is a necessary but hardly a sufficient reason for attributing to the abnormality any particular importance, much less a pathogenetic significance. However, when independent evidence suggests that the abnormality found might help explain changes known to occur early in the disease, then further studies are especially indicated. For example, muscle of children with Duchenne dystrophy or of mice with genetically determined muscular dystrophy is known to relax slowly.[17] Our knowledge of the mechanism of relaxation of muscle suggests a number of possible explanations for a delayed relaxation. Relaxation depends on the energy-dependent accumulation of calcium by the sarcoplasmic reticulum surrounding each myofibril. Recently the calcium-accumulating capacity of sarcotubular vesicles (fragmented sarcoplasmic reticulum) isolated from patients with Duchenne dystrophy and from dystrophic mice was noted to be decreased.[18-22] This abnormality was an important finding because it could help explain the delayed relaxation of muscle in these dystrophies. However, these and subsequent studies were hampered by the absence of a proper reference base. In this case the investigators found that the total amount of calcium which could be accumulated per milligram (mg) of protein in a given fraction, (sarcotubular vesicles) isolated by differential centrifugation from a homogenate of dystrophic muscle, was less than that which could be accumulated per mg protein of the "same" fraction isolated from normal muscle. The important, unsupported assumption here is that the fractions from both normal and dystrophic muscle contain the same ratio of sarcotubular vesicle protein/total protein. If, however, the dystrophic fraction contains more nonvesicle protein than does the fraction from normal muscle then the decreased capacity for calcium accumulation per mg protein in the dystrophic fraction may simply manifest contamination of the dystrophic fraction by nonvesicle protein and hence a lower total capacity for calcium accumulation per mg protein in the fraction, but not necessarily a lower total capacity per mg of actual sarcotubular vesicle protein. Examination of certain of the data[22] indicates that maximal rate of Ca^{++} uptake and total capacity for Ca^{++} uptake were both decreased to the same extent in studies of vesicles from patients with DMD. As explained above contamination of the dystrophic vesicle fraction by nonvesicle protein is a reasonable explanation of such changes. On the other hand, our studies show a significant abnormality in calcium affinity of sarcotubular vesicles in Duchenne dystrophy.[23] The affinity assay avoids the difficulties mentioned above because the total capacity for calcium accumulation per mg protein of a given fraction is first determined. Then the conditions for the calcium affinity assay are adjusted so that the initial ratio of Ca^{++}/mg protein is less than one-third of the total calcium-accumulating capacity. Under these conditions the apparent Michaelis constants for calcium transport are increased in vesicles isolated from children with Duchenne dystrophy. The abnormal Michaelis constants are largely independent of the actual amount of vesicle protein present, and the same abnormal Km's provide a reasonable explanation for the slowed relaxation of muscle in Duchenne dystrophy.[23, 24]

Summary

I have outlined a few of the biochemical approaches to the study and classification of muscle disease and have tried to stress difficulties which are peculiar to each of these approaches as well as some general problems in all such approaches. The investigator who wishes to study muscular dystrophies of humans must continually bear these and other considerations in mind. He must be able to analyze and, if necessary, to adapt basic biochemical technics which, although entirely satisfactory for study of normal muscle, may give misleading or ambiguous results if applied without further consideration to the study of diseased muscle.

REFERENCES

1. Heyck, H.; Laudahn, G. and Lüders, C. J.: Fermentaktivitätsbestimmungen in der gesunden menschlichen Muskulatur und bei Myopathien. II. Enzymaktivitätsveränderungen im Muskel bei Dystrophia musculorum progressiva. *Klin. Wschr.* **41**:500, 1963.
2. Heyck, H. and Laudahn, G.: Muscle and serum enzymes in muscular dystrophy and neurogenic muscular atrophy. A comparative study, in *Exploratory Concepts in Muscular Dystrophy and Related Disorders*, ed, A. T. Milhorat. International Congress Series No. 147 Excerpta Medica Foundation, Amsterdam, 232, 1967.
3. Pennington, R. J.: Biochemical aspects of muscular dystrophy in *Biochemical Aspects of Neurological Disorders*, eds, John N. Cumings and Michael Kremer. F. A. Davis Co., Philadelphia, 28, 1965.
4. Schapiro, G. and Dreyfus, J. D.: Biochemistry of progressive muscular dystrophy, in *Muscular Dystrophy in Man and Animals*, eds, G. H. Bourne and M. N. Golary. Hafner Publishing Co., New York, 48, 1963.
5. Peter, J. B.: Recent research in muscle and its diseases, in *Vistas in Connective Tissue Diseases*, ed, J. C. Bennett. Charles C Thomas, Springfield, 215, 1968.
6. Nihei, T. and Monckton, G.: Some aspects of ribosomal and nuclear activity in normal and dystrophic muscle, in *Progress in Neurogenetics*, eds, Andre Barbeau and Jean-Réal Burnette. Excerpta Medica Foundation, Amsterdam, 23, 1967.
7. Monckton, G.: Personal communication, 1969.
8. Kakulas, B. A.; Papadimitriou, J. M.; Knight, J. O. and Mastaglia, F. L.: Normal and abnormal human muscle in tissue culture. *Proceedings of the Australian Association of Neurology* **5**:79, 1968.
9. Kakulas, B.: Personal communication, 1969.
10. Swift, M. R. and Finegold, M. J.: Myotonic muscular dystrophy: abnormalities in fibroblast culture. *Science* **165**:294, 1969.
11. Prosser, E. J.; Murphy, E. G. and Thompson, M. W.: Intelligence and the gene for Duchenne's muscular dystrophy. *Arch. Dis. Childh.* **44**:221, 1969.
12. Peter J. B.: Studies of human skeletal muscle mitochondria. *Biochemical Medicine* **2**:179, 1968.
13. Furukawa, T. and Peter, J. B.: Troponin activity of skeletal muscle in muscular dystrophy and other myopathies. *Clin. Res.* XVIII:140, 1970.
14. Schapira, F.: Ontogenic evolution and pathologic modifications of multiple forms of lactate dehydrogenase, creatinekinase and aldolase, in *Homologous Enzymes and Biochemical Evolution*, eds, N. V. Thoai and J. Roche. Gordon and Breach, New York, 151, 1968.
15. Brody, I. A.: The significance of lactate dehydrogenase isozymes in abnormal human skeletal muscle. *Neurology (Minneap.)* **14**:1091, 1964.

16. Cosmos, E.: Ontongeny of red and white muscles. A study of the enzymic profile and the lipid distribution of immature and mature muscles of normal and dystrophic chickens, in *The Physiology and Biochemistry of Muscle as a Food II*, eds, E. J. Brishey and R. G. Cassens. The University of Wisconsin Press, Madison, in press, 1970.

17. Roe, R. D.; Yamaji, K. Y. and Sandow, A.: Contractile responses of dystrophic muscles of mouse and man, in *Exploratory Concepts in Muscular Dystrophy and Related Disorders*, ed, A. T. Milhorat. International Congress Series No. 147, Excerpta Medica Foundation, Amsterdam, 299, 1967.

18. Sugita, H.; Okimoto, K. and Ebashi, S.: Some observations on the microsome fraction of biopsied muscle from patients with muscular dystrophy. *Proc. Japan Acad.* **42**:295, 1966.

19. Sugita, H.; Okimoto, K.; Ebashi, S. and Okinaka, S.: Biochemical alterations in progressive muscular dystrophy with special reference to the sarcoplasmic reticulum, in *Exploratory Concepts in Muscular Dystrophy and Related Disorders*, ed, A. T. Milhorat. International Congress Series No. 147, Excerpta Medica Foundation, Amsterdam, 321, 1967.

20. Sreter, F. A.; Ikemoto, N. and Gergely, J.: Studies on the fragmented sarcoplasmic reticulum of normal and dystrophic mouse muscle, in *Exploratory Concepts in Muscular Dystrophy and Related Disorders*, ed, A. T. Milhorat. International Congress Series No. 147, Excerpta Medica Foundation, Amsterdam, 289, 1967.

21. Martonosi, A.: Sarcoplasmic reticulum, VI. Microsomal Ca^{++} transport in genetic muscular dystrophy of mice. *Proc. Soc. exp. Biol. (N.Y.)* **127**:824, 1968.

22. Samaha, F. J.; Gergely, J.: Biochemical abnormalities of the sarcoplasmic reticulum in muscular dystrophy. *New Engl. J. Med.* **280**:184, 1969.

23. Peter, J. B. and Worsfold, M.: Muscular dystrophy and other myopathies: Sarcotubular vesicles in early disease. *Biochemical Medicine* **2**:364, 1969.

24. Worsfold, M.; Peter, J. B. and Dunn, R. F.: Duchenne muscular dystrophy: distinctive biochemical and electron microscopic abnormalities of the sarcotubular vesicle fraction. International Congress on Muscle Diseases, Milan, Italy, In press, 1970.

25. Peter, J. B.; Stempel, K. and Armstrong, J.: Biochemistry and Electron Microscopy of Mitochondria in Muscular and Neuromuscular Diseases. Proceedings of the International Congress on Muscle Disease—Milan, Italy, 19–21 May, in press, 1970.

26. Peter, J. B.; Verhaag, D. and Stempel, K.; Fatty acid oxidation by mitochondria from normal and dystrophic skeletal muscle, in preparation, 1970.

27. Ionasescu, V.; Luca, N. and Vuia,O.: Respiratory control and oxidative phosphorylation in the dystrophic muscle. *Acta Neurologica Scandinavica*, **43**:564, 1967.

28. Lin, C. H.; Hudson, A. J. and Strickland, K. P.: Fatty Acid Metabolism in Dystrophic Muscle *In Vitro. Life Sciences*, **8**: 21, Part II, 1969.

29. Banker, B. Q.: A Phase and Electron Microscopic Study of Dystrophic Muscle. II. The Pathological Changes in the Newborn Bar Harbor 129 Dystrophic Mouse. *J. Neuropath. exp. Neurol.* **27**:183, 1968.

Glycogen Storage Diseases of Muscle*
Problems in Biochemical Genetics

LEWIS P. ROWLAND, M.D.; SALVATORE DIMAURO, M.D.
AND WILLIAM J. BANK, M.D.

The glycogen storage diseases of muscle are the only inherited diseases of muscle in which the biochemical abnormalities are known. Despite impressive advances in knowledge during the past decade there are vital gaps in understanding. In none of these diseases is treatment satisfactory. In none of these disorders can theory relate the symptoms of the disease (weakness, cramps, myoglobinuria) to the enzymatic defect. In several there are biochemical abnormalities that do not permit explanation in terms of the enzymatic defect. Individual patients and families do not fit into simple schemes of genetic and biochemical analysis. Different proteins have the same enzymatic activities in different organs, apparently under separate genetic control. One enzyme in particular, acid maltase, plays an uncertain role in the normal metabolism of glycogen; lack of this enzyme in the infantile Pompe's disease and myopathies of later onset are of uncertain significance. For these reasons, and others, there is much to be learned about these diseases we know best. About more common diseases like the muscular dystrophies, we know even less. It is one thing to deliver medical care and something else to have medical care to deliver.

Introduction

During the past decade, widespread application of biochemical technics has had a major impact on medicine and many new syndromes have been recognized. Out of the morass of all-inclusive designations, such as "cerebral palsy" and "mental retardation," have come precisely delineated biochemical syndromes, some with distinctive clinical features that were recognized only when the biochemical abnormality was understood. Implicit in this activity was the hope that recognition of an abnormal metabolite would be followed by identification of the missing enzyme, and then rational therapy could be devised. In the realm of muscle disease, we still

Rowland—Professor and Chairman, Department of Neurology,
Dimauro—Associate in Neurology,
Bank—Assistant Professor of Neurology,
The Neurological Clinical Research Center and Spiller Neurological Unit, Hospital of the University of Pennsylvania, Philadelphia.
* Supported by NIH Grant NB-08075 and a Grant from the Muscular Dystrophy Associations of America.

await some clue to the nature of the most common disorders, the muscular dystrophies. But there has been progress among a group of rare disorders in which glycogen metabolism is abnormal. The advances have been impressive, but it is useful to consider the problems that remain; a review of the problems would be helpful to focus attention upon what has yet to be done, but is especially pertinent now, in these days of diminishing support for medical research. If we are so limited in understanding and treating the diseases we know best, there is still a very long way to go for the more common disorders.

The missing enzyme has been identified in seven diseases in which glycogen accumulates in affected tissues.[1-4] Of these, four affect muscle. In Type II (Pompe's disease), the missing enzyme is amylo-1,4-glucosidase or acid maltase, a lysosomal enzyme. Glycogen accumulates in many tissues, but especially motor neurons, muscle and heart; the typical disease is fatal in the first year of life. (An atypical form will be discussed later.) In Type III, Cori's dis-

Birth Defects: Original Article Series. Vol. VII, No. 2; February 1971

43

tine phosphate would disappear, creatine and inorganic phosphate concentrations in the muscle would increase proportionately, and ATP would ultimately vanish. We tested this hypothesis in two patients. In one of them, there was no change in any of these metabolites in muscle obtained at the peak of contracture. In the other patient, there was a 50% decline in the concentration of creatine phosphate, with the expected increases in creatine and phosphate, but there was no change in the content of ATP.[27]

In explaining this deviation from expected results, we were forced to conclude that if the total muscle ATP did not change, there must have been depletion of the nucleotide in some local pool, such as the SR. There are other reasons to suspect this. In ultrastructural studies of muscle obtained during contracture, Schotland[19] found surprisingly little morphologic evidence of shortening of muscle. Apparently not all sarcomeres shorten completely, even during a vigorous and painful contracture. In one area, however, he found that the I-band had disappeared into the A-band and the Z-lines were thickened. Here, and here only, the SR was dilated. This is a nonspecific finding, encountered in many myopathic disorders not characterized by cramps, but the striking localization to shortened muscle in this case suggested that there might have been some structural injury. Physical injury, requiring repair, would also explain why the cramp does not recover clinically for an hour or longer; in one case the cramp persisted for 24 hours.[25] Results consistent with this view were obtained by Gruener *et al*[28] in a different kind of study of fibers from a patient lacking PPL. After removing the sarcolemma, these fibers first contracted and relaxed normally after exposure to calcium, but after several applications, relaxation was defective. If the muscle had been stimulated electrically prior to treatment with calcium, residual contractures were more apt to develop, even after the first application. Shortened fibers relaxed promptly in a solution containing ATP and a chelating agent that binds calcium. They suggested that calcium "reaccumulation by the SR becomes defective during vigorous exercise."

DiMauro, Bank and Rowland[31] recently studied this problem in another way. Calcium-binding by isolated SR fragments obtained from PPL-deficient muscle before and after contracture bound calcium, and there was only a slight decline in activity after contracture. In a lighter fraction of vesicles however, there was a marked increase in binding activity. This might be explained by physical disruption of the SR during the contracture, yielding lighter fragments after homogenization of the muscle. Since this was only a single experiment, however, it requires confirmation, and other tests of the biologic activity of SR need to be devised.

Energy for Muscular Work: It has long been known that muscular work is dependent upon its stores of glycogen to supply the energy for muscular work. In man, Hultman and his associates[20, 32, 33] have shown a direct proportionality between muscle glycogen content and capacity to work. Blood glucose and the free fatty acids of serum are also used by normal exercising muscle.[34, 35] The ability of patients lacking PPL and PFK to do any work at all implies that glycogen stores cannot be limiting for light work, but their inability to sustain heavy work, and particularly prolonged contractions, implies that under certain circumstances, muscle glycogen makes an essential contribution. The mechanisms that convert muscle metabolism from glycolysis to oxidation of fatty acids remain to be elucidated.

Relationship of Enzymatic Defect to Biochemical Abnormalities

Control of Glycogen Metabolism: It is not clear why glycogen accumulates in all these diseases, nor why the tissue concentrations are so much higher in some forms than others. For instance, although there is variation among patients with the same enzymatic abnormality, muscle glycogen concentrations in Pompe's disease are usually about ten times normal, whereas in PPL and PFK deficiency they are usually only four times normal. A complex control mechanism normally maintains muscle glycogen below 1 gm glycogen/100 gm muscle. In storage diseases the thermostat is set higher, but glycogen does not accumulate indefinitely in any of these conditions; there is an upper limit of concentration. In their remarkable studies of Scandinavian athletes, Bergstrom *et al*[32, 33] found that muscle glycogen could be depleted by strenuous skiing or cycling, and that after such exercise a diet high in carbohydrate led to replenishment in excess, the level approximating that in storage diseases (up to 4.7 gm glycogen/100 gm muscle in these normal subjects).

Little is known of the enzymatic controls that regulate glycogen concentration, but glycogen itself may regulate its own biosynthesis.[36] Increased concentrations of the polysaccharide are associated with decreased proportions of the active form of the biosynthetic enzyme, UDPG-glycogen transferase, and of increased proportions of the active form of the principal degradative enzyme, phosphorylase. It has not been possible to show this relationship in normal man, but in muscle excised from patients with storage diseases, DiMauro[27] found shifts in the anticipated direction. Yet there are undoubtedly other influences, and Piras[38] has shown the important effects of phosphorylated intermediates. Among these is glucose-6-phosphate, essential for the activity of the "dependent" form of the synthetase and a metabolite that accumulates in PFK deficiency because of the metabolic block. For this reason, the proportion of the "independent" form of the synthetase may not be decreased in PFK deficiency as it is in other storage diseases.[37, 39]

Acid Maltase: Amylo-1,4-glucosidase, the enzyme that is lacking in Pompe's disease was discovered by Hers in the search for an enzyme that might explain the accumulation of glycogen in this disease.[40] He found a hydrolase that was active at pH 4.0 and that sedimented with cell fragments otherwise identified as lysosomes.[41] This enzyme was lacking in Pompe's disease, and in the liver, the accumulated glycogen seemed to be largely confined to membrane-bound aggregates.[15] Thus was born the concept of lysosomal disease,[41] a concept now extended to storage diseases involving mucopolysaccharides and lipids.

But the concept has limitations. The role of acid maltase in the normal economy of glycogen metabolism is not clear. Moreover, there is a problem in the identification of two alternative pathways for the degradation of glycogen (the normal pathway through PPL, and the side path through acid maltase). If both are truly important, then blockade of either one should not lead to accumulation since the other pathway would be open. If, on the other hand, only the PPL pathway is practically effective, then loss of the maltase should have no impact. It is argued that PPL, a sarcoplasmic enzyme, cannot enter the lysosome and act on the enclosed glycogen. This might be a satisfactory explanation of Pompe's disease, but why then does acid maltase not compensate for lack of PPL or PFK?

DiMauro, Mellmann[43] and their associates have used skin fibroblasts grown in tissue culture to study glycogen metabolism in Pompe's disease. These cells normally contain the acid amylo-1,4-glucosidase and the enzyme is lacking in cells taken from affected individuals. Although the enzyme is lacking, the resting content of glycogen is not significantly higher than control cells. When grown in a medium containing large amounts of glucose, glycogen accumulates in the control cells and even more in the enzyme-deficient cells. But when glucose is withdrawn from the medium, the intracellular glycogen is degraded as rapidly and as completely in cells lacking the enzyme as in controls. It is conceivable that these dividing cells do not have time enough to store the polysaccharide, but it is clear that the glycogen is accessible to degradative enzymes.

There are other problems, too. In muscle, glycogen accumulates with little evidence of membrane-bound particles; there is little difference in the ultrastructure of Pompe's disease and McArdle's disease.[17, 18] In normal muscle, lysosomes are difficult to find and in Pompe's disease most of the glycogen particles are free. This does not, of course, refute the lysosomal concept, but makes it the more difficult to accept.

There have been few determinations of the activities of other lysosomal enzymes in tissues lacking acid maltase, but if lysosomes do accumulate, activity of other lysosomal enzymes might be increased.[44, 45] In preliminary studies we have found increased activities of acid phosphatase in muscle of a child with Pompe's disease. Platt and Platt[46] found increased activity of two other lysosomal enzymes (β-glucuronidase and β-acetylglucosaminidase), but they also found a marked deficiency of hyaluronidase.

It is clear that much remains to be done to elucidate the role of amylo-1,4-glucosidase. The enzyme has been lacking in every case of infantile Pompe's disease reported since Hers' original description; it must have something to do with the basic defect. Yet all these bothersome facts impede development of a coherent theory of the disease based upon the assumption that lack of acid maltase is the fundamental abnormality. The variety of clinical syndromes attributed to late onset acid maltase deficiency increases these doubts. Perhaps lack of this enzymatic activity is not the primary fault, but merely a consequence of the basic abnormality.

Amyl-1,6-glucosidase: This is the debrancher, the enzyme lacking in type III or Cori's disease. Phosphorylase attacks the outer branches of glycogen, peeling off one glucosyl unit at a time, until the branch is about five units long. There, presumably for steric reasons, phosphorylase can no longer act. A transferase then removes an oligosaccharide of four units, leaving one unit at the branch point that is split by amylo-1,6-glucosidase. These two activities 1-4,transferase and 1-6,glucosidase, have very different enzymatic requirements, yet the two activities have never been separated and it is not clear whether one or two enzyme proteins are involved.[47] This is important in human genetics, because Hers has described patients lacking one activity but not the other,[48, 49] implying that the two enzymes are distinct and different proteins. The assays for the two activities separately are still very difficult, requiring special substrates and open to multiple interpretations. One enzyme or two, it is difficult to understand why glycogen should accumulate in abnormal amounts. There may be an indigestible core but phosphorylase can attack the outer branches.

Unknown Defects: It seemed for a while that there would be a disease for each of the metabolic steps in glycogen metabolism, but this neat arrangement has been sullied by cases and families which do not fit. Many of these are liver glycogen diseases, but the muscular disorders have been involved, too. There have been cases of glycogen storage in which no enzymatic defect could be identified,[50-56] cases in which more than one enzyme seemed to be lacking[51, 57, 58] or in which glycogen structure seemed to be abnormal without enzymatic explanation,[59] and families in which one sib seemed to lack one enzyme while another sib was affected by quite a different deficiency.[60-62] There are cases in which some of the biochemical abnormalities suggested insufficiency of phosphoglucomutase[63] or phosphohexoseisomerase,[64] but in which the enzymatic defect was not proved. And there are cases which resemble PPL or PFK deficiency in one way or another, yet no defect of glycogen metabolism could be demonstrated.[65-69] Moreover, Engel *et al*[70] described a family apparently lacking muscle phosphorylase but with late onset of weakness, and no cramps or myoglobinuria, a syndrome so different from the others that a different genetic disorder must be suspected. In a family with central core disease phosphorylase was deficient in biochemical tests but normal histochemically.[71] Larner and Oliner[72] described a patient with late-onset myopathy, lacking debrancher. These aberrant cases are not easily dismissed on technical grounds. Moreover, in Pompe's disease a nonglycogen polysaccharide may accumulate and its relation to the fundamental abnormality is not known.[73]

The Flat Lactate Response: The simplest way to identify patients with PPL or PFK deficiency is the ischemic work test, devised by McArdle himself and the first clue that there might be an abnormality of glycogen metabolism in a human disease. When normal individuals exercise forearm muscles with a cuff occluding arterial circulation, there is a sharp increase in venous lactate content when the cuff is subsequently released. In patients lacking PPL or PFK this response is totally absent. There have been patients with other conditions whose lactate response was similar but who did not experience the cramp that ensues after ischemic work in patients with PPL and PFK deficiency. The flat response in these other patients has been taken to indicate some abnormality of glycogen metabolism, yet in none of these other conditions has a true abnormality been identified. Some of these abnormal lactate results may have been artifacts. Coleman *et al* described a patient whose response was clearly abnormal on one occasion yet normal on another.[74] Flat curves have been reported in thyrotoxic myopathy[75] and alcoholic myopathy.[76] We have been asked to study several patients whose test was abnormal in another center, but proved normal in ours. Since we have encountered anomalous results in some otherwise normal individuals, we have considered these abnormalities spurious, although lacking adequate explanation. In some cases, arterial occlusion may not be complete.

Genetic Heterogeneity

In PFK and PPL deficiency the clinical manifestations are reasonably constant, although there is variation in exercise tolerance. These syndromes are virtually identical clinically, however, and indicate

that biochemical identification is mandatory. Clinical identity does not preclude biochemical diversity.

The clinical patterns of Type III disease, due to lack of the debranching system, are not so clear, however. Most patients seemed to be affected by a liver disease, some with both liver and muscle disease, and some with muscle disease alone.[48] How often each form occurs, or why, has not been explained.

The problem of genetic heterogeneity, however, is most marked in relation to acid maltase deficiency. The clinical picture of the classical disease is uniform, and all patients have died by age one year. Recently, however, there have been reports of ten patients with a milder myopathy, starting later in childhood and extending into adult life.[77-84] These cases have been identified first by histologic evidence of glycogen accumulation, and then by biochemical analysis. In almost all of them, there was biochemically proven accumulation of glycogen and lack of the enzyme. It has been implied by almost all authors, or frankly stated, that these cases are merely variants of Pompe's disease, a milder form of the same genetic defect.

Despite the biochemical evidence, it is difficult to believe that Pompe's disease and late acid maltase deficiency are really the same disease. There has never been a family in which one sib had the typical infantile form and another the milder late form. Moreover, the two syndromes are clinically distinct, not only in severity. The heart and neurons are regularly affected in the infantile form, never in the late cases. The infantile form is constant in clinical manifestations. The late form varies so much even among the few cases reported, in age of onset, severity, and distribution of weakness, that more than one cause is implied. In one boy the clinical syndrome was that of Duchenne dystrophy[83]; in a girl, the picture was that of a relatively mild congenital myopathy.[82] One boy died at age ten years,[80] while in another patient weakness commenced in the fifth decade.[82, 84] The infantile form is clearly inherited as an autosomal recessive disease, and this kind of variation of mild and severe forms of a disease is more characteristic of dominantly inherited disorders. Taken with the dubious role of acid maltase in normal glycogen metabolism, it is difficult to believe that late acid maltase deficiency is really the same disease as the infantile form, or that these are merely different expressions of the same genetic fault. The glycogen accumulation in these late cases, and the lack of this enzymatic activity pose unanswered problems.

Isozymes and the Identification of Heterozygotes

In recent years, considerable attention has been given to proteins that differ in physical properties yet have the same enzymatic activities. Experience with PPL and PFK deficiency indicates that these distinctions may be of clinical importance. In both of these syndromes, only skeletal muscle may be affected, with no evidence of disorder of liver, heart, or brain, even though these tissues contain the same enzymatic activities. There are isozymes in these other tissues, and they can be identified directly,[84, 85] but the human disease implies that the enzymes in the other tissues are under separate genetic control. There is another form of PPL deficiency in which only liver is affected, muscle being spared. Because these isozymes indicate physical differences, it might be anticipated that genetic disease might arise from a mutant protein that lacked enzyme activity, but in both PPL[86] and PFK[12, 13] deficiency, the protein seems to be totally lacking.

The activity of isozymes can be used for both diagnostic and genetic studies. In Pompe's disease, enzymatic activity is lacking in leukocytes as well as muscle (and at autopsy in other tissues as well).[87, 88] Skin fibroblasts also lack the enzyme.[89, 90] In amylo-1,6-glucosidase deficiency the enzyme is lacking in erythrocytes and leukocytes, in most but not all cases.[90-102] Whether these differences imply genetic heterogeneity is not clear. In PPL deficiency of muscle, there is no abnormality of enzymatic activity of blood cells, but in the liver disease, enzymatic activity is also lacking in leukocytes.[102-105] In PFK deficiency of muscle, there is also decreased activity in erythrocytes, and immunological studies imply that the residual enzyme differs structurally from the normal erythrocyte enzyme.[106, 107]

Genetic studies of these accessible blood cells are not so clear. Because of inconsistencies in the activity of acid maltase in leukocytes from the heterozygote parents of patients with Pompe's disease, lymphocyte stimulation by phytohemagglutinin has been used to accentuate differences from normal.[108] The presence of the enzyme in amniotic fluid and cells permits detection of the disease *in utero*.[109] Because all these diseases seem to be inherited in autosomal recessive patterns,[110] because heterozygotes may not be identified readily or reliably, and because effective treatment seems elusive, termination of pregnancy may be the only way to control lethal forms of these diseases.

REFERENCES

1. *Carbohydrate Metabolism and Its Disorders*, eds, F. Dickens, P. J. Randle and W. J. Whelan, Academic Press, New York, 1968.
2. Hers, H. G.: Glycogen storage diseases. *Adv. Metab. Disord.* 1:2, 1964.
3. Field, R. A.: Glycogen deposition diseases. In *The Metabolic Basis of Inherited Disease*, eds, J. B. Stanbury, J. B. Wyngaarden and D. S. Fredrickson. McGraw-Hill, New York, 1966.
4. *Control of Glycogen Metabolism*, eds, W. J. Whelan and M. P. Cameron. Ciba Foundation Symposium, Little, Brown & Co., Boston, 1964.
5. Hug, G. and Schubert, W. K.: Lysosomes in type II glyco-
genosis. Changes during administration of extract from Aspergillus niger. *J. Cell. Biol.* 35:C1, 1967.
6. Lauer, R. M.; Mascarinas, T.; Racela, A. S. and Diehl, A. M.: Administration of a mixture of fungal glucosidases to a patient with type II glycogenosis (Pompe's disease). *Pediatrics* 20:672, 1968.
7. Schmid, R. and Mahler, R.: Chronic progressive myopathy with myoglobinuria. Demonstration of a glycogenolytic defect in the muscle. *J. clin. Invest.* 38:2044, 1959.
8. Pearson, C. M.; Rimer, D. G. and Mommaerts, W. F. H. M.: A metabolic myopathy due to absence of muscle phosphorylase. *Amer. J. Med.* 30:502, 1961.
9. Layzer, R. B.; Bank, W. J. and Rowland, L. P.: (Unpublished data).
10. Porte, D., Jr.; Crawford, D. W.; Jennings, D. B.: Alber, C. and McIllroy, M. B.: Cardiovascular and metabolic responses to exercise in a patient with McArdle's syndrome. *New Engl. J. Med.* 275:406, 1966.
11. Pernow, B. P.; Hause, R. J. and Jennings, D. B.: The second wind phenomenon in McArdle's syndrome. *Acta med. scand. Suppl.* 472:194, 1967.
12. Tarui, S.; Okuno, G.; Ikura, Y.; Tanaka, T.; Suda, M. and Nishikawa, M.: Phosphofructokinase deficiency in skeletal muscle. A new type of glycogenosis. *Biochem. biophys. Res. Commun.* 19:517, 1965.
13. Layzer, R. B.; Rowland, L. P. and Ranney, H. M.: Muscle phosphofructokinase deficiency. *Arch. Neurol.* 17:512, 1967.
14. Cardiff, R. D.: A histochemical and electron microscopic study of skeletal muscle in a case of Pompe's disease (glycogenosis II). *Pediatrics* 37:249, 1966.
15. Baudhuin, F.; Hers, H. G. and Loeb, H.: An electron microscopic and biochemical study of type II glycogenosis. *Lab. Invest.* 13:1140, 1964.
16. Sacerdoti, F. F.; DiMauro, S. and Dorbrilla, C. A.: Un case di glicogenosi tipo II (m. di Pompe). Studio clinico, morfologico e biochimico. *Acta paediat. lat.* 20:651, 1967.
17. Escourolle, R.; Berger, B. and Poirer, J.: Etude ultrastructurale d'une biopsie musculaire au cours d'une glycogénose type II. *Path. Europ.* 2:447, 1967.
18. Garancis, J. C.: Type II glycogenosis. Biochemical and electron microscopic study. *Amer. J. Med.* 44:289, 1968.
19. Schotland, D. L.; Spiro, D.; Rowland, L. P. and Carmel, P.: Ultrastructural studies of muscle in McArdle's disease. *J. Neuropath. exp. Neurol.* 24:629, 1965.
20. Hultman, E.: Studies on muscle metabolism of glycogen and active phosphate in man with special reference to exercise and diet. *Scand. J. clin. Lab. Invest.* Suppl. 44, Vol. 19, 1967.
21. Lowry, O. H.; Passoneau, J. R.; Hasselberger, F. X. and Schulz, D. W.: Effect of ischemia on known substrates and cofactors of the glycolytic pathway in brain. *J. biol. Chem.* 239:18, 1964.
22. Mancall, E. L.; Aponte, G. E. and Berry, R. G.: Pompe's disease (diffuse glycogenosis) with neuronal storage. *J. Neuropath. exp. Neurol.* 24:85, 1965.
23. Hogan, G. R.; Gutmann, L.; Schmidt, R. and Gilbert, E.: Pompe's disease. *Neurology* 19:894, 1969.
24. Resibois-Gregoire, A. and Dourov, N.: Electron microscopic study of a case of cerebral glycogenosis. *Acta neuropath.* 6:70, 1966.
25. Tobin, R. B. and Coleman, W. A.: A family study of phosphorylase deficiency in muscle. *Ann. intern. Med.* 62:313, 1965.
26. Rowland, L. P.; Lovelace, R. E.; Schotland, D. L.; Araki, S. and Carmel, P.: The clinical diagnosis of McArdle's disease. Identification of another family with deficiency of muscle phosphorylase. *Neurology* 16:93, 1966.
27. Rowland, L. P.; Araki, S. and Carmel, P.: Contracture in McArdle's disease. Stability of adenosine triphosphate during contracture in phosphorylase-deficient muscle. *Arch. Neurol.* 13:541, 1965.
28. Gruener, R.; McArdle, B.; Ryman, B. E. and Weller, R. O.: Contracture of phosphorylase-deficient muscle. *J. Neurol. Neurosurg. Psychiat.* 31:268, 1968.
29. Dorland, W. A. N.: *The American Illustrated Medical Dictionary*, W. B. Saunders Company, Philadelphia.
30. McArdle, B.: Myopathy due to a defect in muscle glycogen breakdown. *Clin. Sci.* 10:13, 1951.
31. DiMauro, S.; Bank, W. J. and Rowland, L. P.: Function of sarcoplasmic reticulum during contracture in phosphorylase-deficient muscle. (In preparation).
32. Hultman, E.: Physiological role of muscle glycogen in man.

with special reference to exercise. *Circulat. Res.* **20-21 (suppl. 1)**:99, 1967.

33. Bergstrom, J.; Hermansen, L.; Hultman, E. and Saltin, B.: Diet, muscle glycogen and physical performance. *Acta physiol. scand.* **171**:129, 1967.
34. Carlson, L. A.: Lipid metabolism and muscular work. *Fed. Proc.* **26**:1755, 1967.
35. Johnson, R. H.; Walton, J. L.; Krebs, H. A. and Williamson, D. H.: Metabolic fuels during and after severe exercise in athletes and non-athletes. *Lancet* **ii**:452, 1969.
36. Danforth, W. H.: Glycogen synthetase activity in skeletal muscle. Interconversion of two forms and control of glycogen synthesis. *J. biol. Chem.* **240**:588, 1966.
37. DiMauro, S. and Rowland, L. P.: Control of glycogen metabolism in human muscle: evidence from storage diseases. (In preparation).
38. Piras, R.; Rothman, L. B. and Cabib, E.: Regulation of muscle glycogen synthetase by metabolites. Differential effects on the I and D forms. *Biochemistry* **7**:56, 1968.
39. Okuno, G.; Kisukuri, S. and Nishikawa, M.: Activities of glycogen synthetase and UDPG-pyrophosphorylase in muscle of a patient with a new type of glycogenosis caused by phosphofructokinase deficiency. *Nature* **212**:1490, 1966.
40. Hers, H. G.: α-glucosidase deficiency in generalized glycogen storage disease (Pompe's disease). *Biochem. J.* **86**:11, 1963.
41. Hers, H. G.: Inborn lysosomal disease. *Gastroenterology* **48**:625, 1965.
42. Lejeune, N.; Thines-Sempoux, D. and Hers, H. G.: Tissue fractionation studies. Intracellular distribution and properties of α-glucosidases. *Biochem. J.* **86**:16, 1963.
43. DiMauro, S.; Mellman, W.; Oski, F. and Baker, L.: Glycogen and hexose metabolism in fibroblast cultures from galactosemic and glycogenosis type II patients. *Ped. Res.* **3**:368, 1969.
44. Öckerman, P. R.: Lysosomal enzymes in juvenile amaurotic idiocy. *Acta paediat. scand.* **57**:537, 1968.
45. Van Hoof, F. and Hers, H. G.: The abnormalities of lysosomal enzymes in mucopolysaccharidoses. *European J. Biochem.* **7**:34, 1968.
46. Platt, D. and Platt, M.: Glykogenose Typ II (Pompesche Krankheit) mit α-Amylase- und Hyaluronidase-mangel. *Dtsch. med. Wschr.* **94**:1414, 1969.
47. Nelson, T. E.; Kolb, E. and Larner, J.: Purification and properties of rabbit muscle amylo-1,6-glucosidase oligo-1,4-1,4-transferase. *Biochemistry* **8**:1419, 1969.
48. Van Hoof, F. and Hers, H. G.: The subgroups of type III of glycogenosis. *European J. Biochem.* **2**:265, 1967.
49. Hers, H. G.; Verhue, W. and van Hoof, F.: The determination of amylo-1,6-glucosidase. *European J. Biochem.* **2**:257, 1967.
50. Hers, H. G.: Future trends in the investigation of glycogen storage disease. *Israel J. med. Sci.* **1**:6, 1965.
51. Brown, B. I. and Brown, D. H.: Glycogen storage diseases: types I, III, IV, V, VII and unclassified glycogenosis. In *Carbohydrate Metabolism and Its Disorders*, eds, F. Dickens, P. J. Randle and W. J. Whelan. Academic Press, N. Y. 124, 1968.
52. Antopol, W.; Boas, E. P.; Levison, W. and Tuchman, L.: Cardiac hypertrophy caused by glycogen storage in a 15 year old boy. *Amer. Heart J.* **20**:546, 1940.
53. Holmes, J. M.; Houghton, C. R. and Woolf, A. L.: A myopathy presenting in adult life with features suggestive of glycogen storage disease. *J. Neurol. Neurosurg. Psychiat.* **23**:302, 1960.
54. Lehoczky, T.; Halassy, M.; Simon, G. and Harmos, G.: Skeletal muscle glycogenosis in identical twins. *J. Neurol. Sci.* **2**:366, 1965 and *Brit. med. J.* **2**:802, 1964.
55. DiSant Agnese, P. A.; Anderson, D. H. and Metcalf, K. M.: Glycogen storage disease of the muscles. *J. Pediat.* **61**:438, 1962.
56. Krivit, W.; Polgase, W. J.; Gunn, F. D. and Tyler, F. H.: Studies in disorders of muscle. IV. Glycogen storage disease primarily affecting skeletal muscle and clinically resembling amyotonia congenita. *Pediatrics* **12**:165, 1953.
57. Gutman, A.; Rachmilewitz, E. Z.; Stein, O.; Eliakim, M. and Stein, Y.: Glycogen storage disease: report of a case with generalized glycogenosis without demonstrable enzyme defect. *Israel J. med. Sci.* **1**:14, 1965.

58. Moses, S. W.; Levin, S.; Chayoth, R. and Steinitz, K.: Enzyme induction in a case of glycogen storage disease. *Pediatrics* **38**:111, 1966.
59. Smith, H. L.; Amick, L. D. and Sidbury, J. B., Jr.: Type II glycogenosis. Report of a case with four year survival and absence of acid maltase associated with an abnormal glycogen. *Amer. J. Dis. Child.* **111**:475, 1966.
60. Eberlein, W. R.; Illingworth, B. A. and Sidbury, J. B.: Heterogeneous glycogen storage disease in siblings and favorable response to synthetic androgen administration. *Amer. J. Med.* **33**:20, 1962.
61. Field, J. B. and Drash, H. L.: Studies in glycogen storage diseases II. Heterogeneity in the inheritance of glycogen storage diseases. *Trans. Ass. Amer. Phycns.* **80**:284, 1967.
62. Ozand, P.; Tokatli, M. and Amiri, S.: Biochemical investigation of an unusual case of glycogenosis. Deficient hepatic glucose-6-phosphatase and muscle amylo-1,6-glucosidase with severe myopathy. *J. Pediat.* **71**:225, 1967.
63. Thomson, W. H. S.; McLaurin, J. C. and Prineas, J. W.: Skeletal muscle glycogenosis: an investigation of two dissimilar cases. *J. Neurol. Neurosurg. Psychiat.* **26**:60, 1963.
64. Satoyashi, E. and Howa, H.: A myopathy due to glycolytic abnormality. *Arch. Neurol.* **17**:248, 1967.
65. Sltowiner, P.; Song, S. K. and Maker, H. S.: Myopathy resembling McArdle's syndrome. *Arch. Neurol.* **20**:586, 1969.
66. Brody, I. A.: Muscle contracture induced by exercise. A syndrome attributable to decreased relaxing factor. *New Engl. J. Med.* **281**:187, 1969.
67. Bethlem, J.; van Gool, J.; Hulsmann, W. C. and Meijer, A. E. F. H.: Familial nonprogressive myopathy with muscle cramps after exercise. A new disease associated with cores in muscle fibers. *Brain* **89**:569, 1966.
68. Rowland, L. P.; Fahn, S.; Hirschberg, E. and Harter, D. H.: Myoglobinuria. *Arch. Neurol.* **10**:537, 1964.
69. Larsson, L. E.; Linderholm, H.; Müller, R.; Ringqvist, T. and Somas, R.: Hereditary myopathy with paroxysmal myoglobinuria due to abnormal glycolysis. *J. Neurol. Neurosurg. Psychiat.* **27**:361, 1964.
70. Engel, W. K.; Eyerman, E. L. and Williams, H. E.: Late-onset type of skeletal muscle phosphorylase deficiency. A new familial variety with completely and partially affected subjects. *New Engl. J. Med.* **268**:135, 1963.
71. Engel, W. K.; Foster, J. B.; Hughes, B. P.; Huxley, H. E. and Mahler, R.: Central core disease. An investigation of a rare muscle cell abnormality. *Brain* **84**:167, 1960.
72. Larner, J.: Glycogen storage disease type V. In *Control of Glycogen Metabolism*, eds, W. J. Whelan and M. P. Cameron. Ciba Foundation Symposium. Little, Brown & Co., Boston, 1964.
73. Wolfe, H. J. and Cohen, R. B.: Nonglycogen polysaccharide storage in glycogenosis type II (Pompe's disease). *Arch. Path.* **86**:579, 1968.
74. Coleman, R. F.; Nienhuis, A. W.; Brown, W. J.; Munsat, T. L. and Pearson, C. M.: New myopathy with mitochondrial enzyme hyperactivity. *J. Amer. med. Ass.* **199**:624, 1967.
75. Araki, S; Terao, A.; Matsumoto, I.; Narazaki, T. and Kuroiwa, Y.: Muscle cramps in chronic thyrotoxic myopathy. *Arch. Neurol.* **19**: 315, 1968.
76. Perkoff, G. T.: Reversible acute muscular syndrome in chronic alcoholism. *New Engl. J. Med.* **274**:1277, 1966.
77. Courtecuisse, V.; Royer, P.; Habib, R.; Monnier, C. and Demos, J.: Glycogenose musculaire par deficit d'alpha 1,4-glucosidase simulant une dystrophie musculaire progressive. *Arch. franç. Pédiat.* **22**:1153, 1965.
78. Zellweger, H.; Brown, B. I.; McCormick, W. F. and Tu, J. B.: A mild form of muscular glycogenosis in two brothers with alpha 1,4-glucosidase deficiency. *Ann. paediat.* **205**:413, 1965.
79. Isch, R.; Juif, J. G.; Screz, R. and Thiebaut, F.: Glycogenose musculaire à forme myopathique par déficit en maltase acide. *Pédiatrie* **21**:71, 1966.
80. Smith, J.; Zellweger, H. and Affife, A. K.: Muscular form of glycogenosis type II (Pompe). Report of a case with unusual features. *Neurology* **17**:537, 1967.
81. Badoual, J.; Lestradet, J.; Wilde, J. L. and Ploussar, D.: Une forme atypique de glycogénosis par déficit en maltase acide. *Sem. Hôp. Paris* **43**:1427, 1967.
82. Hudgson, P.; Gardner-Medwin, D.; Warsfold, M.; Penning-

ton, R. J. T. and Walton, J. N.: Adult myopathy from glycogen storage disease due to acid maltase deficiency. *Brain* **91**:435, 1968.

83. Swaiman, K. F.; Kennedy, W. R. and Sauls, H. S.: Late infantile acid maltase deficiency. *Arch. Neurol.* **18**:642, 1968.

84. Engel, A. G. and Dale, A. J. D.: Autophagic glycogenosis of late onset with mitochondrial abnormalities: light and electron microscopic observations. *Mayo Clin. Proc.* **43**:233, 1968.

85. Layzer, R. B.; Rowland, L. P. and Bank, W. J.: Physical and kinetic properties of human phosphofructokinase from skeletal muscle and erythrocytes. *J. biol. Chem.* **244**:3823, 1969.

86. Dawson, D. M.; Spong, F. L. and Harrington, J. F.: McArdle's disease. Lack of muscle phosphorylase. *Ann. intern. Med.* **69**:229, 1968.

87. Huijing, F.; van Creveld, S. and Losekoot, G.: Diagnosis of generalized glycogen storage disease (Pompe's disease). *J. Pediat.* **63**:984, 1963.

88. Steinitz, K.: Laboratory diagnosis of glycogen diseases. *Advanc. clin. Chem.* **9**:228, 1968.

89. Nitowsky, H. M. and Grunfeld, A.: Lysosomal α-glucosidase in type II glycogenosis: activity in leucocytes and cell cultures in relation to genotype. *J. Lab. clin. Med.* **69**:472, 1967.

90. Dancis, J.; Hutzler, J.; Lynfield, J. and Cox, R. P.: Absence of acid maltase in glycogenosis type 2 (Pompe's disease) in tissue culture. *Amer. J. Dis. Child.* **117**:108, 1969.

91. Sidbury, J. B., Jr.; Cornblath, M.; Fisher, J. and House, E.: Glycogen in erythrocytes of patients with glycogen storage diseases. *Pediatrics* **27**:103, 1961.

92. Sidbury, J. B., Jr.; Gitzelmann, R. and Fisher, J.: The glycogenoses. Further observations on glycogen in erythrocytes of patients with glycogenosis. *Helv. paediat. Acta* **16**:506, 1961.

93. Steinitz, K.; Bodur, H. and Arman, T.: Amylo-1,6-glucosidase activity in leucocytes from patients with glycogen storage disease. *Clin. chim. Acta* **8**:807, 1963.

94. Huijing, F.: Enzymes of glycogen metabolism in leucocytes in relation to glycogen storage disease. In *Control of Glycogen Metabolism*, ed, W. J. Whelan. Academic Press, N. Y. 115, 1968.

95. Huijing, F.: Amylo-1,6-glucosidase activity in normal leucocytes and in leucocytes of patients with glycogen storage disease. *Clin. chim. Acta* **9**:269, 1964.

96. Huijing, F.; Klein-Obgink, H. J. and van Creveld, S.: The activity of debranching enzyme system in leucocytes. A ge-

netic study of glycogen storage disease type III. *Acta genet. (Basel)* **18**:128, 1968.

97. Chayoth, R.; Moses, S. W. and Steinitz, K.: Debrancher enzyme activity in blood cells of families with type III glycogen storage disease; a method for diagnosis of heterozygotes. *Israel J. med. Sci.* **3**:422, 1967.

98. Van Hoof, F.: Amylo-1,6-glucosidase activity and glycogen content of the erythrocytes of normal subjects, patients with glycogen storage diseases and heterozygotes. *European J. Biochem.* **2**:271, 1967.

99. Williams, H. E.; Kendig, E. M. and Field, J. B.: Leucocyte debranching enzyme in glycogen storage disease. *J. clin. Invest.* **42**:656, 1963.

100. Williams, C. and Field, J. B.: Studies in glycogen storage disease. III. Limit dextrinosis: a genetic study. *J. Pediat.* **72**:214, 1968.

101. Moses, S. W.; Chayoth, R.; Levin, S.; Lazarowitz, E. and Rubinstein, D.: Glucose and glycogen metabolism in erythrocytes from normal and glycogen storage disease type III subjects. *J. clin. Invest.* **47**:1343, 1968.

102. Essman, V.; Habboth, N. and Jorgensen, J. I.: Heredity of leucocyte phosphorylase and amylo-1,6-glucosidase deficiency. *J. Pediat.* **74**:90, 1969.

103. Hulsmann, W. C.; Ooei, T. I. and van Creveld, S.: Phosphorylase activity in leucocytes from patients with glycogen storage disease. *Lancet* **ii**:581, 1961.

104. Williams, H. E. and Field, J. B.: Low leucocyte phosphorylase in hepatic phosphorylase-deficient glycogen storage disease. *J. clin. Invest.* **40**:1841, 1961.

105. Williams, H. E. and Field, J. B.: Further studies on leucocyte phosphorylase in glycogen storage disease. *Metabolism* **12**:464, 1963.

106. Layzer, R. B.; Rowland, L. P. and Bank, W. J.: Isoenzyme abnormality in human muscle phosphofructokinase deficiency. *Clin. Res.* **10**:152, 1968.

107. Tarui, S.; Kono, N.; Nasu, T. and Nichikawa, M.: Enzymatic basis of the coexistence of myopathy and hemolytic disease in inherited muscle phosphofructokinase deficiency. *Biochem. biophys. Res. Commun.* **34**:77, 1969.

108. Hirschhorn, K.; Nadler, H. L.; Waithe, W. I.; Brown, B. I. and Hirschhorn, R.: Pompe's disease: Detection of heterozygotes by lymphocyte stimulation. *Science* **196**:1632, 1969.

109. Nadler, H. L. and Massina, A. M.: In utero detection of type II glycogenosis (Pompe's disease). *Lancet* **ii**:127, 1969.

110. Sidbury, J. B., Jr.: The genetics of the glycogenoses. In *Exploratory Concepts in Muscular Dystrophy*, ed, A. T. Milhorat. Excerpta Medica, Amsterdam, 83, 1967.

Genetic Approaches to the Nosology of Muscle Disease: Myotonias and Similar Diseases*

PROF. P. E. BECKER

Besides myotonic dystrophy some generalized myotonias exist, until now mostly diagnosed as "Thomsen's disease." It is questionable whether the dominant "myotonia congenita" is homogeneous. Surely there is at least one recessive type of generalized myotonia, which is also clinically different from Thomsen's disease. Paramyotonia congenita Eulenburg is a genetically independent type separated from paralysis periodica paramyotonia. Further diseases with myotonia and some other diseases of differential diagnostic importance with regard to myotonias are mentioned.

Previously, I presented a survey of genetic approaches to the nosology of nervous system diseases. I now want to speak about myotonias and those diseases which are of differential diagnostic relevancy to them. As far as possible, my conclusions will be supported by my own genetic investigations.

During the past years I have collected about 500 propositi with the diagnosis of myotonic dystrophy, as well as approximately 240 cases of nondystrophic myotonia, most of which have been diagnosed as Thomsen's disease. I became aware of these cases through an inquiry which was carried out among neurologists and internists in the German Federal Republic and in Berlin.

Myotonic dystrophy is a disease entity separate from other myotonic diseases. As this is generally accepted, and as there are several thorough genetic investigations of this dystrophic form, I shall speak only about the other myotonic types.

I was able to examine 24 families with Thomsen's disease in the Federal Republic. In these families, including the original pedigree of Dr. Julius Thomsen (Fig. 1), I counted 124 patients and 132 unaffected among the children of affected persons. This number coincides with the ratio of one to one, expected in regularly dominant transmission. Never was a generation skipped. The disease, as the term

Becker—Professor, Director Institut, fur Humangenetik, Universität Göttingen.

* The investigations of myotonias were supported by the "Deutsche Forschungsgemeinschaft," "Fritz Behrens-Stiftung," and the "Eugenie-Deutsch-Stiftung."

BIOGRAPHIC DATA

Professor P. E. Becker, born in Hamburg in Western Germany, received his neurologic training from Professor Pette in Hamburg and Professor Beringer in Freiburg i.Br. Professor F. Lenz was his instructor in human genetics. After about ten years neurologic practice and as Assistant Professor and then Associate Professor of Neurology and Psychiatry at the University of Freiburg i.Br., he was appointed Director of the "Institut für Humangenetik" in Göttingen in 1957 and in 1962 full Professor at the University of Göttingen.

His special interests are in the fields of neurologic genetics and of hereditary muscular diseases.

"congenita" expresses, is already noticeable after birth. Myotonia is often generalized. Sometimes, however, it manifests itself only slightly. Cold temperatures increase the symptoms of myotonia. Myotonic contraction disappears gradually after repeated muscular action. A strongly developed muscular hypertrophy is rarer than is expected according to illustrations in texts and handbooks. Figure 2 shows the propositi of some families with dominant

Birth Defects: Original Article Series. Vol. VII, No. 2; February 1971

52

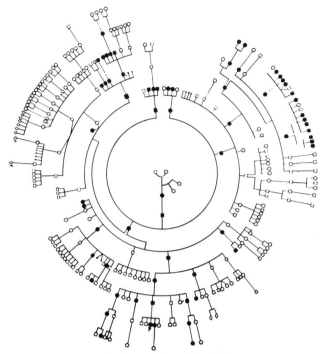

Fig. 1. Pedigree of Dr. Julius Thomsen.

characteristics. The degree of severity can vary considerably among the families; however, the variability of severity seems to be more limited within a family. This may indicate different dominant types of Thomsen's disease.* I am, however, not yet quite certain on that point.

Figure 3 shows the geographic distribution of the birthplaces of the oldest known affected persons in each family.

The families with Thomsen's disease in two or more successive generations constitute only a small proportion of all cases with generalized nondystrophic myotonia which were diagnosed by colleagues as "Thomsen's disease." Table I shows that 62 propositi are sporadic and that in 39 cases only sibs are affected. In 101 families, in other words, generalized myotonia occurs only in one generation as against 24 families with patients in two or more generations. One could suppose that the sporadic cases are new mutants of Thomsen's disease. This hypothesis, however, has to be discarded since the mutation rate would then be improbably and inexplicably high, that is if all sporadic cases or the majority of them were new mutants. The numerous sib cases would also need to be explained. Therefore, the only plausible explanation is that the diagnosis "Thomsen's disease" is applied to heterogeneous cases and that there exists, in addition to the dominant Thomsen's disease, a recessive type of generalized myotonia.

* Perhaps a dominant "myotonia levior" exists besides the real Thomsen's disease.

The existence of the recessive type is confirmed by the proportion of affected to nonaffected among the sibs of the 101 propositi with healthy parents and children. The value is between 18% and 28%. This is in agreement with the expected 25% in recessive inheritance. In connection with this, I checked to see whether sporadic cases were in excess or whether they were as frequent as expected. The 62 observed cases corresponded exactly to the expectation. This means that there are no, or only very few, new mutants of the dominant Thomsen's disease among the sporadic cases. The recessive type is further indicated by the average number of consanguineous marriages among the parents of patients. They occur in 14% of these, 5% of which are first cousin marriages. This is at least ten times the frequency of first cousin marriages in the random population.

After having shown the existence of a recessive type of generalized myotonia, one could expect that there may also be clinical differences between the recessive type and the dominant Thomsen's disease. Myotonia congenita bears the term "congenita" for a good reason, whereas the recessive generalized myotonia has its onset in the course of childhood and in individual cases even later as Figure 4 demonstrates. The onset is gradual and often barely noticeable. In most cases, the legs are the first to be affected and after some years the hands and arms; finally, the chewing muscles, the levator palpebrae and the orbicularis oculi are also involved. Patients with the recessive type are, as a rule, more severely affected than those of real Thomsen's disease (Fig. 5). I believe that muscle hypertrophy is more pronounced in the recessive type (Fig. 6). Aggravation of myotonic symptoms through cold seems to be more frequent in the real Thomsen's disease than in the recessive gen-

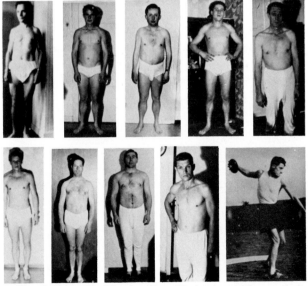

Fig. 2. Propositi of ten families with dominant Thomsen's disease.

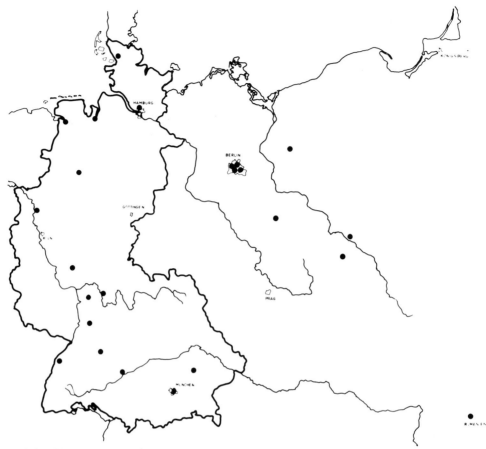

Fig. 3. Birthplaces of the oldest known affected persons of families with Thomsen's disease living in the German Federal Republic.

TABLE I
PATIENTS DIAGNOSED AS "MYOTONIA CONGENITA (THOMSEN)"

24 Families with patients in successive generations
  12   Families with patients in 2 generations
   7   Families with patients in 3 generations
   2   Families with patients in 4 generations
   2   Families with patients in 5 generations
   1   Family with patients in 8 generations
	62 Families with
	sporadic cases
		39 Families with sib
		cases (only brothers
		and sisters)

160 Patients	62 Patients	98 Patients

eralized myotonia. A further important difference concerns muscle strength. In the recessive type, muscular weakness is striking although there is hypertrophy of the muscles. Besides, I observed in several cases a remarkable diminution of muscular volume in the lower third of the forearms. There was only in rare cases a distinct atrophy of the forearms and of the sternomastoid muscles and only very rarely of the small hand muscles (Fig. 7). Leg muscles and shoulder girdle muscles are generally hypertrophic. In the biopsy of the forearm muscles, we often found dystrophic fibers scattered among

normal fibers (Fig. 8). The EMG of the extensors of the forearm often shows dystrophic potentials, considerable phase abbreviation, and lower amplitude potentials without an increase of interference density. In most cases, as Doctor Prill has shown, stimulation with frequencies up to 50 seconds caused a noticeable diminution of the amplitude of the action potentials within the first seconds of stimulation and this is related to the stimulus frequency. The hypertrophic muscles are usually firm even when relaxed. The dorsal flexion of hands and feet is usually limited. Hollow feet (pes cavus) often occur.

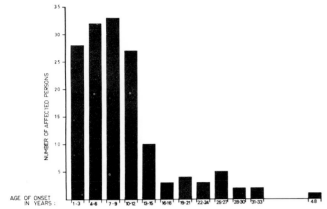

Fig. 4. Age of onset in recessive generalized myotonia.

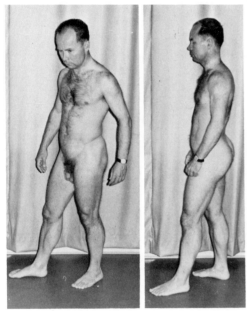

Fig. 5. Recessive generalized myotonia. The first steps are stiff and clumsy, then the gait becomes easier but not completely free.

Recessive myotonia is much more common than the dominant Thomsen's disease. Figure 9 shows the birthplaces of the patients of 101 families with recessive myotonia. One can see that they are almost equally distributed throughout the Federal Republic. Apparently these families are only a small proportion of the actual number of affected families in Western Germany. During the investigation, it was found that persons suffering from myotonia try to conceal their ailment even from physicians. Most of them have experienced that they were regarded as simulants ("fakers," "goldbrickers").

It can be assumed, therefore, that a large number of affected persons in Germany have never come to medical notice. An approximate estimate of the real frequency can be derived by estimating the gene frequency with the aid of the frequency of first cousin marriages. If one assumes that the estimate of 5% for

first cousin marriages is correct and that the corresponding value is 0.5% for the general population, one arrives at a frequency of recessive myotonia of 35 patients per million. In other words, there should be about 2,100 persons affected with myotonia of the recessive type in the Federal Republic and Berlin, whereas I have found only about 160 patients.

Another form of myotonia is paramyotonia congenita (Eulenburg). Until today, some authors have the opinion that paramyotonia congenita and myotonia congenita (Thomsen) are one and the same disease. Others suggest that paramyotonia congenita and adynamia episodica hereditaria may be identical conditions. Starting from 23 propositi, I was able to collect 18 pedigrees (Figs. 10, 11) with 308 cases of paramyotonia. One hundred fifty-seven out of 164 living persons affected with paramyotonia could be examined. The transmission is dominant without any skipping of generations. The geographic

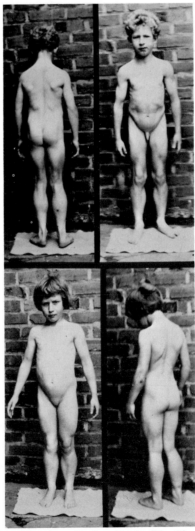

Fig. 6. Recessive generalized myotonia. Sibs (the boy is nine, the girl ten years old) with marked hypertrophy of muscles.

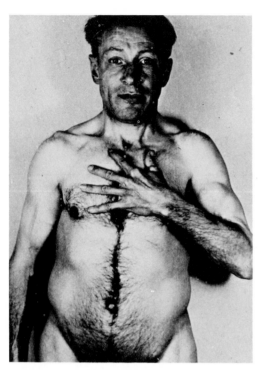

Fig. 7. Recessive generalized myotonia. Atrophy of the small hand muscles and diminution of the volume of the lower third of the forearm and sternomastoid muscles. Hypertrophy of the muscles of the shoulder girdle and of the legs.

distribution is remarkable. The residences of the eldest known paramyotonic patients of each family are pointed out on the map of the Federal Republic (Fig. 12). The genealogic investigations suggest that all affected persons, those living near Bielefeld in the Ravensberger Land as well as the one from Vörden and the one from Dortmund, originate from the same mutated ancestor. One may assume that this is also true for the paramyotonic patients in the western part of Nordrhein-Westfalen as well as for those in Hessen. Outside of a relatively small region in the central part of the Federal Republic, no cases of paramyotonia could be detected either by my own investigations or in the literature. One could, therefore, assume that all affected persons in the German Federal Republic derive from one and the same mutant. The mutation must have arisen before the second half of the 17th century. The only exception is one sporadic propositus in the far northern part of Germany presumably carrying a new mutation.

One can assume under these circumstances that the cases of paramyotonia which I have examined are genetically homogeneous, and the large number of affected may give a good estimate of the variability of the disease.

Paramyotonia is congenital. The facial muscles, when exposed to cold, become rigid and show tonic contractions which relax only in warmth, usually within a few minutes (Fig. 13). The hands become "clumsy" from the cold and the fingers are flexed

and abducted. This is due to the tonic contraction of the intrinsic muscles of the hand and perhaps of the muscles of the forearm. After a short time, the stiffness of the hands progresses to weakness and paralysis (Fig. 14) which gradually disappears in warmth from half an hour to several hours. The legs are less affected and their stiffness is not so impressive. Only three patients had sporadically experienced generalized weakness similar to periodic paralysis. On the other hand, in cases described in literature, attacks of general weakness are more often reported. These cases apparently represent a selection according to severity. This is the reason for the erroneous impression that a severe paramyotonic affection including the legs and with longer lasting weakness is typical. However, this is not true.

The laboratory investigations have not been able to demonstrate any significant abnormality with the exception of the potassium level in blood serum. The results, however, are not uniform. In our experience, it seems that generalized weakness or paralysis in the rare severe cases is associated with lowered serum potassium level and that elevated serum potassium level may be connected with generalized stiffness of the muscles.

Paramyotonia is dominant and, therefore, differs from recessive myotonia. An impressive dependency upon cold, the so-called "paradoxical myotonia" and the subsequent "cold paresis," make, among other signs, a quite different disease entity from Thomsen's disease.

Frequent short-lasting attacks, which are generally independent of cold and usually occur during the day, differentiate hyperkalemic periodic paralysis from Eulenburg's paramyotonia. It is still doubtful whether a special type of "hyperkalemic periodic paralysis with myotonic signs" exists or whether slight myotonic signs are occasionally found in some cases of hyperkalemic periodic paralysis (adynamia episodica hereditaria).[1]

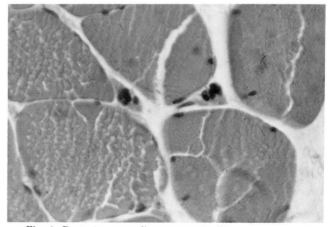

Fig. 8. Recessive generalized myotonia. Biopsy specimen of an extensor muscle of the forearm. Some dystrophic fibers are scattered among normal fibers.

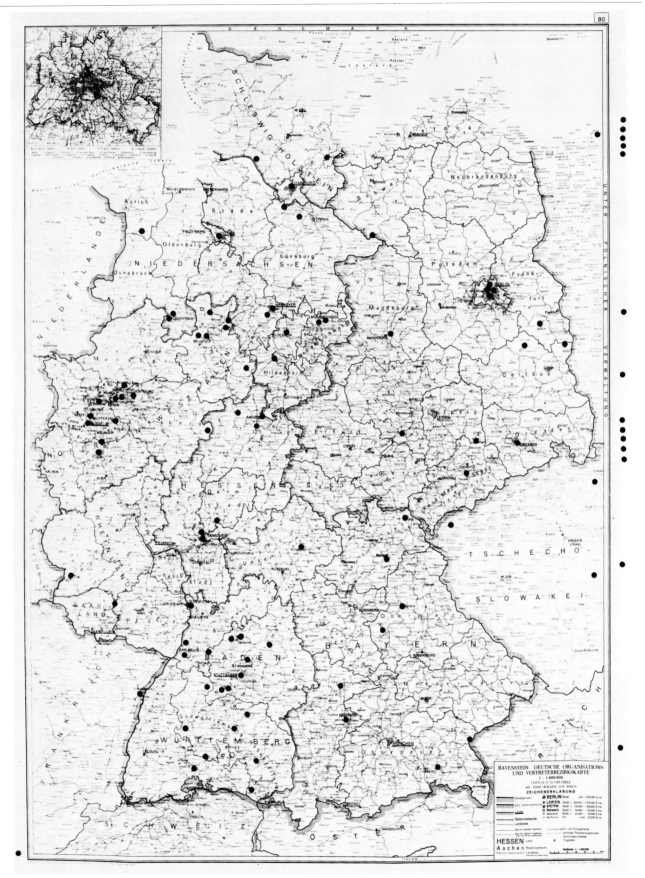

Fig. 9. Birthplaces of the propositi with recessive generalized myotonia living in the German Federal Republic.

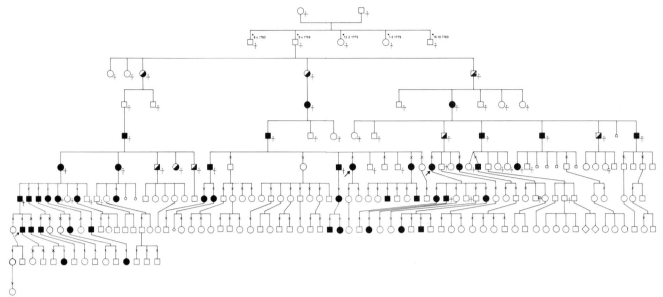

Fig. 10. Pedigree Sch.-Z.-D. with paramyotonia congenita (Eulenburg). ↗ Propositi

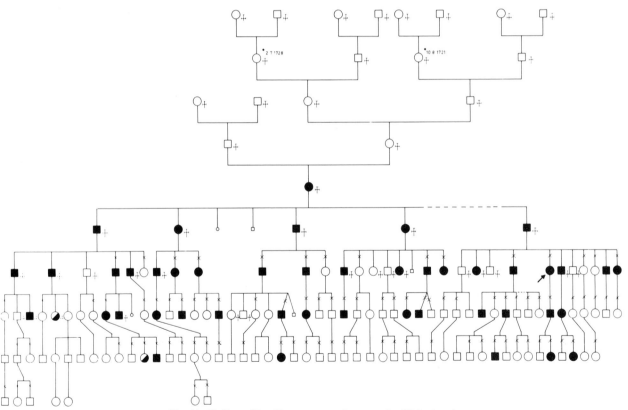

Fig. 11. Pedigree P. with paramyotonia congenita (Eulenburg)

However, another genetically independent type exists which is different from the one just mentioned. It is characterized by the combination of paramyotonia or paradoxical myotonia occurring at warm temperatures, not only in the cold (Fig. 15). In addition, one observes prolonged attacks of weakness usually occurring during the night or early in the morning being independent of exposure to the cold. I should like to name this type "paralysis periodica paramyotonica." In this type, potassium intake leads to attacks of paresis or paralysis while in Eulenburg's paramyotonia congenita, potassium aggra-

Fig. 12. Map of the German Federal Republic. ● Birthplaces of the eldest known affected members of the 23 families with paramyotonia congenita. ○ Birthplace of the eldest known affected members in the families reported by Hollmann (Barmen) and Hübner (Bonn).

Fig. 14. Paramyotonia congenita (Eulenburg). After a short exposure to cold the fingers become stiff and then weak and paralyzed.

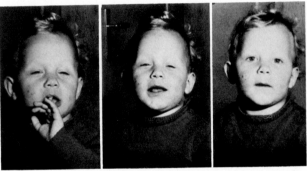

Fig. 15. After closing the eyes, they can be opened again after one half to two hours even in warm temperatures.

Fig. 13. Paramyotonia congenita (Eulenburg). After intensive cooling of the face for three minutes, the patient was asked to close his eyes tightly. The paramyotonic contraction relaxed within eight to ten minutes.

vates paramyotonic stiffness at least in some cases but causes no weakness.

I observed two families of this type, one with four and the other with seven affected persons. One family lives in southern and the other in northern Germany. Both are originally from Landsberg an der Warthe in Poland. Transmission is dominant. Several families of this type have been written about in the literature.

Last year Saunders *et al*[2] described three affected persons, a father and his two sons, in a family whose clinical picture is very similar to the aforementioned "paralysis periodica paramyotonica." They coined the term "familial myotonic periodic paralysis with muscle wasting." These persons show, in addition, permanent weakness of extensor muscles of the forearms with atrophy of the sternomastoid muscle, the small muscles of the hands and of the forearm muscles in differing degrees. Administration of potassium provokes paralysis. Muscle wasting has also been reported in other cases of paralysis periodica paramyotonica. It is still undecided whether these cases represent a special type different from those without muscle wasting. The transmission is also dominant.

Apparently, further diseases with myotonia exist. Some years ago, I examined a male patient about 40 years old who displayed a so-called paradoxical myotonia characterized by increasing myotonic contractions appearing with repeated muscle action and leading to weakness (Fig. 16). This weakness can be pronounced after strong muscle action, and cold has an unfavorable effect on the myotonia. The face muscles get stiff in a manner similar to paramyotonia. However, contrary to paramyotonia, the paramyotonic behavior in this case is also present at warm temperatures. Slight weakness is permanent. Doctor Kuhn examined this patient in his clinic. Glucose-insulin infusion (150g and 20U insulin) enhanced the muscular weakness at a time when the serum potassium values again reached an almost normal level. The excretion of potassium in the urine decreased and muscle contraction led to an increase of myotonia and to a decrease of muscle strength. This weakness diminished after oral administration of 5g of potassium chloride. The symptoms and findings in this case are different from paralysis periodica paramyotonica and also from Eulenburg's paramyotonia. The patient is the only one in his family. Recently, Isch et al described a mother and her daughter whose clinical picture and findings are in some respects similar to this patient.[3]

Another syndrome with myotonic myopathy, dwarfism, chondrodystrophy, ocular and facial abnormalities has been described by Aberfield et al in a brother and sister.[4] Besides myotonic myopathy, the progressive disorder is characterized by dystrophy of epiphyseal cartilages, joint contractures, blepharophimosis, myopia and pigeon breast. To me, this observation is unique.

It was while studying Thomsen's disease that a family was encountered with nine affected members, six males and three females, in four generations clearly showing dominant transmission. The myotonic signs were Thomsen-like; but in addition, all affected persons suffered from painful cramps of muscles, especially in the calves, neck and arms which were elicited by a strong movement and which lasted from less than a minute to several minutes or even longer. This is probably a separate disease entity (Fig. 17).

Some diseases of differential diagnostic importance with regard to the myotonias should be mentioned.

Bethlem et al described a "nonprogressive myopathy with muscle cramps after exercise" in four patients in four successive generations.[5] Contrary to the aforementioned syndrome of myotonia and muscle cramps, the cramps in this disease were painless and there was no evidence of myotonia. Urinary creatine excretion was greatly increased. Muscle biopsies showed cores in the muscle fibers. In the cores, the activity of the oxidative enzymes was greatly diminished. The ATP-ase activity of the myosin contained in the cores was also greatly diminished. Probably the same disease, affecting a father, two sons and a daughter has already been described by Bumke in 1911[6] in a paper entitled "Observations of a myotonia-like familial form of intention spasms."

Gamstorp and Wohlfart[1] described three unrelated male patients with "a syndrome characterized by myokymia, myotonia, muscular wasting and increased perspiration." The onset is in childhood or juvenile age. In one case, the parents were first cousins. Grund has given a report of two brothers with myokymia, myotonia and muscular wasting of the distal parts of the arms and legs.[7] I examined a sporadic male patient with myotonia, muscular hypertrophy, myokymia and increased perspiration. The myotonic troubles occurred periodically and lasted some months. In the meantime, myotonic signs disappeared but myokymia was still present.

These cases remind one of the "syndrome of continuous muscle-fiber activity" described by Isaacs in Johannesburg.[8] As the clinical description of the aforementioned cases is not always complete, it is impossible to decide whether they are clearly different from the Isaacs syndrome. This does not seem to be an inherited disease while, on the other hand, at least one case of Gamstorp and Wohlfart and the cases of Grund would seem to indicate a recessive transmission. The possible genetic background and

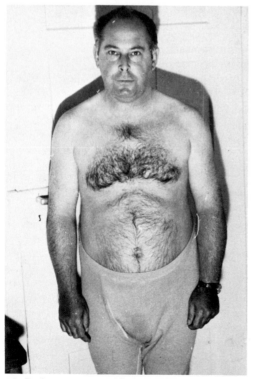

Fig. 16. Patient, 40 years old, with paradoxical myotonia and weakness increasing with muscle action.

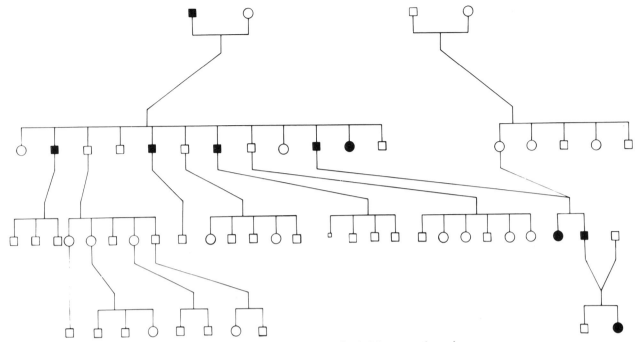

Fig. 17. Pedigree with myotonia and painful cramps of muscles.

the finding of myotonic signs—if they are real—in the last cases would speak in favor of different syndromes.

"Continuous muscle-fiber activity" is a well-defined entity with clear-cut symptoms. The entire musculature may be abnormally stiff at night and during the day. The stiffness is aggravated by movements and is slightly enhanced by cold. After strong voluntary contractions, there is sustained shortening of the muscle outlasting the initial stimulus. All motion is viscous. The first movement is usually the most difficult to overcome but occasionally eases on repetition; whereas, at other times, the first few movements are relatively free and repetition gets more difficult up to a point after which movements become easier. The onset is in childhood up to late adult age. Three patients have been described by Isaacs[8, 9] and three others have been published by Mertens.[10] This author entitled the disease "neuromyotonia" (Fig. 18), but the resemblance to myotonia is only superficial. Myotonic response to percussion is absent but obvious fasciculations involve all muscles in varying degrees. The electromyogram shows continuous high-voltage electric activity at rest recruiting with voluntary effort; but on relaxation, the activity continues for some time well above the normal pattern which was present before the voluntary contraction. Altogether, four males and two females have been reported. As far as I can see, the disease is not as rare as it seems. While studying a large number of people with myotonia, I encountered several suspect cases but the diagnosis could not be confirmed since clinical investigations were

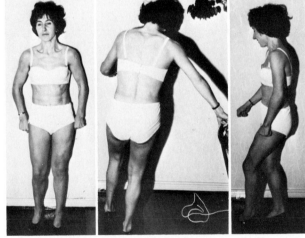

Fig. 18. Female patient with continuous muscle-fiber activity[8, 9] or neuromyotonia.[10]

not yet possible. All cases are sporadic. Blood relationship of parents is not known. Apparently, continuous muscle-fiber activity is exogenous; the cause is unknown up to now. Hyperactivity of peripheral γ-motoneurones is known to bring about the Isaacs syndrome.

Another probably exogenous disease is the so-called stiff-man syndrome[11] characterized by generalized muscle stiffness and painful muscle spasm. There is some reason to suppose that at least in several cases an abnormal activity of the γ-motoneurones is present. There has been an attempt to explain the permanent activity of the anterior horn cells by a lack of inhibitory activity of the Renshaw cells.[12]

Furthermore, in respect to differential diagnosis, I should like to mention "pseudomyotonia," well known as a common feature of myxedema. On the other hand, Thomsen's disease, as well as paramyotonia congenita, may be markedly aggravated by a hypofunction of the thyroid gland.

Finally, I would like to make some genetic remarks about the McArdle syndrome. This myopathy is characterized by lack of muscle phosphorylase. In the last few years, another enzyme defect has been found in the glycolytic cycle, namely, phosphofructokinase deficiency, indistinguishable from the classical McArdle syndrome. In the brothers described by Satoyoshi and Kowa[13] with similar symptoms but late onset, a further metabolic defect in glycolysis, probably at the level of phosphohexose isomerase, is suspected but not yet confirmed. Engel[14] described a woman with late-onset myopathy and total absence of skeletal muscle phosphorylase but this patient was clinically different from cases with early onset so that the authors rightly assume a new variant of muscle phosphorylase deficiency. Strugalska-Cynowska in Poland observed a boy with the McArdle syndrome.[15] The histochemical examination of a muscle biopsy did not indicate a complete lack of activity of phosphorylase but disturbances in the activation of its inactive form "b" to the active form "a" through phosphorylase-b-kinase.

A remarkable observation was recently made by Schimrigk et al[16] about a female patient, 46 years old, and her mother who have suffered from McArdle's disease since childhood. In addition to the typical symptoms, they have had chronic obstipation since childhood and spastic uterine inertia. A complete absence of phosphorylase activity has been shown in the daughter by histochemical and biochemical means. Since both mother and daughter are clinically equally affected, one cannot suppose homozygous manifestation in the one and heterozygosity in the other. One must rather suppose that this is an enzyme defect with dominant inheritance. In general, enzyme defects are recessive because only in the homozygous state the enzyme is nonexistent or noneffective while in heterozygotes, the enzyme level, depending on the normal allele, is generally sufficient to guarantee a nearly normal enzymatic process. In contrast, most dominant diseases are structural abnormalities of tissues and organs. One could imagine that the abnormal gene product has been inserted into the tissue along with the normal product of the allele (Lenz).[17] In the case of Schimrigk and colleagues, however, it is difficult to imagine that a structural abnormality could have caused a complete enzyme defect. The electron microscopic changes of muscle tissue found in this case seem to be secondary. Another possible hypothetical explanation is an "uninducible or superrepressed mutation" utilizing the "operon" system of Jacob and Monod. According to this hypothesis the loci of phosphorylase are under the control of an operator gene. If in an inducible system the regulator gene produces an altered repressor which inhibits the operator gene but which cannot be transformed in an inactive form by an inducer, then the production of phosphorylase is inhibited. This mutation of the regulator gene must be dominant. This hypothesis may be an interesting approach but it is not yet open to any experimental verification.

To conclude, McArdle syndrome is heterogeneous. It is the first myopathy in which the genetic approach has reached the molecular level. In myotonias we are still far distant from this to date.

REFERENCES

1. Gamstorp, I. and Wohlfart, G.: A syndrome characterized by myokymia, myotonia, muscular wasting and increased perspiration. *Acta Psychiat. scand.* **34**:181, 1959.
2. Saunders, M.; Ashworth, B.; Emery, A. E. H. and Benedikz, J. E. G.: Familial myotonic periodic paralysis with muscle wasting. *Brain* **91**:295, 1968.
3. Isch, F.; Stoebner, P. and Warter, J. M.: Paramyotonie congénitale de von Eulenburg: Etude des observations d'une enfant et de sa mère. *Rev. neurol.* **118**:214, 1968.
4. Aberfield, D. C.; Hinterbuchner, L. P. and Schneider, M.: Myotonia, dwarfism, diffuse bone disease and unusual ocular and facial abnormalities (a new syndrome). *Brain* **88**:313, 1965.
5. Bethlem, J.; von Gool, J.; Hülsmann, W. C. and Meijer, A. E. F. H.: Familial non-progressive myopathy with muscle cramps after exercise. A new disease associated with cores in the muscle fibres. *Brain* **89**:569, 1966.
6. Bumke, O.: Uber eine der myotonischen ähnliche, familiär auftretende Form von Intentionskrämpfen. *Z. ges. Neurol. Psychiat.* **4**:645, 1911.
7. Grund, G.: Uber genetische Beziehungen zwischen Myotonie, Muskelkrämpfen und Myokymie (zugleich ein Beitrag zur Pathologie der neuralen Muskelatrophie). *Dtsch. Z. Nervenheilk.* **146**:3, 1938.
8. Isaacs, H.: A syndrome of continuous muscle-fibre activity. *J. Neurol. Neurosurg. Psychiat.* **24**:319, 1961.
9. Isaacs, H.: Continuous muscle fibre activity in an Indian male with additional evidence of terminal motor fibre abnormality. *J. Neurol. Neurosurg. Psychiat.* **30**:126, 1967.
10. Mertens, H.-G. and Zschocke, S.: Neuromyotonie. *Klin. Wschr.* **43**:917, 1965.
11. Moersch, F. P. and Woltman, H. W.: Progressive fluctuating muscle rigidity and spasm ("stiff-man-syndrome"): Report of a case and some observations in 13 other cases. *Proc. Mayo Clin.* **31**:421, 1956.
12. Heitmann, R.: Das Stiff-Man-Syndrom. *Fortschr. Neurol. Psychiat.* **36**:82, 1968.
13. Satoyoshi, E. and Kowa, H.: A myopathy due to glycolytic abnormality. *Arch. Neurol. (Chic.)* **17**:248, 1967.
14. Engel, W. K.: The essentiality of histo- and cytochemical studies of skeletal muscle in the investigation of neuromuscular disease. *Neurology* **12**:778, 1962.
15. Strugalska-Cynowska, M.: Disturbances in the activity of phosphorylase-b-kinase in a case of McArdle myopathy. *Folia Histochem. et Cytochem.* **5**:151, 1967.
16. Schimrick, K.; Mertens, H. G.; Ricker, K.; Führ, J.; Eyer, P. and Pette, D.: McArdle-Syndrom (Myopathie bei fehlender Muskelphosphorylase). *Klin. Wschr.* **45**:1, 1967.
17. Lenz, W.: Medizinische Genetik. Thieme, Stuttgart, 1961.

Reprinted from MUSCLE, Birth Defects, Original Article Series, February 1971, Vol. VII, No. 2.

Hereditary Ptosis

DONALD C. ABERFELD, M.D.

Weakness of the external eye muscles was believed to be of genetic origin in 94 of 97 patients studied and was familial in 73 patients. Thirty patients had congenital ptosis alone or with weakness of other ocular muscles. The lack of progression and high incidence of other congenital anomalies suggested that congenital ptosis had in most instances a developmental etiology. Neurogenic congenital ptosis was documented in one instance and was suspected in another patient. The most common causes of progressive ophthalmoplegia with onset after birth was myotonic dystrophy and ocular muscle dystrophy. On clinical and genetic grounds, ptosis associated with retinitis pigmentosa was considered as a distinct disease and there was no conclusive evidence that ocular muscle dystrophy and oculopharyngeal dystrophy were separate diseases. The relatively high incidence of familial myasthenia gravis was probably due to the selection of the patients. Two pairs of sibs with "chondrodystrophic myotonia" were included in the study. Progressive external ophthalmoplegia with onset after birth was neurogenic in three instances. It accompanied motor neuron disease, Kugelberg-Welander disease and an undetermined disease affecting the central and peripheral nervous system, each in one patient.

The data presented are based on the study of 94 patients with weakness of the external eye muscles believed to have a genetic etiology and three patients with familial nongenetic ptosis. The patients selected had familial disease or clinical and pathologic features similar to those of patients with observed or reported familial disease.

About one-third of the patients had congenital ptosis, which was familial in 80%. The remaining patients had disease with onset after birth and 73% had familial disease. There was a high incidence of various forms of muscular dystrophy among patients with sporadic ptosis with postnatal onset and, therefore, the genetic etiology of the disease was considered with greater confidence than in patients with sporadic congenital ptosis. As has been reported in previous studies, congenital ptosis was more

common in men, and was accompanied by weakness of the oculomotor muscles in over 20% of the cases. The common occurrence of other associated congenital anomalies suggested that congenital ptosis frequently had a developmental origin. In four patients, congenital ptosis was associated with disease of the nervous system (two) and of the neuromuscular junction (two). One patient with transient, unilateral congenital ptosis had a family history of ocular muscular dystrophy. In two brothers, unilateral congenital ptosis was associated with hereditary hemorrhagic telangiectasia. The association was only coincidental, since their father had only unilateral ptosis and their mother only hereditary hemorrhagic telangiectasia. The familial occurrence of congenital ptosis and abnormalities of the mandibular arch or pes planus were observed each in one family. One of the two first cousins with congenital ptosis had two sibs with retinitis pigmentosa and heart block, without ptosis, and one other sib with heart block but no ophthalmologic abnormalities. Ptosis associated with plagiocephaly, microcephaly and mul-

Aberfeld—Assistant Attending (Medicine/Neurology), Maimonides Hospital; Associate Director (Neurology) Coney Island Hospital and Assistant Attending, The Lutheran Medical Center, Brooklyn, also St. Clare and New York Polyclinic Hospitals, New York.

Birth Defects: Original Article Series. Vol. VII, No. 2; February 1971

63

BIOGRAPHIC DATA

Dr. Donald C. Aberfeld received his M.D. degree with honors from Faculty of Medicine, Bucharest, in 1957. He was guest physician, neuro-psychiatric clinic of the University of Vienna from 1957 to 1958 and served his internship at Reddy Memorial Hospital, Montreal. He received training in neurology at Metropolitan Hospital, Bronx Municipal Hospital, The Jewish Chronic Disease Hospital and a postgraduate course at New York Polyclinic Hospital.

Dr. Aberfeld received his New York State License in 1964 and his appointments in Medicine/Neurology include Maimonides Hospital, Coney Island Hospital, The Lutheran Medical Center, all in Brooklyn, and St. Clare and New York Polyclinic Hospitals in New York. He is the author of numerous scientific publications.

TABLE I

Congenital ptosis + weakness of the oculomotor muscles

Patients studied and affected relatives: 30
  a. familial: 24, 80%
  b. sporadic: 6, 20%
1. Unilateral ptosis with no other abnormality: 4
   a) father and son
   b) father of two sons (see 2a) with unilateral congenital ptosis and hereditary hemorrhagic telangiectasia
   c) child with transient unilateral ptosis and family history of ocular muscular dystrophy
2. Unilateral ptosis and hereditary hemorrhagic telangiectasia: 2
   a) two brothers whose father had unilateral ptosis only (see 1b), and their mother had hereditary hemorrhagic telangiectasia
3. Unilateral ptosis and epicanthus, together with plagiocephaly, microcephaly, multiple joint contractures and mental defect: 1
4. Ptosis and weakness of the superior recti: 3
   a) patient with sporadic disease
   b) two first cousins with family history of retinitis pigmentosa and heart block
5. Retinitis pigmentosa and family history of congenital ptosis: 2
   a) two sibs with retinitis pigmentosa and heart block and no weakness of the oculomotor muscles, whose sister and first cousin had congenital ptosis (4b)
6. Ptosis and pes planus: 9 (all members of one family)
7. Ptosis and abnormal development of the mandibular arch: 3
   a) father and two sons
8. Ptosis, blepharophimosis, microtrigonocephaly, malformed ears, spina bifida, pes equinovarus, bifid ureter and mental defect: 1
9. Ptosis, weakness of the oculomotor muscles, facial diplegia, epilepsy and mental defect: 1 (with electromyographic evidence of denervation of the facial muscles)
10. Ptosis and facial dysostosis: 1
11. Ptosis and diffuse neurofibromatosis: 1
12. Congenital familial myasthenia gravis: 1
13. Neonatal myasthenia: 1

tiple joint contractures, or with blepharophimosis, microtrigonocephaly, malformed ears, spina bifida, pes equinovarus, bifid ureter and mental defect, or with facial dysostosis, occurred each in one instance (Table I).

After birth, the most common causes of hereditary ptosis and weakness of the oculomotor muscles, occurring together or separately, were myotonic dystrophy, ocular muscular dystrophy and familial myasthenia gravis, in this order (Table II).

Ptosis with or without weakness of the oculomotor muscles was a more common feature of myotonic dystrophy, but one patient had weakness of the oculomotor muscles and no ptosis.

Two different forms of ocular muscular dystrophy were encountered among the patients studied, one featuring muscular dystrophy as the only abnormality, and the other, featuring muscular dystrophy together with retinitis pigmentosa. A third form of disease, in which the affected muscles respond to prostigmine or exhibit sensitivity to curare has been described in the literature but did not occur in any of the patients studied. Involvement of the pharyngeal and limb muscles were variable features among patients with ocular muscular dystrophy with or without retinitis pigmentosa and, in some instances, belonging to the same family seemed to be related to the duration of the disease. There was no evidence that oculopharyngeal muscular dystrophy is a separate disease. Weakness of the pharyngeal muscles was also present in a patient with muscular dystrophy, hypokalemic periodic paralysis and corneal dystrophy. Occasionally, patients with ocular muscular dystrophy had weakness of the oculomotor muscles without ptosis. In one instance, electromyography of the limb muscles revealed a myopathic pattern in the absence of any clinical abnormality of the muscles studied.

Patients with familial myasthenia gravis included in this study were selected from among 761 patients

TABLE II

Ptosis ± weakness of the oculomotor muscles, with onset after birth

---

Patients studied and affected relatives: 67
    a. familial: 49, 73.1%
    b. sporadic: 18, 27.3%
1. Myotonic dystrophy: 19 patients in 13 unrelated families
    a. familial: 11
    b. sporadic: 8
        a. Ptosis ± weakness of the oculomotor muscles: 18
        b. Weakness of the oculomotor muscles without ptosis: 1
2. Ocular muscular dystrophy: 18 patients in 6 unrelated families
    a. familial: 15
    b. sporadic: 3
        a. Ptosis ± weakness of the oculomotor muscles: 16
        b. Weakness of the oculomotor muscles without ptosis: 1
3. Ocular muscular dystrophy and pigmentary degeneration of the retina:
    a. familial: 7
    b. sporadic: 2
        9 patients in 3 unrelated families
        a. Ptosis and retinitis pigmentosa: 3
        b. Ptosis only, and family history of ptosis associated with retinitis pigmentosa: 4
        c. Weakness of the oculomotor muscles, without ptosis, and family history of ptosis associated with retinitis pigmentosa: 2
4. Sporadic myasthenia gravis in the mother of a child with neonatal myasthenia: 1
5. Familial myasthenia gravis: 11 patients in 4 unrelated families
6. Muscular dystrophy associated with corneal dystrophy and hypokalemic periodic paralysis: 1
7. Facioscapulohumeral muscular dystrophy, juvenile cataract and weakness of the oculomotor muscles, without ptosis: 1
8. Chondrodystrophic myotonia: 4 patients in two unrelated families
9. Kugelberg-Welander disease: 1
10. Spinal muscular atrophy: 1
11. Central nervous system disease and chronic sensory neuropathy: 1

---

with myasthenia gravis, so that the actual incidence of familial myasthenia gravis among patients with hereditary ptosis must be lower than this study would suggest.

Four of the patients studied, who were brother and sister in two unrelated families, had chondrodystrophic myotonia (myotonia of early onset, dwarfism, diffuse bone disease and oculofacial abnormalities), which is probably transmitted as an autosomal recessive trait. Two of these patients had intermittent ptosis, and the two remaining patients had microcornea and probable microphthalmus and pseudoptosis.

One patient with features of facioscapulohumeral muscular dystrophy and juvenile cataract had weakness of the oculomotor muscles without ptosis, and, myotonic dystrophy was ruled out clinically and electromyographically.

Three patients had disease of the nervous system. Kugelberg-Welander disease and spinal muscular atrophy each occurred in one patient. The remaining patient, whose parents were first cousins, had a chronic organic mental syndrome, ptosis, facial weakness and sensory neuropathy of the legs with mal perforans.

Although this study illustrates many of the clinical settings, within which hereditary ptosis can occur, the list of hereditary diseases with which ptosis can be associated is much longer.

A Brief Review of Inherited Hypertrophic Neuropathy

PETER J. DYCK, M.D.

Introduction

In 1893, Déjérine and Sottas[1] described two sibs with hypertrophic neuropathy of infancy. The features of the disorder were clubfoot, kyphoscoliosis, weakness and atrophy of skeletal muscles (most marked distally in the limbs), fasciculation, decreased reactivity of muscles to electrical stimulation, areflexia, marked sensory loss (particularly distally in the limbs), incoordination of the arms, Romberg's sign, miosis, and nystagmus. The disorder began in infancy in one of the sibs and at the age of 14 years in the other. Both parents were unaffected. Of the sibs, five had died during infancy and two were without neurologic abnormality. Fanny Roy, the person who had the disorder since infancy, died at the age of 45 years. At postmortem examination, peripheral nerves were increased in size, with marked hypertrophy of the interstitial connective tissue and with fusiform cells surrounding nerve fibers. The myelin sheath was found to be very thin or totally absent, leaving a denuded axis cylinder. Onion-bulb formations were seen.

Earlier, Gombault and Mallet[2] had described the histologic features of hypertrophic neuropathy in a patient considered by them to have had tabes dorsalis. In many of the subsequent articles[3-16] on hypertrophic neuropathy, the emphasis was on the pathologic alteration. Generally it was agreed that onion-bulb formations developed particularly around myelinated fibers. Additionally, most authors thought that the lamellae of the onion-bulb formation were Schwann cell in origin. The endoneurium also was thought to be increased in this disorder. The "hallmark" of the disorder was the onion-bulb formation. It is apparent that disorders with diverse natural histories have been reported under the term "hypertrophic neuropathy"[17, 18]; such reports have not separated recessively inherited severe hypertrophic neuropathy from dominantly inherited mild hypertrophic neuropathy and from other sporadic

Dyck—Associate Professor of Neurology, Mayo Graduate School of Medicine, University of Minnesota, Rochester; Consultant, Department of Neurology, Mayo Clinic and Mayo Foundation, Rochester.

BIOGRAPHIC DATA

Dr. Peter J. Dyck was born in Gorgiensk, Russia. He attended the Hepburn Public School in Saskatchewan, Canada and in 1948 enrolled in the University of Saskatchewan, from which he obtained his B.A. degree in 1951. He then became a student at the University of Toronto Faculty of Medicine where he received his M.D. degree in 1955. He served a rotating internship at the University of Saskatchewan Hospital in Saskatoon until 1959 when he came to the Mayo Graduate School of Medicine as a resident in neurology. In 1963 he was appointed to the staff of the Mayo Graduate School of Medicine as Instructor in Neurology and in 1967 became Assistant Professor.

Dr. Dyck was certified as a Specialist in Neurology in 1962 by the American Board of Psychiatry and Neurology, Inc. He became a fellow of the American College of Physicians in 1964 and is a member of the American Medical Association, the American Academy of Neurology and other professional organizations. He has maintained a special interest in studies of the peripheral nerves and the diseases thereof, in hereditary neuropathies, in experimental production of the "onion-bulb" phenomenon in neural tissues and in investigation of neural tissues with the aid of the electron microscope.

types. It also seems likely that kinships with peroneal muscular atrophy have been described in which the hypertrophic neuropathy went unrecognized because it now is known[17] that even very careful search for it will only reveal it in low numbers in affected persons.

The view that the onion-bulb formation might not be specific for one disease process but is a pathologic

Birth Defects: Original Article Series. Vol. VII, No. 2; February 1971

66

reaction common to different disorders had been suggested by a few workers.[14, 19, 20] This view was strengthened by the observation that in Refsum's disease, a recessively inherited disorder with the abnormal finding of phytanic acid in the serum, a hypertrophic neuropathy of the nerves was found.[21] Furthermore, it was found that hypertrophic neuropathy could be produced experimentally by the injection of phenanthracene into nerve,[13] by the production of lead neuropathy,[22] and by the repeated applications of a tourniquet cuff.[23] It has been suggested that[23]:

> The probable sequence of histologic events in the genesis of onion-bulb formation includes the following: 1) partial or complete demyelination of an internode; 2) mitosis of the Schwann cell associated with the demyelinated internode; 3) capture of the demyelinated internode by one of the two newly formed Schwann cells, with outward displacement of the other; 4) circumferential orientation (influenced by the second-order basement membrane) and further mitosis of the displaced Schwann cell and 5) successive outward displacement of layers of basement membranes and Schwann cells with repeated segmental demyelination and remyelination. Additional Schwann cells may be attracted to the demyelinating internode from other regions.

There are at least three distinct genetic types of hypertrophic neuropathy.[17] By far the most common variety is dominantly inherited—the hypertrophic neuropathy of the Charcot-Marie-Tooth type (HN-CMT). The second type is extraordinarily uncommon and is similar to the syndrome described by Déjérine and Sottas (hypertrophic neuropathy of the Déjérine-Sottas type; HN-DS). The third type was first described by Refsum and is known to be associated with the presence of phytanic acid in the serum (hypertrophic neuropathy of the Refsum type). In addition, there are probably several noninherited forms of hypertrophic neuropathy. Relapsing neuropathy, which is presumably a segmentally demyelinating disease on a hyperimmune basis, is often associated with hypertrophic neuropathy. Hypertrophic neuropathy also may occur in older age groups, as described by Roussy and Cornil.[24] Stewart[25] described a hypertrophic neuropathy associated with acromegaly. I think that the list of diseases associated with hypertrophic neuropathy will lengthen.

Hypertrophic Neuropathy of the Charcot-Marie-Tooth Type

Historical

Based on the type of inheritance, the natural history, the characteristics of the conduction velocities of nerve, and the pathologic alterations in nerve biopsies, there are at least three disorders commonly identified by neurologists as peroneal muscular atrophy.[17, 18] The first and most common is the HN-CMT. The second is a neuronal disorder (neuronal type of Charcot-Marie-Tooth disease). The third is a progressive spinal muscular atrophy (progressive muscular atrophy form of Charcot-Marie-Tooth disease). I will discuss only the first type; for a discussion of the other types see Reference 18.

In reviewing the historic accounts of sporadic and inherited peroneal muscular atrophy and of hypertrophic neuropathy, it is often difficult to classify them. Most reports were published prior to the availability of studies of conduction velocity of nerves. Also, the clinical determination of enlargement of nerves is uncertain,[17] and pathologic examination of nerves was often unavailable.

One of the earlier accounts of inherited peroneal muscular atrophy was that of Eichhorst[26] in 1873. He described affected persons in six generations. Patients with peroneal muscular atrophy also were described by Virchow,[27] Eulenburg,[28] Friedreich,[29] and others.[30]

In 1886, Charcot and Marie[31] and Tooth[32] described a slowly progressive muscular atrophy which usually began in the feet and legs and particularly affected the peroneal muscle group. The disorder was familial and, in both of the reports, was transmitted directly from one generation to the next through affected persons. In the muscles, fasciculations and the reaction of degeneration were found. Vasomotor abnormalities also occurred in atrophic muscles. In the opinion of Charcot and Marie, the disorder was either a myelopathy or a neuropathy, but they favored the former. Tooth correctly concluded that the disorder affected the peripheral nerves. Since that time, there have been numerous descriptions of kinships with this disorder. It should be pointed out that nerve enlargement was not noted by these early workers. Biemond,[33] Thévenard and Berdet,[34] and Dyck and co-workers[16, 35, 36] drew attention to the enlargement of the greater auricular nerve, the median nerve, and other peripheral nerves in some persons with typical familial disorders of this type. Lambert[37] first noted low conduction velocities in the peripheral nerves in patients with this type of neuropathy.

The syndrome described by Roussy and Lévy[38] was like the disorder described by Eichhorst,[26] by Charcot and Marie,[31] and by Tooth[32] in the following features: dominant inheritance, clubfoot, weakness and minimal atrophy of the distal limb muscles, hyporeflexia or areflexia, decreased excitability of muscles to galvanic and faradic stimulation, and distal sensory loss. Additionally, these patients had what we now would interpret as a static tremor of the hands, voice, and head. Roussy and Lévy stressed the absence of cerebellar signs, Babinski's sign, and nystagmus. In subsequent literature and in textbooks, inherited disorders with the features of peroneal muscular atrophy, sensory loss, and cerebellar ataxia were named the Roussy-Lévy syndrome. These latter cases should be grouped with the spinocerebellar degenerations. Recently, Yudell and associates[39] studied a kinship with the Roussy-Lévy syndrome (with the features described by the original authors) and asked the question, "Could this disorder be the result of a combination of two dominant genes—one for Charcot-Marie-Tooth disease and one for essential tremor?" This did not appear to be the case. A striking feature of the disorder was the low conduction velocities of peripheral nerve. It has become apparent that the cases described by Roussy and Lévy have essentially the same inheritance pattern, natural history, electrophysiologic characteristics, and pathologic alterations as those included in the category of hypertrophic neuropathy of the Charcot-Marie-Tooth type.

Marie[40] and Marie and Bertrand[41] described two sibs with hypertrophic neuropathy of infancy. In addition to peroneal muscular atrophy, pes cavus, hyporeflexia, enlargement of nerves, and tremor, they had a slight degree of exophthalmus. Unfortunately, there is not enough information about parents and sibs or about the natural history to decide whether they should be included with the HN-DS or the HN-CMT or considered to be a separate group. In the opinion of Marie and of Déjérine, these cases belonged in the HN-DS group. The pathologic changes in peripheral nerve are more like those we have come to associate with HN-DS than with HN-CMT.

Clinical Features

In a recent report,[17] Lambert and I described our evaluation of 204 persons from 21 kinships with this disorder; 38 males and 29 females were affected. The earliest evidence of the disorder, on the basis of clinical examination, usually was a foot deformity or an abnormal gait. By history, many patients stated that they had always had high arches and curled-up toes; corns, callouses, and difficulty in obtaining properly fitting shoes were further common symptoms. However, affected patients may have normal arches or even flat feet. Of our 67 affected persons, only 2 gave a history of having had an ulcer of the foot. Usually the abnormality in gait does not develop until the second decade, but in two of our patients it began in the first decade. The gait is described as "awkwardness," "clumsiness," "the family walk" or in similar terms. Characteristically, the knees are raised higher than normal and in this posture the foot assumes a marked pes equinovarus deformity.

A few persons with well-developed disease have, in addition to this, a slapping gait and difficulty in

maintaining their balance on standing still. This probably is not due to a loss of kinesthetic sensation but rather to weakness of the muscles stabilizing the ankle. Some patients are able to maintain their balance in this position by bending their knees and locking their ankle joints. Others tend to shift their feet to maintain balance. Some of the patients have difficulties of digital manipulations such as turning a key in a lock or holding small objects tightly. Although some of the patients describe discomfort, by far the majority do not. When it occurs, foot pain is usually explained by the presence of corns and callouses. Numbness, prickling pain, and lancinating pain are absent. Coldness of the feet is a common complaint and, in patients who have lost considerable muscle bulk, the skin temperature over the feet often is considerably lower than it is in normal persons. Ichthyosis, retinitis pigmentosa, miosis, nystagmus, and cerebellar ataxia are not found.

We found that weakness occurred first in small muscles of the foot and in peroneal muscles. In affected persons, some weakness usually was noticeable within the second decade. Subsequently, weakness of the plantar flexor muscles of the ankle and of the intrinsic muscles of the hand was found. Affected persons often could be recognized by their inability to walk on their heels. Muscle atrophy of a marked degree is not common in these patients. The "stork legs" associated with Charcot-Marie-Tooth disease usually do not occur in this disorder but rather in the neuronal or in the progressive muscular atrophy type. We found that the muscle stretch reflexes disappeared in the following sequence: Achilles, quadriceps, and upper limb. Hyperreflexia, the Babinski sign, and cerebellar ataxia were not seen.

A few affected persons from several kinships had a tremor which had the characteristics of an essential tremor. This tremor is present when the patient holds his hands outstretched in a static position, and it disappears when the hands are at rest. An oscillatory tremor of the head and of the voice also may be present. The tremor is particularly noticeable during tension. The tremor does not have the characteristics of cerebellar ataxia. Touch-pressure, joint position and motion, and vibration sensations usually are abnormal. In early or mild cases, quantitative sensory tests may be needed to demonstrate an abnormality. Temperature and pain sensations probably are not affected or affected only slightly. The sensory loss is greatest in the feet.

Evidence that sensory nerves are affected comes also from electrophysiologic studies. The action potential may be delayed or absent from electrodes overlying the median and ulnar nerves at the wrist (stimulation of digital fibers). Low conduction velocities and decreased amplitude also have been demonstrated in myelinated fibers of cutaneous nerves stimulated *in vitro*.[36] The amplitude and conduction velocity of the C fiber potential have not been abnormal. Enlargement and increased firmness of the following peripheral nerves have been noted: greater auricular, anterior cervical, median, ulnar, terminal twigs of the radial nerve at the wrist, and peroneal nerves. In our examination of the 67 persons with this disorder, only 17 had unequivocal enlargement of nerves.

Genetic Features

In the 21 kinships examined, a direct line of inheritance could be established either by direct examination of the parents and children or by the history; 42% of the children with one affected parent had the disorder. There was considerable variability in the expressivity. Several affected persons without neurologic signs are known to be affected on the basis of low conduction velocities of nerves.

Conduction Velocity Studies

On the average, the conduction velocities of the ulnar, median, and peroneal nerves of the affected persons were less than half those of their unaffected relatives.[17] Additionally, the amplitude of the muscle action potential was decreased by more than one half and the distal latencies were increased almost threefold. No affected person in these kinships had normal conduction velocities but several persons with low conduction velocities did not have evidence of the disorder on the clinical examination; however, subsequent examination of two of three such persons revealed the disorder in typical form. The third person, a 43-year-old woman, had a son with the disorder in typical form and had evidence of a mild hypertrophic neuropathy on nerve biopsy. In affected persons, digital nerve action potentials could not be detected or, if they were present, they had a small amplitude and a long latency. The compound action potential of the sural nerve *in vitro* is abnormal.[36] The conduction velocity and amplitude of unmyelinated fibers has not been abnormal.

Histologic Studies

My associates and I have done extensive biopsy studies of the greater auricular, anterior tibial, and sural nerves in this disorder. At biopsy, enlargement of the nerve is apparent. A better indication of the size of the nerve, however, is the transverse fascicular area: it has been greater in nerves from patients with this disorder than in healthy nerves. The enlargement is from an increase in the endoneurial area, not from an increase in the amount of perineurium or epineurium. The increase in the endoneurial

area is thought to be due to an increase in the number of nuclei of Schwann cells and of collagen. Obviously, onion-bulb formations are more prominent in more severely affected persons. The morphology of the onion-bulb formation has now been extensively studied under the electron microscope.[9-16] Usually, at the center of an onion-bulb formation there is a myelinated fiber, a demyelinated portion of a myelinated fiber, or no fiber. The lamellae of the onion-bulb formation are made up of circumferentially directed Schwann cells with attenuated cytoplasmic processes which lie in layers around the central structure. Between the lamellae of the Schwann cells are collagen fibrils directed longitudinally. Occasionally, at the outer edge of an onion-bulb formation is a circumferentially directed fibroblast.

In transverse sections there is a decrease in the number of myelinated fibers per nerve or per square millimeter of transverse fascicular area.[16] In part this decrease is spurious because demyelinated regions of myelinated fibers would not be seen in transverse sections and would not be counted. Therefore, quantitative measurements were made of the percentage of the length of teased myelinated fibers which were demyelinated. Even when the numbers of myelinated fibers per nerve and per unit of transverse fascicular area were recalculated, using a correction factor for demyelinated portions, the numbers of fibers were still low. However, it is possible that some formerly myelinated fibers become totally demyelinated and therefore would not be recognized in the teased-fiber preparation. The presence of muscle atrophy, denervation, fasciculation, and a low Meissner corpuscle count[42] also favors the concept that the numbers of myelinated fibers are decreased. Almost all fibers which were teased for a distance of approximately 6 to 8 mm had portions along their length which were demyelinated.[16] In addition, intact internodes of myelin were abnormally short, suggesting that they had been previously demyelinated and had remyelinated. Unmyelinated fibers have been present in normal numbers. It appears that the main abnormality in this disorder is in the maintenance of myelin, perhaps an abnormality in the metabolism of myelin.

Cerebrospinal Fluid

In most patients with this disorder, the cerebrospinal fluid protein has been normal but occasionally a patient is seen who has a mild increase in protein.

Management

The majority of persons with this disorder probably do not require surgery of the feet, special shoes, or specific treatment. Proper hygiene of the feet, especially to keep the skin of the sole soft, and wide, properly fitted shoes to prevent callous formation are important. Foot-drop springs, braces to stabilize the ankle, and similar devices should be used only when they benefit the patient to his satisfaction. In patients with very high degrees of pes cavus and marked degrees of hammertoes, foot surgery such as triple arthrodesis seems to be worthwhile. Furthermore, foot surgery should be considered when there is marked inversion of the foot at the ankle. Medication for discomfort probably has little or no place in this disorder because, if discomfort is marked, attention should be paid to the pressure points and callouses of the feet.

Hypertrophic Neuropathy of the Charcot-Marie-Tooth Type—Sporadic, Dominant Inheritance with Poor Expressivity or Recessive Inheritance

Patients are seen who have a slowly progressive hypertrophic neuropathy which, on the basis of neurologic findings or conduction velocity characteristics, cannot be separated from the dominantly inherited group, but their parents cannot be shown to have the abnormality. The possibility exists that the correct parents have not been identified, that one of the parents has the disorder in such a mild form that it cannot be recognized by present methods, or that the disorder is not dominantly inherited. It is also possible that these cases represent mutations.

Hypertrophic Neuropathy of the Déjérine-Sottas Type (HN-DS)

I have seen only five affected persons from four kinships with a disorder[17] which is similar to that described by Déjérine and Sottas. Such persons have a severe sensory motor polyneuropathy, usually present since birth or early childhood. None of the parents of these five had evidence of a peripheral neuropathy (most were examined by clinical and electrophysiologic methods). The development of the syndrome was typical. Walking was delayed in four of the five affected persons and occurred at 15, 33, 36, and 48 months of age; even at the best motor development, none of these four was able to run. Typically, these patients are in a wheelchair by the end of the second decade. Although pes cavus and hammertoes may be seen, these were not prominent features in most of the patients. Muscle weakness was generalized in the limbs but was most severe distally. Muscle weakness was greater in lower limbs than in upper limbs. Tendon reflexes were absent.

Sensory loss was much more severe than in the HN-CMT variety and affected mostly the distal aspects of the limbs but shaded off to normal near the knee. The modalities of sensation affected were mainly touch-pressure, joint position, and vibration. Although miosis and nystagmus have been described in some kinships, these were not present in our patients. These patients did not have retinitis pigmentosa. Cerebrospinal fluid protein was markedly increased. Conduction velocities of peripheral nerves were very low. Values of less than 5 m/sec for the major nerve trunks have been found.

Nerve biopsy has shown that cutaneous nerves are greatly enlarged (in some cases, four to eight times the normal transverse fascicular area).[35, 36] Myelinated fiber counts per nerve or per square millimeter of transverse fascicular area are much decreased; however, in these nerves the greater part of the length of myelinated fibers are demyelinated and therefore these low values are misleading.[16] The fiber spectrum also is markedly abnormal. The largest fibers may only be 4 or 5 μ in diameter. Unmyelinated fibers are present in normal numbers.

There is abundant evidence of an abnormality of myelination in these nerves. Onion-bulb formations are similar to those described in other varieties of hypertrophic neuropathy. Recently, in one patient a systemic abnormality of ceramide hexoses and their sulfates has been postulated.[16] A liver biopsy from a patient with this disorder in typical form was found to have a sixfold increase in ceramide monohexose-sulfate and a great decrease in ceramide dihexose-sulfate and of other complex sulfates. On nerve biopsy, the absence of cerebrosides was thought to be on the basis of the great decrease in the amount of myelin. However, in view of this, the increase in sulfatides and sphingomyelin was impressive.

REFERENCES

1. Déjérine, J. and Sottas, J.: Sur la névrite: interstitielle, hypertrophique et progressive de l'enfance. *C. R. Soc. Biol. (Paris)* **45**:63, 1893.
2. Gombault, A. and Mallet, R.: Un cas de tabès: ayant débuté dans l'enfance—autopsie, *Arch. Méd. exp.* **1**:385, 1889.
3. Déjérine, J.: Contribution a l'étude de la névrite interstitielle hypertrophique et progressive de l'enfance. *Rev. méd.* **16**:881, 1896.
4. Déjérine, J. and Andre-Thomas: Sur la névrite interstitielle hypertrophique et progressive de l'enfance. *Nouv. Iconogr. Salpêt.* **19**:477, 1906.
5. Boveri, P.: De la névrite hypertrophique familiale (type Pierre Marie). *Sem. méd. (Paris)* **30**:145, 1910.
6. Bielschowsky, M.: Familiare hypertrophische Neuritis und Neurofibromatose. *J. Psychol. Neurol. (Lpz.)* **29**:182, 1922.
7. Slauck: Über progressive hypertrophische Neuritis (Hoffmannsche Krankheit). *Zbl. ges. Neurol. Psychiat.* **92**:34, 1924.
8. Wolf, A.; Rubinowitz, A. H. and Burchell, S. C.: Interstitial hypertrophic neuritis of Déjérine and Sottas: a report of three cases. *Bull. neurol. Inst. N.Y.* **2**:373, 1932.
9. Gruner, J. E.: La biopsie nerveuse en microscopie électronique. *C. R. Soc. Biol. (Paris)* **154**:1632, 1960.
10. Dyck, P. J.: Histologic measurements and fine structure of biopsied sural nerve: normal, and in peroneal muscular atrophy, hypertrophic neuropathy, and congenital sensory neuropathy. *Mayo Clinic Proc.* **41**:742, 1966.
11. Garcin, R.; Lapresle, J.: Fardeau, M. and de Recondo, J.:

Étude au microscope électronique du nerf périphérique prélevé par biopsie dans quatre cas de névrite hypertrophique de Déjérine-Sottas. *Rev. Neurol (Paris)* **115**:917, 1966.

12. Webster, H. deF.; Schröder, J. M.; Asbury, A. K. and Adams, R. D.: The role of Schwann cells in the formation of "onion bulbs" found in chronic neuropathies. *J. Neuropath. exp. Neurol.* **26**:276, 1967.

13. Weller, R. O.: An electron microscopic study of hypertrophic neuropathy of Déjérine and Sottas. *J. Neurol. Neurosurg. Psychiat.* **30**:111, 1967.

14. Thomas, P. K. and Lascelles, R. G.: Hypertrophic neuropathy. *Quart. J. Med.* n.s. **36**:223, 1967.

15. Zacks, S. I.; Lipshutz, H. and Elliott, F.: Histochemical and electron microscopic observations on "onion bulb" formations in a case of hypertrophic neuritis of 25 years duration with onset in childhood. *Acta neuropath. (Berl.)* **11**:157, 1968.

16. Dyck, P. J.; Ellefson, R. D.; Lais, A. C.; Smith, R. C.; Taylor, W. F. and Van Dyke, R. A.: Histologic and lipid studies of sural nerves in inherited hypertrophic neuropathy: preliminary report of a lipid abnormality in nerve and liver in Déjérine-Sottas disease. *Mayo Clin. Proc.* **45**:286, 1970.

17. Dyck, P. J. and Lambert, E. H.: Lower motor and primary sensory neuron diseases with peroneal muscular atrophy. I. Neurologic, genetic, and electrophysiologic findings in hereditary polyneuropathies. *Arch. Neurol. (Chic.)* **18**:603, 1968.

18. Dyck, P. J. and Lambert, E. H.: Lower motor and primary sensory neuron diseases with peroneal muscular atrophy. II. Neurologic, genetic, and electrophysiologic findings in various neuronal degenerations. *Arch. Neurol. (Chic.)* **18**:619, 1968.

19. Austin, J. H.: Observations on the syndrome of hypertrophic neuritis (the hypertrophic interstitial radiculo-neuropathies). *Medicine (Baltimore)* **35**:187, 1956.

20. Nichols, P. C.; Dyck, P. J. and Miller, D. R.: Experimental hypertrophic neuropathy: change in fascicular area and fiber spectrum after acute crush injury. *Mayo Clin. Proc.* **43**:297, 1968.

21. Cammermeyer, J.: Neuropathological changes in hereditary neuropathies: manifestation of the syndrome heredopathia atactica polyneuritiformis in the presence of interstitial hypertrophic polyneuropathy. *J. Neuropath. exp. Neurol.* **15**:340, 1956.

22. Lampert, P. W. and Schochet, S. S., Jr.: Demyelination and remyelination in lead neuropathy: electron microscopic studies. *J. Neuropath. exp. Neurol.* **27**:527, 1968.

23. Dyck, P. J.: Experimental hypertrophic neuropathy: pathogenesis of onion-bulb formations produced by repeated tourniquet applications. *Arch. Neurol. (Chic.)* **21**:73, 1969.

24. Roussy, G. and Cornil, L.: Névrite hypertrophique progressive non familiale de l'adulte. *Ann. Méd.* **6**:296, 1919.

25. Stewart, B. M.: The hypertrophic neuropathy of acromegaly: a rare neuropathy associated with acromegaly. *Arch. Neurol. (Chic.)* **14**:107, 1966.

26. Eichhorst, H.: Ueber Heredität der progressiven Muskelatrophie. *Berl. klin. Wschr.* **10**:497, 511, 1873.

27. Virchow, R.: Ein Fall von progressiver Muskelatrophie. *Virchows Arch. path. Anat.* **8**:537, 1855.

28. Eulenburg, M.: Ueber progressive Muskelatrophie. *Dtsch. klin. (Berlin)* **8**:129, 1856.

29. Friedreich, N.: *Ueber progressive Muskelatropie, über wahre und falsche Muskelhypertrophie.* A. Hirschwald, Berlin, 1873.

30. Schultze, F.: Über die vererbbare neurale oder neurospinale Muskelatrophie. *Dtsch. Z. Nervenheilk.* **112**:1, 1930.

31. Charcot, J.-M. and Marie, P.: Sur une forme particulière d'atrophie musculaire progressive souvent familiale: debutant par les pieds et les jambes et atteignant plus tard les mains. *Rev. méd.* **6**:97, 1886.

32. Tooth, H. H.: *The Peroneal Type of Progressive Muscular Atrophy*, thesis, H. K. Lewis & Co., Ltd., London, 1886.

33. Biemond, A.: Neurotische Muskelatrophie und Friedreichsche Tabes in derselben Familie. *Dtsch. Z. Nervenheilk.* **104**:113, 1928.

34. Thévenard, A. and Berdet, H.: Remarques sur l'hypertrophie des nerfs périphériques: intérêt de l'exploration clinique du plexus cervical superficiel en particulier de sa branche auriculaire et de son examen histologique après biopsie. *Presse méd* **66**:529, 1958.

35. Dyck, P. J.; Beahrs, O. H. and Miller, R. H.: Peripheral nerves in hereditary neural atrophies: number and diameters of myelinated fibers. *Clin. Neurophysiol.*, 673, 1965.

36. Dyck, P. J. and Lambert, E. H.: Numbers and diameters of nerve fibers and compound action potential of sural nerve: controls and hereditary neuromuscular disorders. *Trans. Amer. neurol. Ass.* **91**:214, 1966.

37. Lambert, E. H.: Electromyography and electric stimulation of peripheral nerves and muscle. *Sections of Neurology and Section of Physiology, Mayo Clinic and Mayo Foundation: Clinical Examinations in Neurology.* W. B. Saunders, Philadelphia, 287, 1956.

38. Roussy, G. and Lévy, G.: Sept cas d'une maladie familiale particulière: troubles de la marche, pieds bots et aréfléxie tendineuse généralisée, avec, accessoirement, légère maladresse des mains. *Rev. neurol. (Paris)* **1**:427, 1926.

39. Yudell, A.; Dyck, P. J. and Lambert, E. H.: A kinship with the Roussy-Levy syndrome. *Arch. Neurol. (Chic.)* **13**:432, 1965.

40. Marie, M. P.: Forme spéciale de névrite interstitielle hypertrophique progressive de l'enfance. *Rev. Neurol. (Paris)* **14**:557, 1906.

41. Marie, P. and Bertrand, I.: Contribution a l'anatomie pathologique de la névrite hypertrophique familiale. *Ann. Méd.* **5**:209, 1918.

42. Dyck, P. J.; Winkelmann, R. K. and Bolton, C. F.: Quantitation of Meissner's corpuscles in hereditary neurologic disorders: Charcot-Marie-Tooth disease, Roussy-Levy syndrome, Déjérine-Sottas disease, hereditary sensory neuropathy, spinocerebellar degenerations, and hereditary spastic paraplegia. *Neurology (Minneap.)* **16**:10, 1966.

Characteristic Clinical Findings in Some Neurogenic Myopathies and in Some Myogenic Myopathies Causing Muscular Weakness, Hypotonia and Atrophy in Infancy and Early Childhood

INGRID GAMSTORP, M.D.

Some conditions causing neurogenic or myogenic myopathy are reviewed and illustrated by cases of 1) perinatal cervical cord injury; 2) various types of progressive spinal muscular atrophy and 3) congenital muscular dystrophy, Duchenne-like type of muscular dystrophy, limb-girdle type of muscular dystrophy and facioscapulohumeral type of muscular dystrophy. All the cases of muscular dystrophy described here occurred in girls.

Most young infants referred because of muscular weakness and hypotonia are referred under the diagnosis of Werdnig-Hoffman's disease; older children with the same symptomatology are almost always referred under the diagnosis of progressive muscular dystrophy. The diagnostic possibilities are, however, much more varied. In young infants the most common causes are various types of cerebral lesions and diseases, leading later on to obvious mental retardation with or without cerebral palsy syndromes. These infants have as a rule normal or hyperactive muscle reflexes, normal electromyographic findings and normal findings on a histologic examination of a muscle biopsy specimen. These conditions are left out entirely here, and the presentation concerns only diseases affecting the motor unit and thus causing hypoactive or absent muscle reflexes, electrophysiologic abnormalities and histopathologic abnormalities.

The first condition to be considered is a *traumatic lesion of the spinal cord at the cervical level*, which is an easily overlooked or misinterpreted perinatal injury.[1] Its incidence is unknown, as the spinal cord is seldom examined at autopsy of infants dying in the neonatal period. This lesion should be particularly suspected in term infants, born at a difficult delivery and dying from respiratory insufficiency, in whom only small or no brain damage is found at autopsy. If the infant survives, it may present a puz-

Gamstorp—Head, Department of Pediatrics, Central Hospital, Jönköping, Sweden.

Birth Defects: Original Article Series. Vol. VII, No. 2; February 1971

BIOGRAPHIC DATA

Dr. Ingrid Gamstorp, born in Lund, Sweden, received her M.D. degree in 1949 at the Medical Faculty, University of Lund, wrote a thesis in 1956 and was the same year appointed Assistant Professor at the University of Lund. She received her training in Pediatrics at the Department of Pediatrics, Kristianstad from 1951 to 1953 and at the Department of Pediatrics, Lund from 1954 to 1957. She also received training in neurology at the Department of Neurology, Lund from 1957 to 1958. From 1958 to 1960 she was a Jerry Lewis Fellow of the Muscular Dystrophy Association of America working mainly at the Massachusetts General Hospital, Boston in neurologic and neurophysiologic research. Since 1967 she has been the head of the Department of Pediatrics, Central Hospital, Jönköping, Sweden.

zling clinical picture. We have recently had such a case which I would like to describe briefly.

The patient was a boy who was born at term. Delivery was prolonged and difficult and occurred in breech presentation. He was in poor condition in the neonatal period with weakness and muscular hypotonia, respiratory difficulties, cyanotic spells and bouts of unexplained fever. After some months he started to improve, color and respiration became normal and he started to give contact. His motor development was, however, severely retarded. He was first seen when he was 20 months of age. At that age he appeared alert and interested in his surroundings; he could not speak but obviously understood some words. Nothing abnormal was found from eyes, face, pharyngeal muscles or tongue. His neck muscles were weak and he could not lift his head. Arms were very weak and flaccid and muscle reflexes were absent. He could make only gross movements with his arms and had no control over small finger movements. Sensation was obviously impaired and he bit and chewed on his hands (Fig. 1). No diaphragmatic movements were seen on x-ray examination of the lungs. The legs were also weak and fairly flaccid, but muscle reflexes were hyperactive and Babinski's sign was positive. He had normal sphincter control and no signs of a urinary tract infection. Conduction velocity of peripheral nerves was normal; electromyography revealed no abnormalities in leg muscles and signs of severe denervation in arm muscles. Based on the history of a difficult breech delivery followed by respiratory insufficiency and unexplained febrile episodes, and on the signs of an upper motor neuron lesion in the legs and a lower motor neuron lesion and sensory disturbances in the arms, our final diagnosis was a perinatal lesion of the cervical cord. The boy died about half a year later from pneumonia. The pathologist could confirm the clinical diagnosis, as he found an old severe lesion of the cervical cord with gliosis and scar tissue.

The next condition is *progressive spinal muscular atrophy with onset in infancy or early childhood.* The classification of the various types of this condition has been debated in the literature. The first clear descriptions appear during the latter part of the previous century and are by Werdnig[2, 3] and Hoffmann.[4-7] In their case reports both stressed that the patients were healthy during their first half-year and started to show symptoms, ie muscular hypotonia, weakness and atrophy, during their second or third half-year. Soon thereafter cases were reported with onset in the neonatal period or even during fetal life. Otherwise there is very little to add to Werdnig's and Hoffmann's excellent descriptions of the clinical and histopathologic features of the condition which now carries their names. They also found that the disease runs in families and their material suggests an autosomal recessive inheritance which has been confirmed by later studies.

The issue was confused a few decades later by Oppenheim,[8-10] who in short clinical demonstrations presented some children with severe muscular hypotonia with onset in the neonatal period, and

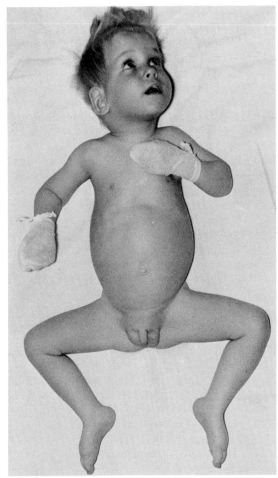

Fig. 1. A 2-year-old boy with a severe perinatal injury to the cervical cord. The hands had to be bandaged, because he bit and chewed on them, presumably as a consequence of probably disturbed sensation. (Courtesy of Läkartidningen)

claimed that these children later on improved. This statement seems to be based exclusively on the fact that this clinical picture is not seen in adulthood; to my knowledge Oppenheim never published a follow-up of his patients. However, for a long while Oppenheim's amyotonia congenita was considered a separate disease with earlier onset and better prognosis than Werdnig-Hoffmann's disease. The diagnostic possibilities in cases of infantile muscular weakness and hypotonia were reviewed by Brandt[11] and by Walton.[12] Both found that most of the patients diagnosed as cases of Oppenheim's amyotonia congenita had Werdnig-Hoffmann's disease, and a large part of the rest had other well-defined neuromuscular or metabolic disorders. It thus appears reasonable to drop Oppenheim's name entirely in this connection.

Another variant of progressive spinal muscular atrophy was described from Sweden by Wohlfart[13] and by Kugelberg and Welander.[14] They described a group of patients who during late childhood started to show weakness, atrophy and fasciculations in proximal limb muscles. The symptoms progressed slowly and the patients were able to walk and also to work at least in early adulthood. The disease was inherited as an autosomal recessive trait. The authors considered the condition a separate disease, distinguished from Werdnig-Hoffmann's disease because of its later onset and slower progress.

However, during the past decade many patients have been reported who seem to represent transitional forms between Werdnig-Hoffmann's disease and Kugelberg-Welander's disease. Many families have been reported with benign cases and more severe cases of progressive spinal muscular atrophy within the same sibship.[15-20]

At least two variants of progressive spinal muscular atrophy can on genetic grounds be separated from the rest. In one type inheritance is dominant; it has usually its onset in early adulthood or adolescence, exceptionally in childhood; its course is benign.[21] In another type, which also has a fairly benign course and to which at least some of Kugelberg and Welander's original patients may belong, a dominant gene seems to play a role together with a recessive one.[22] A distinction between other types of progressive spinal muscular atrophy, with autosomal recessive inheritance and early onset, must wait for a biochemical definition of their cause; it can at present not be done on clinical grounds.

The age of onset appears a particularly unreliable basis for distinguishing, as Kugelberg and Welander suggested, between different diseases. It is a general rule that the pediatrician, used to asking the patient's mother about the onset of the disease, gets an earlier age of onset than does the adult neurologist taking the history from the patient. However, even when the mother is available, is carefully questioned, is observant and cooperative, it may be difficult to get reliable information about the first symptoms of a disease with such an early and insidious onset. The difficulties are well illustrated by one of the families in my material.[17] The oldest child was affected and said to have shown symptoms from age one and a half to two years. When her next child was born healthy, the mother experienced what a healthy infant is supposed to do, and then said that her first child must have had symptoms at least at age one. A third child was born and was affected. In him the mother noted symptoms before he was a month old; in retrospect the mother felt that also her first child had most likely had symptoms from this early age. Thus, the stated age of onset is unreliable and often too high. In my own material of 25 patients with progressive spinal muscular atrophy the onset had been noted before the age of three and had probably occurred during the first year of life in all of them.

The clinical picture and course varied considerably among the 25 patients. Based on the early findings they could be divided in two main groups. One group, which I called Type I, showed in early infancy severe, *generalized* muscular weakness and hypotonia. These infants were unable to lift their heads, elbows or knees from the bed (Fig. 2). They correspond most closely to the condition usually termed Werdnig-Hoffmann's disease; on historic grounds it is, however, debatable if also cases with a very early onset should be included under this heading. Nine of the 25 patients belong to Type I. The prognosis was poor in this group as none of the patients learned to walk or to sit unsupported; four died during the first year and two between one and three years of age. The oldest of the surviving patients was, when last seen, 14 years of age. His mental development is normal. Physically he is severely handicapped, confined to a wheelchair with virtually no strength in proximal muscles, and has severe deformities (Fig. 3). He has tongue fasciculations but no swallowing difficulties.

In the 15 patients considered to belong to Type II the characteristic early finding was *localized* muscular weakness. These infants had no difficulties

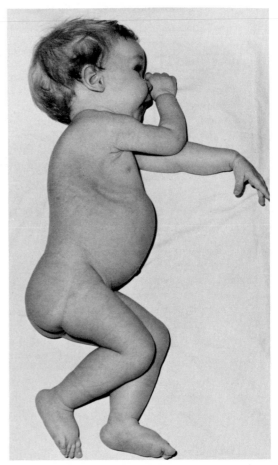

Fig. 2. A 10-month-old boy with progressive spinal muscular atrophy of type I. Note the chest deformity and the protuberant abdomen.

with head lifting or head control and they could use their arms in a normal way. All of them learned to sit unsupported at about seven months of age. Their mothers observed, however, that they had from an early age abnormally thin thighs and weak kicking movements. These abnormalities were noted by observant mothers during the infants' first month of life. They all learned to walk without support although later than healthy children, at the latest in this material about age four. Their gait was waddling, their back hyperlordotic and their abdomen protuberant. The children always had difficulties in getting up from the squatting position or from sitting on the floor and then had to climb on their own knees and thighs (Fig. 4), or on furniture (Fig. 5A). This sign, which reveals weakness of back muscles and hip extensors without telling anything about the cause of the weakness, has erroneously been described as pathognomonic for muscular dystrophy, and this may be the reason why most of these children were referred under a diagnosis of muscular dystrophy. Shoulder muscles were noted to be weak and atrophic at latest when the children were between four and seven years of age (Fig. 5B). The

Fig. 4. A 6-year-old boy with progressive muscular atrophy of type II, climbing up on his knees and thighs to reach erect position.

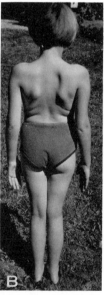

Fig. 5. A 9-year-old girl, sister of the boy in Figure 4. A) She has to use furniture to be able to come up in erect position. B) Weakness and atrophy of shoulder muscles.

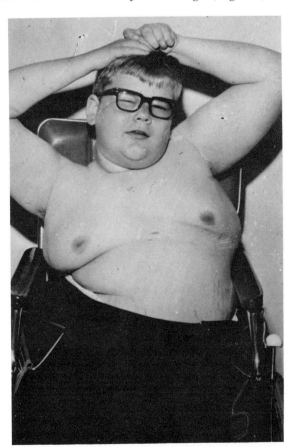

Fig. 3. A 14-year-old boy with progressive spinal muscular atrophy of type I and unusually long survival. Note the obesity, the scoliosis and the weak shoulder and arm muscles which makes it necessary for the boy to rest his hands on his head to be able to keep them above shoulder level.

muscular symptoms progressed slowly and several of the patients became confined to wheelchairs, usually at puberty or during the prepubertal growth spurt. When weakness progressed they also developed contractures and deformities (Figs. 6A and B and 7). Tongue fasciculations were observed in several from age 10 to 12; none had swallowing difficulties. They are all still alive.

The last patient in the material showed the same course of the disease as the 15 patients belonging to Type II. He had, however, also ankle clonus from

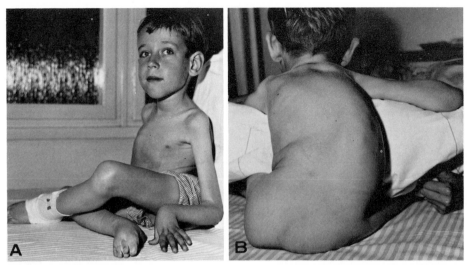

Fig. 6. A) An 8-year-old boy with progressive spinal muscular atrophy of type II. B) Note the deformities and contractures and the severe weakness and atrophy.

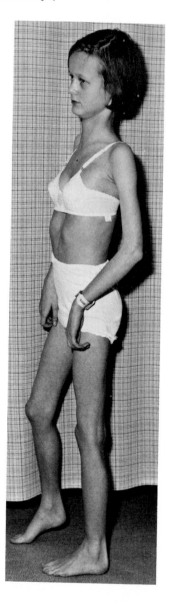

age 14 and a positive Babinski's sign. From that age, he is therefore better classified as a case of juvenile amyotrophic lateral sclerosis than of progressive spinal muscular atrophy. He is the oldest patient in the material. It is conceivable that other patients belonging to Type II will eventually develop cortico-spinal tract signs.

The *chronic peripheral polyneuropathies* in childhood are in my experience[23] often genetically determined, and the clinical picture is dominated by the patients' slow, clumsy movements, general awkwardness, loss of muscle reflexes, and by deformities such as high-arched feet and kyphoscoliosis (Fig. 8). A few of the patients show, however, severe muscular weakness and hypotonia. One of my patients was a newborn boy with severe, generalized hypotonia, inability to move arms and legs and areflexia. Werdnig-Hoffmann's disease was suspected and the parents were told that the prognosis probably was poor. However, when the boy was examined at age five days, the conduction velocity of peripheral nerves was found to be low, between 1 and 5 meter per sec (normal for age 25–35). The final diagnosis was polyneuropathy. The boy improved later. The cause remained unknown in his case; the fact that his mother had taken 17 different and unknown medications during pregnancy may have played a role.

In older children with muscular weakness due to polyneuropathy distal limb muscles seem always to be earlier and more severely affected than proximal limb muscles. Occasionally the weakness of proximal limb muscles is so pronounced that a diagnosis of muscular dystrophy or progressive spinal muscular atrophy may be considered. However, if the weak-

Fig. 7. A 16-year-old girl with progressive spinal muscular atrophy of type II, still able to walk but with difficulty. Note the contractures of hips and elbows.

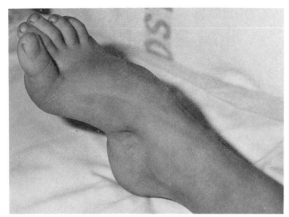

Fig. 8. A pes excavatus of a 7-year-old boy with chronic hereditary polyneuropathy.

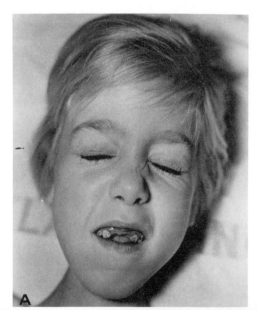

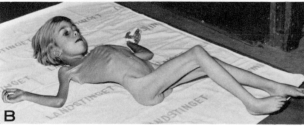

Fig. 9. A 7-year-old girl with severe congenital muscular dystrophy and bilateral facial weakness. A) Note the weakness of eye closure on maximal effort. B) Note the severe muscular atrophy and contractures.

ness is due to polyneuropathy, it is even more pronounced in distal muscles. Another typical clinical feature of polyneuropathy is the early loss of muscle reflexes. If a patient has mild muscular weakness and total areflexia, the likely diagnosis is polyneuropathy; the weakness is usually more pronounced before the muscle reflexes disappear, if the cause of the weakness is spinal muscular atrophy or muscular dystrophy.

Only a few examples of *myogenic myopathies*, illustrating puzzling clinical pictures in girls, will be discussed. In three girls symptoms were noted already in the *newborn period* with profound muscular hypotonia and weakness. All three were first-born children of healthy parents with no known cases of neuromuscular disorders in the family. Two of the girls have no sibs, whereas the third has now a brother and a sister, both healthy.

One of the girls has never been able to lift her head, to sit unsupported or to lift her arms or legs. She has bilateral facial weakness (Fig. 9A) and is unable to chew. Her intercostal muscles are also weak, she has had several attacks of pneumonia, and she has severe deformities (Fig. 9B). External eye muscles, tongue and throat muscles appear to function normally. Her mental development appears entirely normal. She represents a severe variant of congenital muscular dystrophy[24] with facial involvement and a poor prognosis.

The second girl appeared in the newborn period almost as severely affected as the first one. However, the normal development seemed in her to compete to some degree successfully with the progress of the disease. She could sit when she was about a year, she has good head control, she can lift her arms above her head, and she can at age four support her weight on her feet for about a minute. Her face is normal. She has no contractures. She is, however, still very weak with weak intercostal muscles and weak shoulder, arm and neck muscles (Fig. 10). A

Fig. 10. A 5-year-old girl with congenital muscular dystrophy. Note the weakness of neck, shoulder and arm muscles.

short general anesthesia provoked in her a severe episode of respiratory insufficiency during which she had to be treated in a respirator for several weeks. She is a very bright little girl. She must represent a less severe variant of congenital muscular dystrophy[25] with a questionable prognosis. Like girl No. 1 she has no calf muscle hypertrophy.

The third girl appeared less severely affected at birth, she could lift her head and move arms and legs although less actively than her younger sibs. She learned to sit during her second half-year, but she never learned to creep nor to stand. When first seen at age two and a half (Fig. 11) she had severe weakness of proximal leg muscles, flexion contractures of hips, shortened heel cords and calf muscle hypertrophy. Her pectoral muscles were atrophic and her shoulder muscles gave way when she was picked up. Her face was normal. She was followed for a couple of years during which time her condition remained essentially unchanged. Whatever congenital muscular dystrophy[26] may be, this girl also may represent a variant, though less severe than the other two, of this heterogeneous condition. However, her clinical picture also reminds one of the Duchenne-like

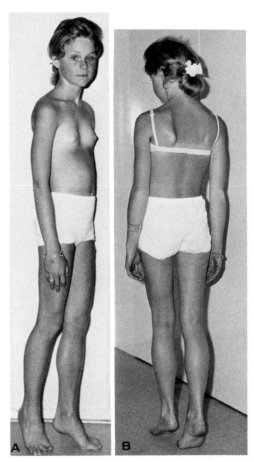

Fig. 12. A 13-year-old girl with the Duchenne-like variant of muscular dystrophy. A) Note the tight heel cords, the hypertrophic calf muscles and the disproportionally severe atrophy of the pectoral muscle and B) of the middle and lower part of the trapezius muscle.

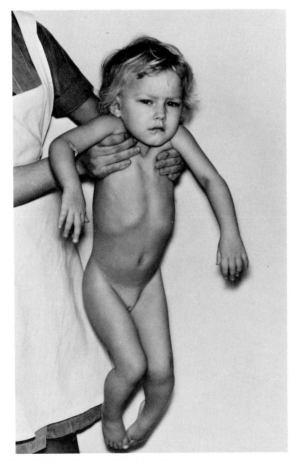

Fig. 11. A 2½-year-old girl with congenital muscular dystrophy. Note the weak shoulder muscles, the hypertrophic calf muscles and the contractures of hips and knees.

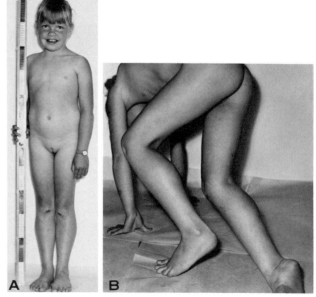

Fig. 13. A 7-year-old girl with the Duchenne-like variant of muscular dystrophy. A) Note the hypertrophic calves and B) her difficulties in getting up from sitting on the floor.

variant of muscular dystrophy, inherited as an auto-somal recessive trait and thus occurring also in girls.

Girl No. 4 was first seen when she was about ten years old. She is the second child of healthy, unre-lated parents; there are no known cases of a neuro-muscular disorder in the family. Her early develop-ment was normal and she started to walk at about age one and a half. When she was two it was noted that she walked on her toes and had difficulty coming down on her heels. At age ten she had short-ened heel cords, hypertrophic calves, weakness of the anterior tibial muscles and particularly of the prox-imal leg and hip muscles. She could not get up from sitting on the floor without climbing on her knees and thighs or on furniture; she could not squat. She also had slight weakness of the shoulder muscles and a definite atrophy of the pectoral muscles. Her con-dition was essentially unchanged at age 13 (Fig. 12A and B). She is a bright and charming young lady. When she was 13 her heel cords were successfully operated on, and her gait improved.

Girl No. 5 was an adopted child with no known cases of neuromuscular disorders in her family. Her early development was normal and she learned to walk when she was about one and a half. She never learned to run and she always had difficulties in climbing stairs. The girl was first seen when she was about seven. She then had weak hip muscles and pelvic girdle muscles, could not get up from sitting on the floor without climbing on her knees and thighs, could not squat, run or climb stairs without the help of her hands (Fig. 13A and B). Her heel cords were tight but she had no fixed contractures. Calf muscles were hypertrophic. Some weakness was found also in the shoulder muscles and pectoral muscles were atrophic. Facial muscles were normal.

These two girls (Nos. 4 and 5) were considered to represent the Duchenne-like type of muscular dystrophy[27, 28] occurring also in girls and suppos-edly inherited as an autosomal recessive trait. The characteristic features are: calf muscle hypertrophy, more severe atrophy of the pectoral muscle and of the middle and lower part of the trapezius muscle than of the rest of the shoulder muscles, normal fa-cial muscles, more severe weakness of the pelvic girdle than of the shoulder girdle. Girl No. 3, de-scribed among the congenital cases, could conceiv-ably also be included here in spite of the remarkably early onset of her symptoms.

Girl No. 6 is the third of four sibs. Parents are unrelated; there are no known cases of neuromus-cular disorders in the family. Her early development was normal and she learned to walk at about 14 months of age. When she was about one year or two it was noted that she kept her head tilted in a pe-culiar way and that she had difficulties in lifting it when she was lying flat on her back. When she was four to five years old her parents noted that she could not run as fast as her peers, that she fell easily and that she had trouble getting up again. She was first seen when she was six years old. She then had severe weakness and atrophy of neck and shoulder muscles (Fig. 14A and B). However, she also had some weakness of pelvic girdle and hip muscles and had to climb on her knees and thighs when getting up from the floor. There was no hypertrophy of calf

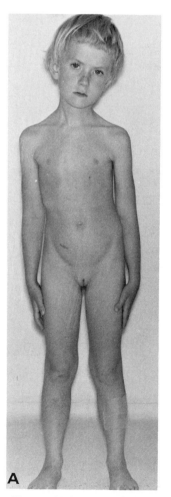

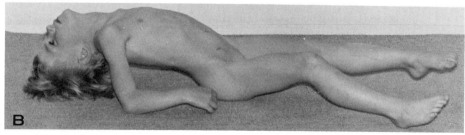

Fig. 14. A) A 6-year-old girl with limb-girdle type of muscular dystrophy. B) Note the atrophy and weakness of neck and shoulder mus-cles and her contracture of neck muscles.

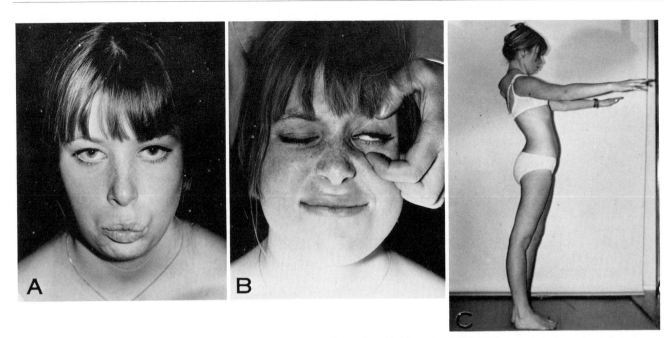

Fig. 15. A 15-year-old girl with facioscapulohumeral muscular dystrophy. A) Note the facial weakness, apparent when she tries to whistle and B) to close her eyes tightly, C) the weakness and atrophy of shoulder muscles, causing winging of scapulae and inability to lift arms above shoulder level, and the weakness of pelvic girdle and hip muscle, causing increased lumbar lordosis and overstretching of knees.

muscles. Facial muscles were normal. She has since been followed for about two years and her condition has remained essentially unchanged. She has been classified as a case of limb-girdle muscular dystrophy. This classification is based mainly on the facts that her shoulder girdle is more severely affected than her pelvic girdle, that she has no hypertrophy of calves, that her face is normal and that there is no evidence of dominant inheritance.

Girl No. 7 was first seen when she was 15 years of age. Her parents had noted weakness of facial muscles since she was a few years old and at about the same time weakness and atrophy of shoulder muscles. From early school-age slowly increasing difficulties in running and climbing stairs were observed. On examination facial weakness was noted and severe atrophy of shoulder muscles (Figs. 15A, B and C). She could not lift her arms up to shoulder level. She had also obvious weakness of pelvic girdle and hip muscles and had to climb on her knees and thighs to get up from sitting on the floor. No calf muscle hypertrophy was present. There was evidence of dominant inheritance, as the girl's mother and maternal grandmother both had the same condition since childhood. The classification of this girl as a case of facioscapulohumeral muscular dystrophy was based on the dominant inheritance and the clinical findings described.

REFERENCES

1. Towbin, A.: Latent spinal cord and brain stem injury in newborn infants. *Develop. Med. Child. Neurol.* 11:54, 1969.
2. Werdnig, G.: Zwei frühinfantile hereditäre Fälle von progressiver Muskelatrophie unter dem Bilde der Dystrophie, aber auf neurotischer Grundlage. *Arch. Psychiat. Nervenkr.* 22:437, 1894.
3. Werdnig, G.: Die frühinfantile progressive spinale Amyotrophie. *Arch. Psychiat. Nervenkr.* 26:706, 1899.
4. Hoffman, J.: Ueber chronische spinale muskelatrophie im Kindesalter, auf familärer Basis. *Dtsch. Z. Nervenheilk.* 3:427, 1893.
5. Hoffmann, J.: Weiterer Beitrag zur Lehr von der hereditären progressiven spinalen Muskelatrophie im Kindesalter. *Dtsch. Z. Nervenheilk.* 10:292, 1897.
6. Hoffmann, J.: Dritter Beitrag zur Lehr von der hereditären progressiven spinalen Muskelatrophie im Kindesalter. *Dtsch. Z. Nervenheilk.* 18:217, 1900.
7. Hoffmann, J.: Ueber die hereditäre progressive spinale Muskelatrophie im Kindesalter. *Münch. med. Wschr.* 47:1649, 1900.
8. Oppenheim, H.: Ueber allgemeine und localisierte Atonie der Muskulatur (Myatonie) im frühen Kindesalter. *Mschr. Psychiat. Neurol.* 8:232, 1900.
9. Oppenheim, H.: Ueber einen Fall von Myatonia congenita. *Berl. klin. Wschr.* 41:255, 1904.
10. Oppenheim, H.: Fall von Myatonia congenita. *Berl. klin. Wschr.* 49:2435, 1912.
11. Brandt, S.: *Werdnig-Hoffmann's Infantile Progressive Muscular Atrophy. Clinical Aspects, Pathology, Heredity and Relation to Oppenheim's Amyotonia Congenita and Other Morbid Conditions with Laxity of Joints and Muscles in Infants.* Munksgaard, Copenhagen, 1950.
12. Walton, J. N.: Amyotonia congenita. A follow-up study. *Lancet* i:1023, 1956.
13. Wohlfart, G.; Fex, J. and Eliasson, S.: Hereditary proximal spinal muscular atrophy—a clinical entity simulating progressive muscular dystrophy. *Acta psychiat. scand.* 30:395, 1955.
14. Kugelberg, E. and Welander, L.: Heredofamilial juvenile muscular atrophy simulating muscular dystrophy. *Arch. Neurol. Psychiat. (Chic.)* 75:500, 1956.
15. Dubowitz, V.: Infantile muscular atrophy. A prospective study with particular reference to a slowly progressive variety. *Brain* 87:707, 1964.
16. Dubowitz, V.: The floppy infant. *Clin. Develop. Med.* Vol. 31, 1969.
17. Gamstorp, I.: Progressive spinal muscular atrophy with onset in infancy or early childhood. *Acta Paediat. Scand.* 56:408, 1967.

18. Hausmanowa-Petrusewicz, I.; Prot, J. and Sawicka, E.: Le problème de formes infantiles et juvéniles de l'atrophie musculaire spinale. *Rev. neurol.* **114**:295, 1966.

19. Martin-Snessens, L. and Radermecker, J.: Amyotrophie neurogène classique (Werdnig-Hoffmann) et pseudomyopathique dans une fratrie. *J. Génét. hum.* **14**:341, 1965.

20. Zellweger, H.; Schneider, H. J.; Schuldt, D. R. and Mergner, W.: Hereditary spinal muscular atrophies. *Helv. paediat. Acta* **24**:92, 1969.

21. Armstrong, R. M.; Fogelson, M. H. and Silberberg, D. H.: Familial proximal spinal muscular atrophy. *Arch. Neurol. (Chic.)* **14**:208, 1966.

22. Becker, P. E.: Atrophia musculorum spinalis pseudomyopathica. Hereditäre neurogene proximale Amyotrophie von Kugelberg und Welander. *Z. menschl. Vererb.-u Konstit.-Lehre* **37**:193, 1964.

23. Gamstorp, I.: Polyneuropathy in childhood. *Acta Paediat. Scand.* **57**:230, 1968.

24. Zellweger, H.; Afifi, A.; McCormick, W. F. and Mergner, W.: Severe congenital muscular dystrophy. *Amer. J. Dis. Child.* **114**:591, 1967.

25. Zellweger, H.; Afifi, A.; McCormick, W. F. and Mergner, W.: Benign congenital muscular dystrophy: a special form of congenital hypotonia. *Clin. pediat.* **6**:655, 1967.

26. Vasella, F.; Mumenthaler, M.; Rossi, E.; Moser, H. and Wiesmann, U.: Die kongenitale Muskeldystrophie. *Dtsch. Z. Nervenheilk.* **190**:349, 1967.

27. Heyck, H. and Laudahn, G.: *Die Progressiv-Dystrophischen Myopathien.* Springer-Verlag, Berlin, Heidelberg, New York, 1969.

28. Walton, J. N., ed: Classification of the neuromuscular disorders. *J. neurol. Sci.* **6**:165, 1968.

The Genetic Heterogeneity of Spinal Muscular Atrophy (SMA)*

HANS ZELLWEGER, M.D.

The clinical picture of the spinal muscular atrophy varies greatly with respect to age of onset, speed of progression, severity and distribution of muscular atrophy, weakness and contractures, yet cases occurring within a family usually show concordant clinical features. Thus, genetic heterogeneity has to be assumed. This is supported by the various genetic transmission patterns (autosomal dominant, recessive, X-linked recessive) found by accurate pedigree analysis.

Clinicians and clinical geneticists are often divided into lumpers and splitters as our Chairman, Dr. Victor McKusick, so vividly illustrated in his introductory remarks to the first of these conferences in 1968.[1] The history of the SMA's shows that—with respect to these conditions—at times splitters prevailed, while at other times investigation tended to lump these conditions together. For many years the early infantile progressive SMA, also called Werdnig-Hoffmann's disease (W.H.) was differentiated from the pseudomyopathic juvenile SMA or Kugelberg-Welander's disease (K.W.). More recently a third form of SMA, namely congenital arthrogryposis multiplex due to anterior horn cell disease was stipulated.[2] An increasing number of observations made in recent years revealed cases with overlapping clinical features which did not fit in any one of these categories.[3-10] Analysis of 46 cases followed in the Iowa University Hospital (Fig. 1) showed all sorts of clinical conditions making a clear-cut delineation between the three forms of SMA impossible.[11] The disease apparently can begin at any age from prenatal life on to early childhood and perhaps even later. I emphasize that late recognition of the disease is not identical with late beginning. The disease often develops so slowly and insidiously that considerable periods of time, perhaps even years, elapse before it becomes noticeable. Seventeen of our cases obviously had a prenatal beginning; some of them were arthrogrypotic, others were extremely flaccid. One baby showed arthrogryposis in one limb and muscular hypotonia and articular hy-

BIOGRAPHIC DATA

Dr. Hans Zellweger, born in Switzerland in 1909, received his medical education at Zurich University Medical School, Hamburg University Medical School, University of Rome Medical School and Berlin University Medical School. He has held appointments in pathology and obstetrics at the Kantonsspital Lucerne, was a co-worker of Dr. Albert Schweitzer, Hospital of Lambaréné, French Equatorial Africa (now Republic of Gabon); Resident, Chief Resident, and Associate Professor, Department of Pediatrics, Kinderspital, Zurich; General Secretary, Sixth International Congress of Pediatrics, Zurich, in 1950 and Fellow, Rockefeller Foundation, New York in 1951. From 1951 through 1959 he was Professor and Head, Department of Pediatrics, American University of Beirut. From 1957 to 1958 he was Research Professor, and since 1959 has been Professor, Department of Pediatrics, University of Iowa.

Dr. Zellweger is a member of a number of professional societies in this country, a corresponding Member of the Swiss Pediatric Society and Honorary Member of the Lebanese Pediatric Society.

Zellweger—Professor of Pediatrics, Pediatric General Hospital, University of Iowa, Iowa City.
* Supported in part by Public Health Service Grant NB 05489-03 from the National Institutes of Health and a grant from the National Foundation for Neuromuscular Diseases.

perlaxity in the other three limbs. Many of the cases with prenatal beginning died in early infancy but a few cases with either arthrogryposis or muscular

Birth Defects: Original Article Series. Vol. VII, No. 2; February 1971

82

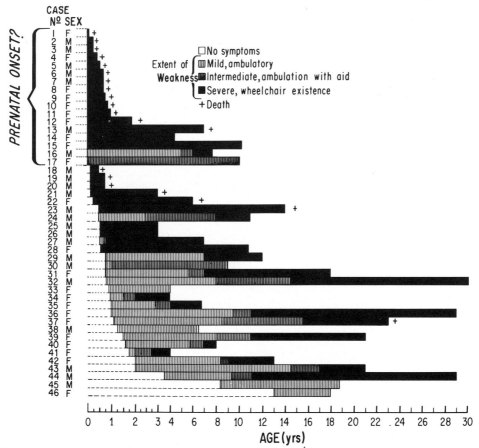

Fig. 1. Clinical Course of 46 Cases of SMA: Each horizontal column represents one case. The columns of 17 cases start at birth although the disease obviously began earlier. In the remaining 29 cases the columns begin at the age when the first signs of muscular weakness were noticed. This age is not necessarily identical with the real onset of the disease. It may well be that the SMA in many of these cases begins at a much younger age, possibly at birth as indicated by the broken line. The diagnosis of all cases was confirmed by muscular biopsy or postmortem examination of muscle and spinal cord. (From *Helv. paediat. Acta* Vol. 24, No. 1, p. 96, 1969, with permission of the author and publisher.)

hypotonia survived for more than a decade. In 29 patients, weakness was noticed several months or years after birth. Some of them developed severe weakness within a short time, others took a long time before a state of severe weakness was reached, and again others never developed more than mild to moderate weakness. Our observations confirmed that SMA forms a wide-ranging continued spectrum of clinical conditions which are all due to the abiotrophy of the anterior horn cells in the spinal cord.[12]

The question then arose whether or not all these different phenotypic manifestations were indeed variants of one disease entity. If they were different expressions of a pleiotropic gene, it should be possible to encounter them within the same family. Intrafamilial variability of the clinical picture is rare and, if it occurs, it does not span over the whole range of the possible clinical pictures.[13-17] The intrafamilial variability was quite pronounced in a family presented in Figure 2.[15, 16] In most instances of familial SMA, course and manifestations of affected

relatives were quite similar; in our series we had seven sibships with more than one affected sib and one family with SMA in two generations (mother and three daughters). In all these observations the clinical picture was astonishingly alike for all members of the same family. On the other hand, the clinical picture differed greatly from one family to the other. Thus intrafamilial concordance prevails over intrafamilial variability while intrafamilial variability is rather limited. These findings suggest genetic heterogeneity. SMA may be caused by different genes or perhaps different alleles. However, one could object that in some instances the effect of the mutant gene could be modified by other genes or by environmental factors. Such modifications could account for the rarely observed intrafamilial variability of the clinical picture, although they could not explain the discrepancy between inter- and intrafamilial variability.

Investigations of the genetics of SMA yielded further support of its genetic heterogeneity. SMA in

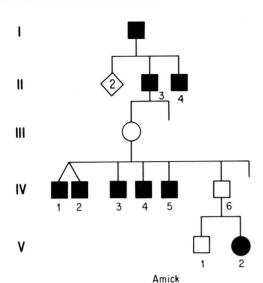

Amick

Fig. 2. SMA; Genetic Pleiotropism (modified from Amick *et al*[15] and Hogenhuis and Engel[16]): The patients IV$_1$ and IV$_2$ were identical twins who, at the age of three years, were noted to have slight difficulties in climbing stairs. The condition progressed slowly. They were wheelchair bound at 14 years of age and severely handicapped but still able to raise their arms to feed and shave themselves at the age of 30 years. The patients IV$_3$, IV$_4$ and IV$_5$ showed severe generalized weakness and atrophy in early infancy and died between two and four years of age. V$_2$, a 22-month-old girl, was able to sit, but could neither creep, stand nor walk. The patients I$_1$, II$_3$ and II$_4$ had progressive impairment of ambulation leading to the use of canes or wheelchair late in life. Deaths occured at 65 (I$_1$), 55 (II$_3$) and 37 (II$_4$) years.

most textbooks is considered as an autosomal recessive condition and indeed most neuropediatricians have witnessed sibships with two or more affected sibs without any evidence of SMA in other relatives. Since in some families SMA patients die before reaching reproductive age, potential autosomal dominance may not be recognized. Hence it may be that autosomal recessive inheritance has been overemphasized.

In accordance with autosomal recessive inheritance of rare genes, parental consanguinity is rather frequent.[18-22] A few representative examples are shown in Figure 3. Brandt[22] reviewed SMA in Denmark and found a consanguinity rate of 5.8% among his SMA cases, which was about eight times higher than the consanguinity rate in the Danish population at large. Becker,[9] by comparing gene frequency of SMA and consanguinity rate at large, came up with an expected consanguinity rate of 9%. The discrepancy between the observed and the expected values indicated that not all familial cases are presumably due to autosomal recessive inheritance (see also Figure 3A). Brandt already suspected "incomplete dominance" as an alternative transmission pattern.

A number of families have been reported displaying an autosomal dominant mode of inheritance.[23-31] A few instances with SMA occurring in two generations (parent and offspring) are listed in

Figure 4. Two families with SMA in three and five generations respectively were reported by Armstrong[28] and by Finkel.[23] Modifications of their pedigrees are presented in Figures 5 and 6. Armstrong's pedigree (Fig. 5) is suggestive of autosomal dominance with complete penetrance. In Finkel's family (Fig. 6), 40 members in five subsequent generations were affected with a late appearing, slowly progressive SMA. The mutant gene did not seem to be completely penetrant. II$_9$ for instance did not show any evidence of disease although she transmitted the mutant gene to two of her offspring, III$_{29}$ and III$_{39}$. Likewise, I$_1$ was not affected, yet had four affected daughters, II$_3$, II$_4$, II$_5$ and II$_7$. It is interesting to note that several affected individuals had only nonaffected children. For instance, III$_9$, III$_{10}$, III$_{11}$, III$_{14}$ and III$_{15}$ together had 51 children. Not a single one of them presented evidence of disease. The two patients III$_8$ and III$_{13}$ were both married twice and had children with SMA from one mating partner only; III$_8$ had seven nonaffected children from another mating partner. III$_{13}$ had six nonaffected children from a second mating partner. These observations are difficult to reconcile with autosomal dominance and incomplete penetrance. An interpretation of these findings will be attempted later on.

Numerous studies revealed an autosomal dominant transmission pattern with incomplete penetrance, of which only two examples are presented in Figure 7. Figure 7A is presented for historic interest. It shows the pedigree of the family G reported by one of the first describers of SMA, Hoffmann.[32] The mother of the proband was perfectly normal, yet seven of her 11 sibs developed progressive muscular atrophy and weakness in late infancy and all died between two and four years presenting clinical features similar to that of her affected children. Figure 7B presents a modification of the pedigree reported by Tsukagoshi *et al*[33] of a family with SMA beginning insidiously in infancy or childhood and leading to more or less severe incapacitation after a steadily progressing course of several decades. The individual III$_5$ of this pedigree did not show any evidence of SMA yet had two affected children IV$_9$ and IV$_{11}$.

Families with SMA have been reported who show a transmission pattern compatible with neither recessive nor dominant inheritance.[12, 30, 34, 35] Four representative examples are shown in Figure 8. In Figure 8B two first cousins only were affected with SMA.[35] All other relatives were not affected. In Figures 8A and 8C second cousins[12] and in Figure 8D two fourth cousins showed SMA without any other affected relatives in between.[34] In all these families, particularly in the three families shown in Figures 8A, C and D there was too long a line of healthy gene carriers between the diseased individuals to warrant autosomal dominance with incomplete penetrance.

Random association of two independent mutant

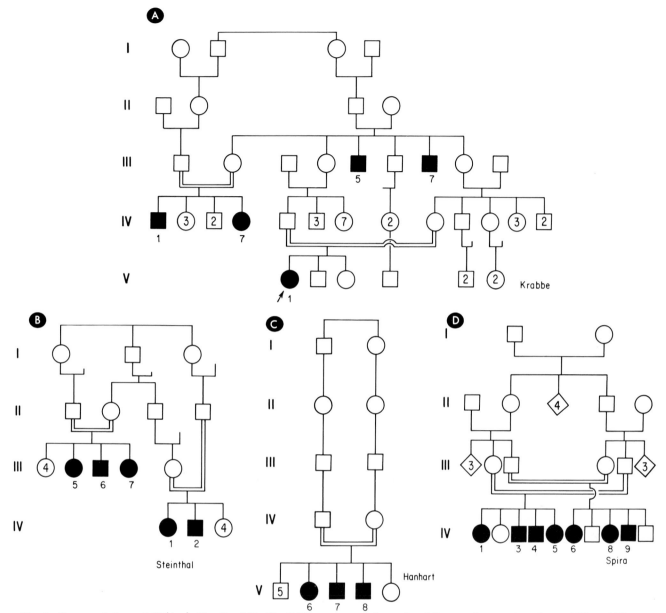

Fig. 3. Consanguinity and SMA: A. Family of Krabbe.[19] The parents of the proband V_1 were first cousins, those of IV_1 and IV_7 were second cousins. The parents of III_5 and of III_7 were not related to each other, which is not fully in keeping with autosomal recessive inheritance and suggests a different transmission pattern. All five affected members of this kinship had a clinical picture of SMA beginning before birth or shortly thereafter; they all had progressive weakness and died in the second half of the first year. B. Family of Steinthal.[20] The parents of III_5, III_6 and III_7 were first cousins as well. All five cases showed the typical picture of infantile SMA. C. Family of Hanhart.[18] Parents of V_6, V_7 and V_8 are third cousins. The three affected children had infantile SMA beginning at birth or in early infancy. They died between five and eight months, two of pulmonary complications, one of bulbar palsy. D. Family of Spira.[21] Parents of both sibships with affected children are first cousins. All affected individuals of both sibships had a slowly progressive SMA involving predominantly the lower limbs. The disease in all of them was noted between two years and eight years. IV_1, IV_3, IV_4 and IV_5 were between three and one-half and nine years, IV_6, IV_8 and IV_9 between 20 and 28 years old. All patients were still ambulatory when last seen.

genes could be assumed notably for the cases shown in Figure 8D and perhaps also for the two first cousins presented in Figure 8B. The patient II_1 of this family (Fig. 8B) showed evidence of mild disease in his fourth year of life. The condition progressed slowly and insidiously and after the age of 17 years he was no longer able to walk. The disease of his

cousin II_2 began much earlier. This girl learned to sit yet was never able to crawl and walk and when last seen at the age of nine years revealed severe generalized weakness, being barely able to move her arms and to feed herself. There are, then, slight phenotypic differences between these two cases, notably with respect to age of onset and rapidity of progres-

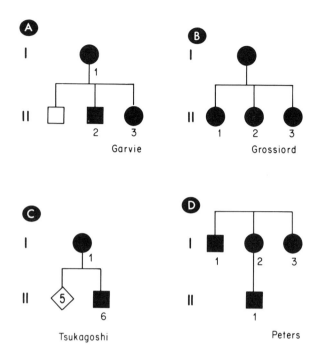

Fig. 4. Autosomal dominant inheritance of SMA with early onset (A, B) and late onset (C, D): A. SMA in mother and two children, very mild proximal weakness first noticed in late infancy and, if any, very slow progression. (Modified from a report by Garvie and Woolf.[26]) B. SMA in mother and three daughters. I[1], 46-year-old woman, mild, barely progressive weakness in proximal musculature since early childhood. SMA in her daughters noticed in early infancy. II[1] died at 24 years of age with bulbar palsy. II[2] and II[3] were 14 and 15 years old and showed proximal compartment weakness and swallowing paresis. (Modified from a report by Grossiord et al.[24]) C. SMA in mother and son. Onset of mother's disease unknown. She was no longer ambulatory at 45 years and died at 52 years. Her son noticed mucular weakness at 38 years. He showed mild spinobulbar involvement at 41 years. (Modified from a report from Tsukagoshi et al.[25]) D. Late onset SMA in three sibs and the son of one of them. Mild weakness noticed at about the 50th year or later. The patient showed mild and barely progressive proximal weakness with mild dysphagia. (Modified from a report of Peters et al.[30])

sion. Whether both patients carry the same—pleiotropic—gene or have two different genes, remains an open question.

Quite informative were the cases presented in Figures 8A and 8C.[12] The identical twins IV[1] and IV[2] of Figure 8A and their second cousin IV[7] revealed impressively similar course and findings. All three patients revealed signs of muscular weakness in the second half of the first year and progressed rapidly to an identical state of severe muscular atrophy and weakness in arms and legs. The three girls IV[9], IV[17] and IV[18] of Figure 8C likewise revealed great similarities. Their disease began in very early infancy. The legs were severely affected while the arms, though being atrophic, could be raised against gravity and some resistance. There was, then, great intrafamilial concordance in both families while the patients of each family showed a phenotypic pattern different from that of the other family (intrafamilial variability). We believe, therefore, that the SMA of the three cases in each family has the same genetic origin. What kind of hereditary pattern was operative in these cases? Autosomal dominance with incomplete penetrance could be excluded since the penetrance fell below a certain percentage, as mentioned by Neel and Schull.[36] An alternative explanation was offered by Becker[9] who assumed that there were at least three allelomorphic genes of the locus of this particular SMA gene, namely:

1) a wild type allele a;
2) an activator allele a';
3) a mutant gene A which however produces phenotypic SMA only in presence of the above activator a'.

The gene combination Aa does not cause manifest disease. Becker assumes that the allele a' is less frequent than a but more frequent than A and frequent

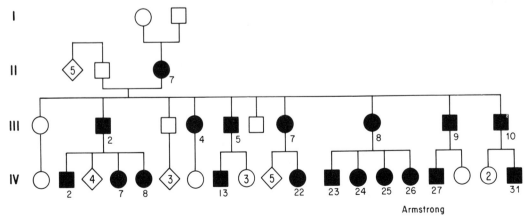

Fig. 5. SMA with autosomal dominance and complete penetrance: First signs of proximal compartment weakness were noticed within the first decade of life in most cases. Very slow progression of the disease. II[7] reached 62 years of age and was still ambulatory at the time she died of heart disease. III[2] to III[10] were between 43 and 27 years of age and still ambulatory. (Pedigree modified from Armstrong et al.[28])

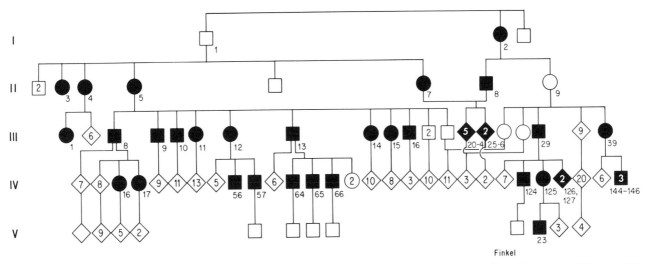

Fig. 6. SMA in 40 members of five generations of a South American family: Onset was noticed only beyond the age of 50 years. The disease consisted of proximal compartment weakness with extremely slow progression. (Modification of a report by Finkel.[23])

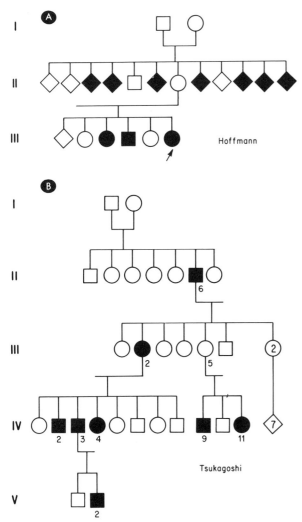

Fig. 7. Two pedigrees of SMA showing autosomal dominance with incomplete penetrance. (Figure A modified from a report by Hoffman[32]; Figure B modified from Tsukagoshi et al.[33])

enough to occur randomly more than once in a wider kindred. The possible phenotypes according to this hypothesis are presented in Figure 8C. The two related grandparents II_{12} and II_{13} as well as the mother III_5 of one patient and the father III_{13} of the two affected girls (Fig. 8C) carry the mutant gene A and the wild type gene a and hence do not show evidence of manifest SMA. The activator gene a' was brought into these families by the two unrelated parents, III_4 and III_{15}. The affected children inherited A from one parent and a' from the other parent. The three other possible phenotypes are indicated for one of the nonaffected sisters IV_{11}. They are $a'a$, Aa and aa. A number of observations correspond with this hypothesis. Furthermore, Becker found the ratio of affected to nonaffected sibs to be about $1:3$, a ratio which would be difficult to reconcile with autosomal dominance, but which is explained by the presented hypothesis. It explains also the surprising observations of Finkel (Fig. 5) of several affected individuals having only nonaffected offspring.

Finally, Kennedy et al[37] in recent months reported two families of late beginning, slowly progressive SMA which affected only males, while females appeared to be heterozygous carriers of the mutant gene. These pedigrees are the first examples known to us of sex-linked recessive inheritance of SMA (Fig. 9).

Summary and Conclusions

1. The clinical features of spinal muscular atrophy (SMA) vary greatly with respect to:
   a) age when muscular atrophy or weakness become clinically apparent;
   b) speed with which the weakness develops;
   c) severity of the clinical picture.
2. Concordance with respect to the clinical picture

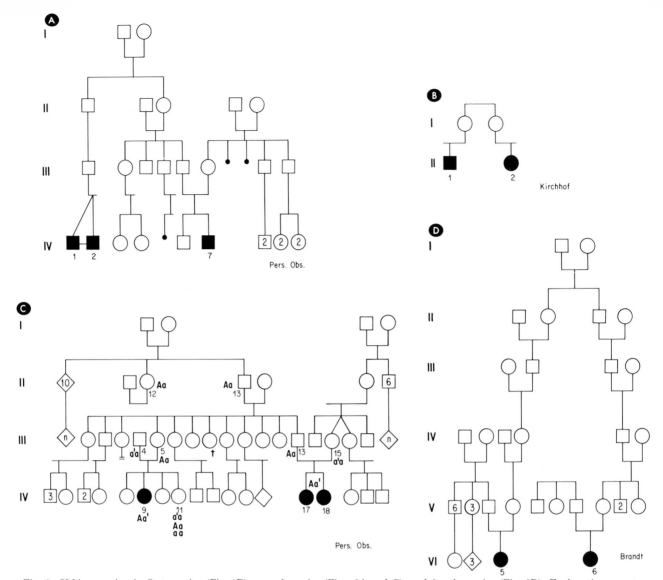

Fig. 8. SMA occurring in first cousins (Fig. 8B), second cousins (Figs. 8A and C), and fourth cousins (Fig. 8D). Explanations, see text. (Figure 8B modified from a report by Kirchhof *et al*[35]; Figures 8A and C, personal observations[12]; Figure 8D modified from a report of Brandt.[34])

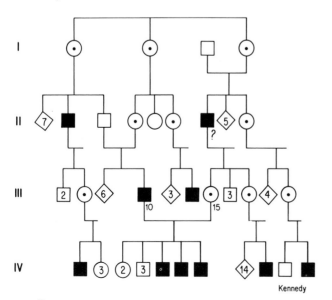

Fig. 9. SMA; X-linked recessive inheritance: Ten males are affected with a progressive spinal and bulbar muscular atrophy. No females are affected, yet females appeared as carriers of the mutant gene. The patient III$_{10}$ had three affected sons, IV$_9$, IV$_{10}$ and IV$_{11}$; however, their mother III$_{15}$ was obviously a carrier of the mutant gene since her father was possibly affected with SMA. SMA of III$_{10}$ is therefore not directly related with the SMA of his three affected sons. (Modification of a report of Kennedy *et al*.[37])

⊙ = Carrier

within a given family is the rule although a certain intrafamilial variability is at times found. The latter is never as pronounced as the interfamilial variability of the clinical picture.

3. These clinical observations suggest that SMA consists of different disease entities (genetic heterogeneity).

4. Genealogic studies revealed several possible modes of heritability, namely:

  a) autosomal recessive inheritance;

  b) autosomal dominant inheritance with either complete or incomplete penetrance;

  c) autosomal inheritance of a mutant gene, which is only pathogenic when linked with an activator allelomorphic gene;

  d) X-linked recessive inheritance.

5. Genetic heterogeneity of SMA is herewith well established.

REFERENCES

1. McKusick, V. A.: On lumpers and splitters, or the nosology of genetic disease. Proc. 1st Conf. on Clin. Delineation of Birth Defects, Part I, *Special Lectures*, Daniel Bergsma, ed. Birth Defects: Orig. Art. Series, The National Foundation, N. Y., Vol. V:23, 1969.

2. Research Group on Neuromuscular Diseases: Classification of the neuromuscular disorders. *J. neurol. Sci.* 6:165, 1968.

3. Martin-Sneessens, L. and Radermecker, J.: Amyotrophie neurogène classique (Werdnig-Hoffmann) et pseudo-myopathique infantile dans une fratrie (discussion de la validité des différentes formes de l'amyotrophie neurogène). *J. Génét. hum.* 14:341, 1965.

4. Hausmanowa-Petrusewicz, I.: Prot, J. and Sawicka, E.: Le problème des formes infantiles et juvéniles de l'atrophie musculaire spinale. *Rev. neurol.* 114:295, 1966.

5. Gross, M.: Proximal spinal muscular atrophy. *J. Neurol. Neurosurg. Psychiat.* 29:29, 1966.

6. Verger, P.; Guillard, J.-M.; Vital, Cl. and Eschapasse, P.: Amyotrophie neurogène pseudo-myopathique infantile. Deux observations nouvelles. *Pédiatrie* 21:585, 1966.

7. De Barsy, Th.; Hariga, J. and Claes, C.: Amyotrophie spinale proximale (Kugelberg-Welander) sporadique à début tardif. Sa place dans le cadre des hérédodégénérésescences. *Rev. neurol.* 114:541, 1967.

8. Gardner-Medwin, D.; Hudgson, P. and Walton, J. N.: Benign spinal atrophy arising in childhood and adolescence. *J. neurol. Sci.* 5:121, 1967.

9. Becker, P. E.: Krankheiten mit hauptsächlicher Beteiligung von Pyramidenbahn, Vorderhorn und bulbären motorischen Kernen (Spastik, spinale Muskelatrophie und Bulbärparalyse). In P. E. Becker ed. *Humangenetik*, Vol. V, part 1, 314. Thieme, Stuttgart, 1966.

10. Munsat, T. L.; Woods, R.; Fowler, W. and Pearson, C. M.: Neurogenic muscular atrophy of infancy with prolonged survival. *Brain* 92:9, 1969.

11. Zellweger, H.; Schneider, H. J.; Schuldt, D. R. and Mergner, W.: Heritable spinal muscular atrophies. *Helv. paediat. Acta* 24:92, 1969.

12. Zellweger, H.; Schneider, H. and Schuldt, D. R.: A new genetic variant of spinal muscular atrophy. *Neurology*, 1969 (in press).

13. Eger, W. and Ohr, A.: Ein Beitrag zur Myatonia congenita Oppenheim. *Arch. Kinderheilk.* 127:1, 1942.

14. Becker, P. E.: Atrophia musculorum spinalis pseudomyopathica. Hereditäre neurogene proximale Amyotrophie von Kugelberg und Welander. *Z. Vereb. -u. Konstit. -Lehre* 37:193, 1964.

15. Amick, L. D.; Smith, H. L. and Johnson, W. W.: An unusual spectrum of progressive spinal muscular atrophy. *Acta neurol. scand.* 42:275, 1966.

16. Hogenhuis, L. A. H. and Engel, W. K.: Early onset chronic motor neuropathies. Clinical and muscle histochemical studies. *Proc. 8th Internat. Congr. Neurol.* 2:499, 1965.

17. Rowland, L. P.; Schotland, D. L.; Lovelace, R. E. and Layzer, R. B.: Neurogenic muscular atrophies. In *Exploratory Concepts in Muscular Dystrophy*. International Congress Series 147, A. T. Milhorat ed. 41. Excerpta Medica Foundation, Amsterdam 1967.

18. Hanhart, E.: Die infantile progressive spinale Muskelatrophie (Werdnig-Hoffmann) als einfach-rezessive, subletale Mutation auf Grund von 29 Fällen in 14 Sippen. *Helv. paediat. Acta* 1:110, 1945.

19. Krabbe, K. H.: Congenital familial spinal muscular atrophies and their relation to amyotonia congenita. *Brain* 43:166, 1920–21.

20. Steinthal, M.: Zur Vererbung der neuralen progressiven Muskelatrophie. *Arch. Rass. Ges. Biol.* 21:425, 1929.

21. Spira, R.: Neurogenic, familial, girdle type muscular atrophy. *Confin. neurol.* 23:245, 1963.

22. Brandt, S.: Hereditary factors in infantile progressive muscular atrophy. *Amer. J. Dis. Child.* 78:226, 1949.

23. Finkel, N.: A forma pseudomiopatica tardia da atrofia muscolar progressiva heredofamilial. *Arch Neuro-psiquiatr.* (S. Paolo) 4:307, 1962.

24. Grossiord, A.; Hariga, J.; Pannier, S. and Gajdos, P.: A propos des frontières de la maladie de Werdnig-Hoffman. *Proc. 8th Internat. Congr. Neurol.* 2:137, 1965.

25. Tsukagoshi, H.; Nakanishi, T.; Kondo, K. and Tsubaki, T.: Hereditary, proximal, neurogenic muscular atrophy in adult. *Arch. Neurol.* (*Chic.*) 12:597, 1965.

26. Garvie, J. M. and Woolf, A. L.: Kugelberg-Welander syndrome (hereditary proximal spinal muscular atrophy). *Brit. med. J.* 1:1458, 1966.

27. Lugaresi, E.; Gambetti, P. and Giovannardi Rossi, P.: Chronic neurogenic muscle atrophies of infancy. Their nosological relationship with Werdnig-Hoffmann's disease. *J. neurol. Sci.* 3:399, 1966.

28. Armstrong, R. J.; Fogelson, H. and Silberberg, D. H.: Familial proximal spinal muscular atrophy. *Arch Neurol.* (*Chic.*) 14:208, 1966.

29. Gamstorp, I.: Progressive spinal muscular atrophy with onset in infancy or early childhood. *Acta Paediat. scand.* 56:408, 1967.

30. Peters, H. A.; Opitz, J. M.; Goto, K. and Reese, H.: The benign proximal spinal progressive muscular atrophies. *Acta neurol. scand.* 44:542, 1968.

31. Magee, K. R. and De Jong, R. N.: Neurogenic muscular atrophy simulating muscular dystrophy. *Arch. Neurol.* (*Chic.*) 2:677, 1960.

32. Hoffmann, J.: Weiterer Beitrag zur Lehre von der hereditären progressiven spinalen Muskelatrophie im Kindesalter. *Dtsch. Z. Nervenheilk.* 10:292, 1897.

33. Tsukagoshi, H.; Sugita, H.; Furukawa, T.; Tsubaki, T. and Ono, E.: Kugelberg-Welander syndrome with dominant inheritance. *Arch. Neurol.* (*Chic.*) 14:378, 1966.

34. Brandt, S.: *Werdnig-Hoffmann's Infantile Progressive Muscular Atrophy*. Munksgaard, Copenhagen, 1951.

35. Kichhof, K. J.; Kumral, K. and Fadiloglu, S.: Späte Manifestation mit protrahiertem Verlauf bei Werdnig-Hoffmannscher spinaler Muskelatrophie (nebst familiärem Tableau). *Nervenarzt* 33:442, 1962.

36. Neel, J. V. and Schull, W. J.: *Human Heredity*, University of Chicago Press, Chicago. 1950.

37. Kennedy, W. R.; Alter, M. and Sund, J. H.: Progressive proximal spinal and bulbar muscular atrophy of late onset. *Neurology* (*Minneap.*) 18:671, 1968.

pathologic picture may stem from a diversity of underlying processes. The following considerations apply to the "neural form" of AMC.

Hereditary Factors

In three cases, a significant family history was elicited. The parents of Bargeton's case were first cousins, and one of the sibs had also been born with AMC.[17] In the case of Coutel and associates, the proband's sib died with AMC and mongolism.[18] An uncle of Brandt's case was reported to have congenital hemiplegia and mental retardation.[19]

Maternal Factors

Three reports include a history suggestive of some abnormality in gestation. In our case,[2] there had been intimate maternal exposure to rubella during the first trimester of pregnancy, although the mother remained asymptomatic. If rubella was indeed responsible for the neuronal damage, one must postulate *inapparent* maternal infection with transplacental passage of the virus infecting the fetus. Viral culture technics have recently established that this can occur.[20] Furthermore, AMC and various abnormalities of the CNS have been reported in the "rubella syndrome."[21, 22] Although prenatal viral infection of the spinal cord is an attractive possibility, it remains to be confirmed by more definitive studies in future cases. In a second case oligohydramnios was reported, and in a third, the infant was the product of a premature delivery.

Werdnig-Hoffmann Disease and AMC

Certain similarities between Werdnig-Hoffmann disease and the "neural form of AMC" are worthy of comment. Both conditions are characterized by loss of motor neurons early in life. In the "congenital" form of Werdnig-Hoffmann disease, the neuronal loss begins prenatally, resulting in congenital joint contractures in about one-third of the cases.[23] By definition, these cases have a neural form of AMC as well as Werdnig-Hoffmann disease. Actually, there is no conflict between the two diagnoses, since "AMC" describes the joint manifestations caused by a heterogeneous group of underlying conditions, while "Werdnig-Hoffmann disease" refers to the specific disorder of motor neurons.

It is not difficult to see how variations in the time of onset and course of the same disease can theoretically result in the typical syndromes of either the neural form of AMC or Werdnig-Hoffmann disease. If the neuronal damage begins relatively early during prenatal life and is severe, the clinical picture at birth will be one of congenital joint deformities. Histologically, the spinal cord may show neuronal loss without much current activity. If, on the other hand, the disorder begins after birth and advances more slowly, it may produce the typical syndrome of Werdnig-Hoffmann disease, with a progressive clinical course, and histologic changes in the spinal cord of continuing neuronal degeneration. Thus, the two conditions are not mutually exclusive; Werdnig-Hoffmann disease appears to be one among the various causes of AMC.

The Möbius Syndrome and AMC

Another disorder in which congenital joint malformations may occur is the Möbius syndrome. This condition is characterized by congenital (often hereditary) paralysis of facial and extraocular muscles, which is due to absence of the motor neurons of the appropriate brain stem nuclei. More than 30% of patients with this disorder have clubfoot or AMC as well.[24] The classification of these cases as the "Möbius syndrome with AMC" rather than AMC with congenital cranial nerve abnormalities, merely reflects the interests of the author. While it seems probable that the anterior horn cells of the spinal cord must be depleted in these cases, further pathologic study is needed.

Miscellaneous

In the majority of cases the anterior horn cell damage cannot be related to any known hereditary or prenatal factors, nor does the disorder fit into one of the disease categories mentioned above. Such cases may be called simply the "neural form" of AMC, but this should not imply that they all stem from the same (unknown) cause.

Summary and Conclusions

Arthrogryposis Multiplex Congenita (AMC) is a syndrome of diverse causes, characterized by congenital rigidity of multiple joints. The joint pathology consists of soft-tissue ankylosis, with all the normal joint elements present. In this respect, it is identical to clubfoot, but by definition, AMC involves more than one joint. The joint malformations result from immobilization of the developing embryo, due to a variety of intra- or extraembryonic factors. This concept of pathogenesis is supported by the fact that experimental paralysis of the developing chick embryo produces a faithful model of AMC and clubfoot.

In man as well, prenatal disorders which are capable of immobilizing the embryo, give rise to AMC. Discrete loss of anterior horn cells, gross damage to the spinal cord, brain damage, muscular dystrophy, oligohydramnios, amnionic bands, etc have all been found in association with AMC. Even the "neural form" of AMC, with discrete loss of anterior horn cells, appears to be a heterogeneous syndrome. This form may result from several different etiologic factors, possibly including prenatal virus infection or a hereditary predisposition, and may be related to Werdnig-Hoffmann disease or the Möbius syndrome is some cases.

Editorial comment: Dr. Drachman's view on the pathogenesis of arthrogryposis is supported by the observation of arthrogryposis in an infant whose mother received tubocurarine in early pregnancy for treatment of tetanus.[25]

V.A.M.

REFERENCES

1. Swinyard, C. A.: Progressive muscular dystrophy and atrophy and related conditions. *Pediat. Clin. N. Amer.* **7**:703, 1960.
2. Drachman, D. B. and Banker, B. Q.: Arthrogryposis multiplex congenita. *Arch. Neurol. (Chic.)* **5**:77, 1961.
3. Rossi, E.: Le syndrome arthromyodysplasique congenital. *Helv. paediat. Acta* **2**:82, 1947.
4. James, T.: Multiple congenital articular rigidities. *Edinb. med. J.* **58**:565, 1961.
5. Hariga, J.; Lowenthal, A. and Guazzi, G. C.: Nosological place and correlations of arthrogryposis "sensu stricto." *Acta neurol. belg.* **63**:766, 1963.
6. Drachman, D. B.: Congenital deformities produced by neuromuscular disorders of the developing embryo. In *Motor Neuron Diseases*. Grune & Stratton, Inc., New York, 1969.
7. Banker, B. Q.: Personal communication, 1967.
8. Drachman, D. B. and Coulombre, A. J.: Experimental clubfoot and arthrogryposis multiplex congenita. *Lancet* **ii**:523, 1962.
9. Drachman, D. B. and Coulombre, A. J.: Method for continuous infusion of fluids into the chorioallantoic circulation of the chick embryo. *Science* **138**:144, 1962.
10. Settle, G. W.: The anatomy of congenital talipes equino-varus: sixteen dissected specimens. *J. Bone Jt. Surg.* **7**:1341, 1963.
11. Browne, D.: The pathology and classification of talipes. *Aust. N. Z. J. Surg.* **29**:85, 1959.
12. Howard, R.: A case of congenital defect of the muscular system (dystrophia muscularis congenita) and its association with congenital talipes equinovarus. *Proc. roy. Soc. Med.* **2**: 157, 1908.
13. Price, D. S.: A case of amyoplasia congenita, with pathological report. *Arch. Dis. Childh.* **8**:343, 1932.
14. Banker, B. Q.; Victor, M. and Adams, R. D.: Arthrogryposis multiplex due to congenital muscular dystrophy. *Brain* **80**: 319, 1957.
15. Pearson, C. M. and Fowler, W. G.: Hereditary non-progressive muscular dystrophy inducing arthrogryposis syndrome. *Brain* **85**:75, 1963.
16. Alberman, E. D.: The causes of congenital clubfoot. *Arch. Dis. Childh.* **40**:548, 1965.
17. Bargeton, E.; Nezelef, C.; Guran, P. and Job, J. C.: Étude anatomique d'un eas d'arthrogrypose multiple congénitale et familiale. *Rev. neurol.* **104**:479, 1961.
18. Coutel, Y.; Toulouse, R.; Grislain, I.; Kerneis, J. P. and Lerous, P.: Arthrogrypose congénitale. *Gynec. et Obstét.* **56**:385, 1956.
19. Brandt, S.: Arthrogryposis multiplex congenita. *Acta Pediat.* **34**:365, 1947.
20. Avery, G. B.; Monif, G. G. R.; Sever, J. L. and Leikin, S. L.: Rubella syndrome after inapparent maternal illness. *Amer. J. Dis. Child.* **110**:444, 1965.
21. Gregg, N. M.: The occurrence of congenital defects in children following maternal rubella. *Med. J. Aust.* **2**:122, 1945.
22. Rudolph, A. J.; Yow, M. D.; Phillips, C. L.; Desmond, M. M.; Blattner, R. J. and Melnick, J. L.: Transplacental rubella infection in newly born infants. *J. Amer. med. Ass.* **191**: 843, 1965.
23. Byers, R. K. and Banker, B. Q.: Infantile muscular atrophy. *Arch. Neurol. (Chic.)* **5**:140, 1961.
24. Henderson, P. L.: The congenital facial diplegiasyndrome. *Brain* **62**:381, 1939.
25. Jago, R. H.: Arthrogryposis following treatment of maternal tetanus with muscle relaxants. *Arch. Dis. Childh.* **45**:277, 1970.

CASE REPORTS

A—Werdnig-Hoffmann Disease

S.L.S. (JHH 1331754) a white male, born November, 1968, was the first and only child of a young and unrelated couple. The father had three brothers who had died in early infancy of uncertain causes, probably not Werdnig-Hoffmann disease. The rest of the family history was noncontributory.

Pregnancy and delivery were normal, birthweight was 6 lb 3 oz and the neonatal course was unremarkable except for a slight degree of hypomobility. At six weeks of age the patient was noted to have decreased use of both lower limbs which progressed over the next several weeks. The hypomobility was accompanied by accentuated hypotonia and by 3 months of age he had very floppy limbs and poor head control.

Examination at that time showed a hypotonic, hypomobile infant with asymmetry of the head (resulting from persistently lying on the same side) and mild substernal retraction. Extraocular movements were intact. He followed light without difficulty. The limbs were flaccid and hypotonic bilaterally, the legs more than the arms. Neck and trunk were very hypotonic and he had no head control at all. Osteotendinous reflexes were hypoactive or absent. There were gross fasciculations of the tongue. No sensorial abnormalities were present. The rest of the clinical examination was normal including respiratory and cardiovascular systems.

An electromyogram was suggestive of a neuropathic alteration; the right median nerve conduction time of 24 meters/sec was considered slow for the patient's age. Serum enzyme levels were SGOT 29 units, SGPT 35 units, LDH 425 units, and CPK 148 units. An intravenous tensilon test failed to produce any muscular improvement. A muscle biopsy showed group atrophy of 90% of the fibers in bundles examined. The atrophic fibers were up to 10 microns in diameter and had large plump nuclei. In each bundle examined there were a few larger, round eosinophilic fibers with peripheral flat nuclei averaging 40 microns in diameter. No significant fibrous reaction was present. These findings, together with the clinical history were interpreted as being consistent with the diagnosis of Werdnig-Hoffmann disease.

When he was reexamined at 6 months of age, a further progression in the muscular weakness was noted. He was almost immobile, completely areflexic, had marked substernal retraction and rales were noted bilaterally in the chest. (Fig. A-1) Tongue fasciculations were still present. He was very alert, however, and able to respond to his parents by smiling; his mental development seemed to be normal.

In follow-up it was learned that the patient had expired in July, 1969 due to massive aspiration. No autopsy was performed.

Victor Penchaszadeh
D. Williams

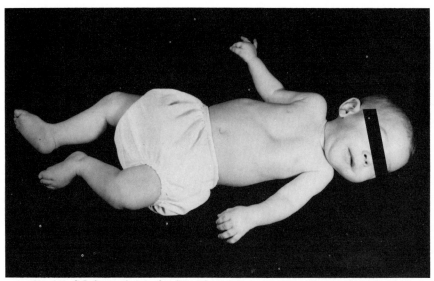

Fig. A-1. *S.L.S.* age six months. Sternal retraction secondary to hypotonia is obvious

B—The Kugelberg-Welander Syndrome (Hereditary Proximal Spinal Muscular Atrophy)

M.R. (JHH 1310826), a white male child, was born 9/24/65 after a 33-week pregnancy. At birth he weighed 4 lbs 5 oz and he spent his first 2 weeks in an incubator. He was not in any way "floppy" or hypotonic, and his subsequent progress was normal until he began to walk at the age of 18 months. His parents then noticed that he had difficulty in rising from a sitting position, and that running or climbing stairs presented considerable problems. His health was otherwise good, and his condition did not progress.

Neither his younger brother nor any other member of the kindred was similarly affected. His parents, who were both in their 20s at the time of conception, were not related. There had been no known exposure to noxious environmental agents during pregnancy.

When examined in 1969, he was a pleasant, intelligent, active boy. (Figs. B-1A, B and C) His gait was lordotic, and he arose from the supine position by rolling over onto his stomach and then "climbing up his legs." He had pronounced symmetric wasting of the quadriceps muscle, and power in the pelvic girdle was diminished. Tendon reflexes were absent at the knees but present at the ankles and the plantar reflexes were flexor. All other aspects of the central nervous system were normal and no abnormality was detected in any other system.

His serum creatinine phosphokinase level was 11.9 sigma units per ml, while those of his mother and brother were 1.6 units and 29.2 units respectively (normal 0–12 units). Serum creatine was 0.6 mg per 100 ml (normal 0.2–1.4 mg) and urinary creatinine was 67.0 mg per 100 ml. Amino acid screening and urinary chromatography revealed no abnormality.

Electroencephalography, electrocardiography and skull and spine radiographs were normal. Electromyography demonstrated electrical silence in the right quadriceps muscle, and biopsy from the same area showed neurogenic atrophy.

The clinical features, the course of the disorder and the laboratory findings supported the diagnosis of the Kugelberg-Welander syndrome.

When seen in follow-up at $4^{5}/_{12}$ years of age the patient had relatively good strength in his arms and shoulders. Muscular weakness was present primarily in the pelvic girdle and lower limbs, particularly in the proximal part of the limbs. He was able to ambulate remarkably well and could even swim.

Comment: The patient's brother was vigorously active at the time blood for a CPK level was obtained. Clinically his brother has remained normal (last examined in January, 1971).

Peter H. Beighton

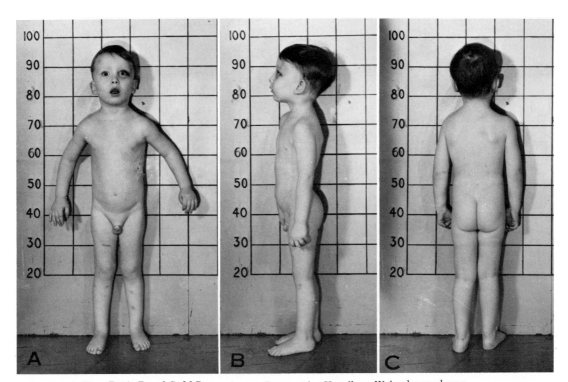

Figs. B-1A, B and C. *M.R.*, age 4 years five months. Kugelberg-Welander syndrome

C—Amyloid Polyneuropathy, Type II (Indiana, or Rukavina Type)

In 11 apparently unrelated kindreds living in Frederick and Washington counties of Maryland and neighboring areas, Mahloudji et al (*Medicine* 48:1, 1969) found dominantly inherited amyloid neuropathy with features like that of the Indiana or Rukavina type: onset in hands, carpal tunnel syndrome, long survival, late and relatively mild visceral manifestations. By geneologic sleuthing it was possible to relate all 11 kindred back to a common ancestor who lived in the 1700s (Table I).

TABLE I
Clinical Features of the Three Types of Hereditary Neuropathic Amyloidosis

Characteristic	Type I Andrade* (Portuguese)	Type II Rukavina** (Indiana)	Type III Van Allen*** (Iowa)
Age at onset	3rd decade	5th decade	4th decade
Site of onset	Feet	Hands	Feet and hands
Gastrointestinal complaints	Common	Rare	Common
Impotence and sphincter disturbances	Common	Rare	Common
Foot ulcers	Common	Rare	Rare
Duration of illness	4–12 years	14–40+ years	12 years (av.)
Nephropathy	Rare	Absent	Invariable

* Andrade, C.: *Brain,* **75**:408, 1952.
** Mahloudji, M., *et al: Medicine,* **48**:1, 1969.
*** Van Allen, M. W., *et al: Neurology,* **19**:10, 1968.

Case 1. A.H. (JHH 1182535), a white, retired cabinet maker born 3/9/03 was in good health until age 55 when he developed numbness and tingling in his fingertips. This started in his right hand and at first occurred mainly at night. Gradually both hands became involved and would become numb while he was driving a car. This numbness could be relieved by allowing his arms to hang at his sides. There was gradual atrophy of the hand muscles particularly those in the thenar area.

The hand problems were followed by numbness in the feet, first the left then the right. His fellow workmen noticed that he walked with a peculiar gait. By age 61 he was unable to dorsiflex his feet.

His major complaint was not the gradual loss of motor function of the arms and legs but the accompanying numbness, tingling and burning primarily over the ball and arch of his left foot. This was particularly distressing at night.

By age 62 ankle edema had become a problem and was worst in the evening. This could be relieved by elevation of his legs. There were no accompanying signs of cardiac failure although diuretics did help to reduce the ankle edema.

At 66 years of age he was able to ambulate only with the aid of crutches for balance and support. He also wore ankle braces to stabilize his ankles. In March 1969 he was hospitalized for 12 days for slowly healing superficial ulcers which developed over his shins.

There was no loss of bladder or bowel control and the only other possible neurologic deficit was a gradual sensorineural hearing loss noted over a number of years.

This man was the proband for a large kindred with peripheral neuropathy due to amyloidosis. (Fig. C-1) In his immediate family his grandfather, father, five paternal uncles and an aunt, nine cousins and four of his thirteen sibs all had a similar problem of varying degrees. He was the oldest child in his family. His next younger brother also in his 60s had only minimal thenar atrophy and no leg problems at all. All affected members had onset in middle or late life and males appeared to be more severely affected than females. The patient had three sons under thirty. All were asymptomatic.

Physical examination in 1968 with follow-up in mid 1969 showed marked weakness and wasting of the small hand muscles (Fig. C-2A and B) and the muscles below the knees. The grip was relatively good but the musculus opponens was severely affected. Proximal muscle strength was well maintained in the arms and legs. There was inability to move the feet. There was absent touch position and vibration sense in the ankles and stocking anesthesia below the knees. The touch sensation was diminished in the hands. Vibration sense was present but diminished in the knees and wrists. Deep tendon reflexes were absent. He could not stand without support.

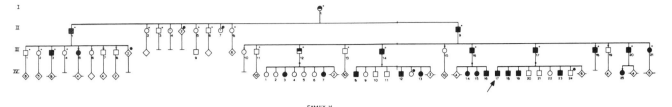

Fig. C-1 Pedigree

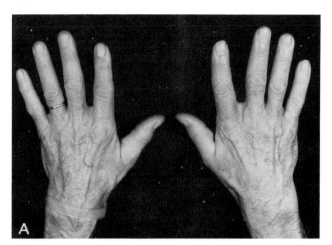
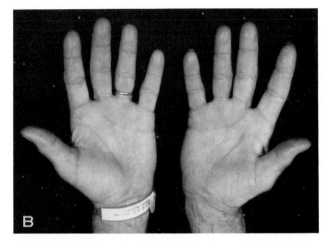

Figs. C-2A and B. Hands in Type II Amyloid Polyneuropathy (*Case 1*)

There was pitting edema of the ankles with overlying stasis dermatitis and shallow healing ulcers. There was bilateral arcus senilis and a large left indirect inguinal hernia. The remainder of the physical examination was normal. The liver and spleen were not enlarged.

Routine hematology, blood chemistries, serum electrophoresis and spinal fluid examination were normal.

Audiometry showed mild sensorineural hearing loss.

Nerve conduction studies showed prolonged distal motor latency determinations in both the median and ulnar nerves.

Amyloid deposits were demonstrated histologically in biopsy material from the gingiva, sural nerve and the atrophic gastrocnemius muscle. In the muscle the amyloid was in the walls of small blood vessels.

Case 2. E.G. (JHH 1204546), a married white farmwife, born 5/31/17, was well until 1962 when she began having tingling and numbness in the fingers of both hands. The paresthesias were worse in the left hand and occurred mostly at night, keeping the patient awake. They increased in frequency and severity, eventually interfering with her farm work. The patient denied cyanosis or weakness, but noted some limitation in apposition of her thumb to the other digits. In July 1966 the patient was evaluated at JHH for possible carpal tunnel decompression.

Past medical history includes 2 hospitals for tubal pregnancies, in 1945 and 1955, the last accompanied by hysterectomy and bilateral oophorectomy. The review of systems is noncontributory. The patient was born in Frederick County, Maryland, attended school through grade 7 and has worked on a farm all her life. She has no children and does not smoke or drink. The family history is positive for paresthesias or numbness in the hands of the father, paternal grandfather, 3 paternal uncles and 2 sisters. The mother has hypertension and one sister has swollen legs and ? renal disease.

Physical examination in 1966 showed an obese white female in no acute distress with stable vital signs. There was bilateral sensory blunting on palms, fingers and dorsum of hands, and a positive Tinel's sign on the left. Motor function was intact and the remainder of the examination was unremarkable except for BP of 164/104. Laboratory data were normal except for nonspecific diffuse elevation of gamma G globulin.

The patient underwent bilateral carpal tunnel decompression on 7/19/66. A specimen of the flexor retinaculum and a gingival biopsy were positive for amyloid.

Postoperatively her paresthesias disappeared and sensory function tests in both hands returned to normal.

The patient was seen again in April, 1969, for follow-up. She had resumed full work activities and denied recurrence of tingling, numbness or pain in her hands. On physical examination there was no thenar or hypothenar wasting. Sensation of pinprick and soft touch was intact in both hands; motor function was grossly intact. Vibratory and position sensation was intact in hands and feet; some decreased sensitivity to vibration in the right palmar area over the metacarpophalangeal joints was noted. The rest of the physical examination was unremarkable.

M. Mahloudji
Jack Nissim

D—Hypertrophic Interstitial Neuropathy of Déjérine-Sottas

W.P. (JHH 398444), a Negro bulldozer operator born in 1920, was well until 1960 when he experienced the onset of clumsiness and trembling of the hands, together with twitching and cramping of the calf muscles. Physical examination at that time revealed mild symmetrical cerebellar dysfunction, complete absence of the tendon reflexes, and weakness, wasting and fasciculation of the calf muscles. A lumbar puncture demonstrated a cerebrospinal fluid protein level of 700 mg per 100 ml, and a muscle biopsy showed focal atrophy, which was considered to be consistent with neuropathic degeneration. He refused myelography and was discharged without a firm diagnosis.

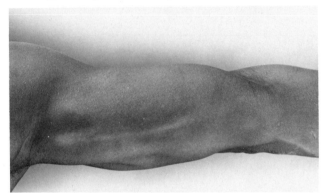

Fig. D-2. View of the left upper arm showing hypertrophy of the nerves.

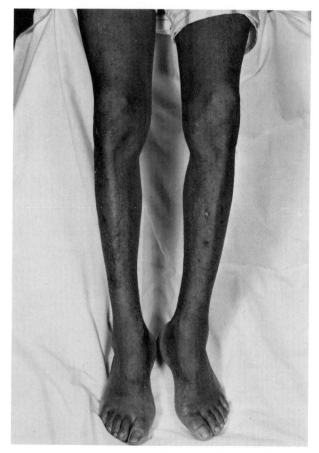

Fig. D-1. *W.P.* age 46 years. Wasting of the lower limb muscles is marked.

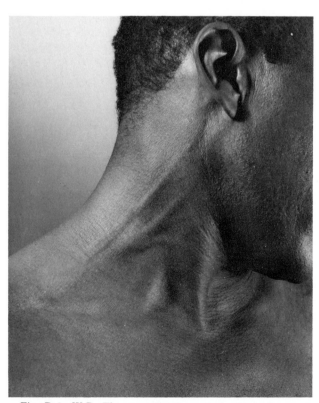

Fig. D-3. *W.P.* The superficial cervical plexus is greatly thickened and is apparent on turning the head to either side.

The disorder slowly progressed, and when seen again in December 1966, he was walking with the aid of a stick. He was still able to operate a bulldozer, but due to the increased weakness of his legs, he had to drag himself on and off the machine. Examination demonstrated that position, vibration and all modalities of sensation were now absent below the knees. The signs of mild cerebellar dysfunction persisted, and the tendon reflexes were still absent. Obvious weakness and wasting of the distal leg muscles (Fig. D-1), with foot drop, had now developed. A tremor was still present in the upper limb, but motor function and sensation were intact in this area.

On myelographic examination, erosion of the posterior aspects of the bodies of all the lumbar vertebras were demonstrated, and the findings were interpreted as being indicative of a large tumor in the lumbar vertebral canal. The rest of the spinal canal was normal in appearance. Laminectomy for decompression revealed nerve roots which were grossly hypertrophied, and nerve biopsy showed Schwann cell infiltration. These changes were considered to be compatible with Dejerine-Sottas hypertrophic interstitial neuritis. Further clinical examination confirmed the presence of thickened median and ulnar nerves (Fig. D-2), as well as the superficial cervical plexus nerves (Fig. D-3).

No immediate improvement took place following the operation, and prednisone therapy was not beneficial.

He was an only child, but his parents and his own two children were apparently unaffected. There was no known consanguinity, and no other members of the kindred had any neurologic disturbance.

The patient died of a gunshot wound, on 12/7/67. A coroner's autopsy was unfortunately limited to observations related to the fatal trauma.

Peter H. Beighton

E—Charcot-Marie-Tooth Syndrome, Dominantly Inherited

J.H. (JHH 389271), an unmarried Negro male pharmacist, was born in 1929 with bilateral pes cavus deformities of the feet. When he was 14 years of age, he began to experience weakness of his ankles towards the end of his daily ten block walk to school. His disorder progressed very slowly, but the hands and forearms became involved, and when he was 27 years old, he had to give up bowling because of loss of strength in the thumbs. At this time, he noticed wasting of the muscles of the limbs and loss of sensation in the hands and feet. Some loss in manual dexterity also occurred, the problems being worse in cold weather. Hyperhidrosis became troublesome, and chronic ulcers developed on the soles of the feet. An unsuccessful attempt at grafting of the ulcers was made when he was 32 years old. A diminution in the hyperhidrosis took place after a left lumbar sympathectomy, and the ulcers then healed on both sides. Triple arthrodesis was later undertaken to correct the foot deformity. At the present time he is in good health, and the ulcers have remained healed. The weakness and sensory changes have progressed only slowly, and they cause no great disability.

His brothers and sisters were unaffected but his father, paternal aunt and paternal grandmother had similar, although less severe involvement (Fig. E-1).

Examination revealed a well built, intelligent male (Fig. E-2A, B and C), with deformed feet and muscular wasting in the distal thirds of all 4 limbs. The interossei muscles were particularly wasted, and weakness of the pinch grip and impairment of dorsiflexion of the hands and feet were prominent features (Fig. E-3A and B). Sensation was blunted in a glove and stocking distribution, up to the midcalf, and over the hands and wrists. Position and vibration sense were diminished in feet, but normal in the hands. (Pretreatment views of the foot ulcers are shown in Figure E-4.)

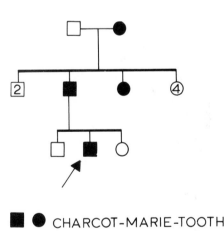

■ ● CHARCOT-MARIE-TOOTH

Fig. E-1. Pedigree

A coarse tremor of moderate degree was present in both hands. His gait was narrow but "flapping," and Romberg's sign was positive. All tendon reflexes were absent, and the plantar reflexes were flexor. There was no palpable thickening of any nerve trunks.

Apart from these findings all other systems were normal.

At lumbar puncture in 1957, the cerebrospinal fluid contained 106 milligrams of protein per 100 ml. The protein level was still elevated when another lumbar puncture was performed in 1963.

Peter H. Beighton

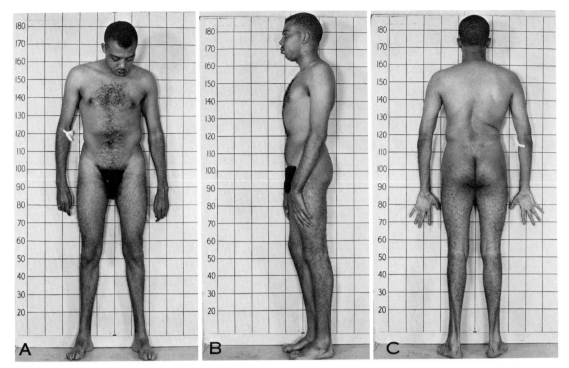

Figs. E-2A,B and C. Note the muscular wasting in the distal portions of the limbs and the deformed feet

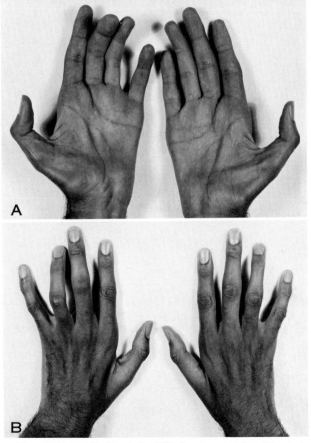

Figs. E-3A and B. Hands in *J.H.* showing atrophy of intrinsic muscles.

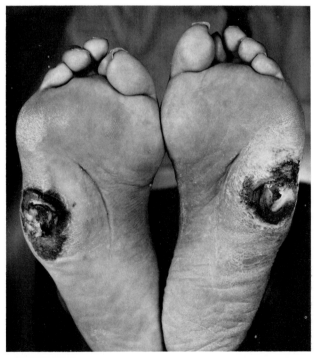

Fig. E-4. Feet in *J.H.* showing the chronic ulcers on lateral borders.

F—Recessively Inherited Charcot-Marie-Tooth Syndrome in Identical Twins

M.S. (JHH 1324080), white male plumber born in 1946, was quite well until the age of 10. He then noticed that his lower legs and ankles were becoming clumsy, and that running was difficult because his feet tended to turn sideways.

The condition progressed slowly, and when he was 16, a bilateral triple arthrodesis was performed. This operation was successful, and he had little trouble with his legs since that time.

Weakness and wasting of the hands and forearms developed during his midteens. Progression was slow, and he was aware of weakness only when carrying out fine movements, such as buttoning up his coat. However, the disability was accentuated in cold weather. His general health has been good, and his condition was little more than a minor nuisance.

Examination revealed a pleasant young man, with pipestem legs, wasting of the distal portions of the forearms and atrophy of the small muscles of the hands. All tendon reflexes were absent, and sensation was impaired over the feet and lower thirds of the legs. There was no tremor, and position, vibration and coordination were all normal. No abnormality was detected in any other system.

His twin brother gave an identical history, and the sibs were virtually indistinguishable on physical examination. Several other persons in the kindred were said to have similar abnormalities and considerable consanguinity was present in this Amish group (Fig. F-1). These facts suggest a recessive mode of inheritance of the condition.

Peter H. Beighton

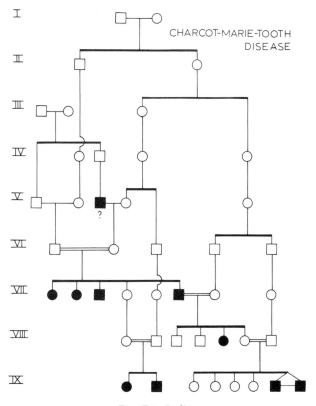

Fig. F-1. Pedigree

G—Roussy-Levy Hereditary Areflexic Dystasia Presenting as Charcot-Marie-Tooth Syndrome

Case 1 (III-2). *S.J.* (JHH 1305124), a white female born in August 1928 was evaluated in 1968 for an hereditary ataxia. The pedigree is shown in Figure G-1. High arches were noted in infancy. An unusual gait was first noticed when she began to walk as her left leg was thrown outward with each step. As a child she had less muscle strength than her playmates and frequently fell while running. Her leg weakness was slowly progressive and when seen at age 40 she was still able to walk without assistance. Hand weakness was first noticed in her midteens while driving a car and was also slowly progressive. Poor balance while walking was particularly troublesome in the dark. The patient had peptic ulcer disease which was controlled by antacid and anticholinergic therapy.

Physical examination showed distal muscular atrophy particularly of the lateral calf muscles (Fig. G-2). There was bilateral pes cavus (Fig. G-3). The wrist and ankle extensors were weak. The deep tendon reflexes were absent in both arms and legs. Light touch, vibration and position senses were diminished at the ankles and below. There was no evidence of cerebellar involvement. A slight tremor was present in the hands at rest.

Nerve conduction studies showed decreased conduction times in the ulnar and median nerves as well as the lower limb nerves.

Case 2 (IV-4). *E.N.* (JHH 1305126), a white girl born in 1956, was the niece of *S.J.* Like several members of her family, her feet had been noted to be high arched at birth. This deformity had caused little trouble, other than some difficulty in fitting shoes, and she had a comparatively normal childhood. At the age of 10, she found that she was unable to run or perform gymnastics as well as her schoolmates. This disability, which was due to muscle weakness, progressed only slowly. She was otherwise well in every way and, in particular, she made no complaint of sensory disturbance.

The patient (Figs. G-4A and B) was a pleasant, intelligent girl, with a marked bilateral pes cavus (Fig. G-5). Her gait was somewhat ataxic, but she had no tremor, and rapid alternating movements, manual dexterity and the heel-to-shin test were all normal. Romberg's sign was negative. There was no muscle wasting, but a mild weakness of extension of both wrists and ankles was present. The tendon reflexes were all absent, and the plantar reflexes could not be elicited. Position, vibration and tactile sensation were all normal. The cranial nerves were intact, and no abnormality could be detected in any other system.

Case 3 (II-1). *A.N.*, a white female born in 1901, was the mother of the four affected sibs in generation III. Weakness of the hands and feet had become apparent in early adult life, and by her 60s, she was able to walk only with the aid of a stick. She had bilateral pes cavus, marked wasting of the peroneal muscles, and gross wasting of the adductor pollicis brevis. The extensors of the wrist, ankles and digits were weak, and all tendon reflexes were absent in the legs. Sensation, vibration and position sense were normal, the cranial nerves were intact and there was no tremor. There were no abnormalities in any other system. Her parents were divorced when she was a child and she lost contact with her father (I-2), but he was said to walk with a peculiar gait. *A.N.* was an only child.

Case 4 (III-1). *E.N.*, a male born in 1925 noticed, at about 8 years of age, that leg weakness made the two-mile walk to school difficult. The weakness was slowly progressive but he was able to fly a plane until age 41. In later years leg pains had become a problem. He had been a diabetic since age 40 and was controlled

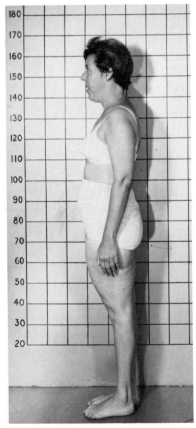

Fig. G-2 Tapering of the lower limbs with atrophy of the lateral calf muscles is demonstrated.

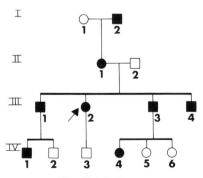

Fig. G-1 Pedigree

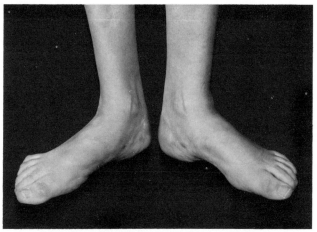

Fig. G-3 Feet showing the pes cavus deformity

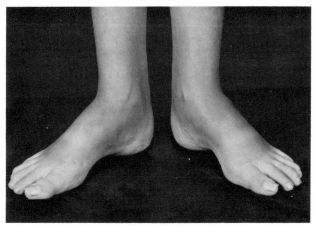

Fig. G-5 Pes cavus in *E.N.*

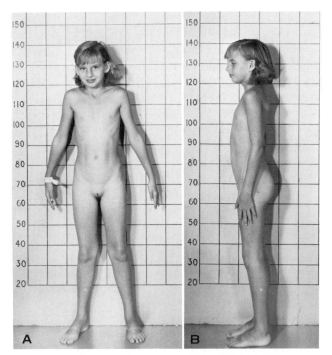

Fig. G-4A,B Front and lateral views of *E.N.* Distal muscular atrophy is not apparent at the age of 12 years.

with 40–50 units of insulin per day. On physical examination the peroneal musculature was atrophic, there was bilateral pes cavus and poor dorsiflexion of the toes. The deep tendon reflexes were absent. Position sense was diminished in the right foot. Moderate thenar atrophy was present.

Case 5 (III-3). *C.N.*, a white male born in 1932, noticed that he was getting slower at baseball when he was 14 years of age. The weakness of his arms and ankles progressed slowly but he was still able to work as a welder in 1968. A mild tremor had been present all his life, but this had been no more than a minor nuisance. He had bilateral pes cavus, pipestem legs, and weakness of the dorsiflexors of the feet. All tendon reflexes were absent, but the modalities of position, vibration and sensation were normal. Cranial nerves and all other systems were normal.

Case 6 (III-4). *W.N.*, the youngest of the four sibs in generation III, was born in 1941. He first noticed leg weakness in mid-childhood and this had slowly become more severe. He also complained of poor balance particularly at night. He was areflexic, had high arches and decreased motor power in his feet with poor dorsiflexion. The right leg was more severely affected than the left. There was minimal peroneal atrophy. A slight tremor was present.

Case 7 (IV-1). *E.N.*, a white male born in 1956, had noticed weakness of his legs when he was five years of age. This disability was slowly progressive, and by the age of 10, weakness had appeared in the hands. For these reasons, he had a low grade in gymnastic classes. He had a mild tremor and weakness of the dorsiflexors of the wrists and ankles. There was no muscle wasting, and no pes cavus. Tendon reflexes were absent in the legs, but all other aspects of the nervous system were normal.

Others: R.N. (IV-2), a male born in 1960, showed no signs of muscle involvement, although he did complain of night pains in his thighs and lower legs. Neurologic examination was normal.

K.J. (IV-3), a male born in 1956, was the son of *S.J.*, the proband. He was not affected.

D.N. (IV-5) born in 1960 and *C.N.* (IV-6) born in 1963 were younger sisters of *E.N.* (JHH 1305726). Neither had muscle weakness nor other symptoms of involvement, although both had diminished deep tendon reflexes in the legs. *D.N.* had slightly high arches. At the time of examination, because of their age, it was impossible to make a final judgment as to whether these girls were affected.

J. Lamont Murdoch
Peter H. Beighton

H—Pseudohypertrophic Muscular Dystrophy of Duchenne with Manifestations in the Heterozygote

G.B. (JHH 1027473), a 10-year-old boy, had been severely disabled with Duchenne muscular dystrophy and in a wheel chair since the age of 7 years. His mother *B.B.* (JHH 1028043) was born 7/25/26, and had shown mild manifestations of the disease since the age of 22 years, with serum muscle enzyme levels intermediate between normal and those of her son. She had one other child by a previous marriage, a daughter aged 20, who had no clinical manifestations of the disease, but who would not consent to muscle biopsy or serum enzyme estimation. Neither husband was available for examination. The mother had no sibs, and did not think that her parents had been affected by any muscle disorder. Details of the two patients are as follows:

Case 1. G.B., a white male born 6/19/58, was the product of a normal pregnancy and delivery in a woman who was 33 years old at the time of his birth. The first abnormality was noted at the age of 14 months, when his mother felt that the arches of his feet were not well developed and bought corrective shoes for him. Developmental milestones were normal, but at the age of 3 years it was observed that he fatigued more easily than his playmates and ran somewhat clumsily. By the age of 3½ years he was walking on his toes, and had great difficulty in rising from the supine position. When he was examined at the age of 4 years pseudohypertrophy of the calves was found, and there was some enlargement of his thighs and biceps (Figs. H-1A–C). General muscular weakness of the face and limbs was noted. Shortening of the Achilles tendons was present, and the tendon reflexes were present but diminished. In April 1963 at the age of 4 years and 10 months he had surgery for bilateral lengthening of the Achilles tendon, with some temporary improvement in his walking. His progressive deterioration continued, however, and by the age of 6 years he was unable to walk without support, and the following year became completely chair bound. Examination in February, 1969, showed a somewhat obese boy, who still had slight hypertrophy of the calves, although this was of a lesser degree than previously (Fig. H-2). He was able to make weak extension movements of both knees, but otherwise had no movement of the legs. Talipes equinovarus was present. His arms were paralyzed, but he could move his neck. The face showed some myopathic weakness, particularly on the right side. Sensation was normal, but the deep tendon reflexes were absent.

Serum enzymes (at age 4 years); CPK 10.6 units (normal up to 4 units); SGOT 134 units (normal up to 50 units) and SGPT units (normal up to 50 units).

EKG, S T depression and T wave inversion in the right precordial leads suggested possible myocardial involvement.

Muscle biopsy: Fiber hypertrophy with increased central nuclei, diffuse endomyseal fibrosis and focal fiber necrosis with abortive regeneration.

Case 2. B.B., the 42-year-old mother of the above patient, had first noted difficulty in climbing stairs and also in rising from a chair at the age of 22 years. These symptoms worsened over the

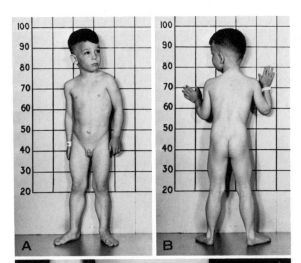

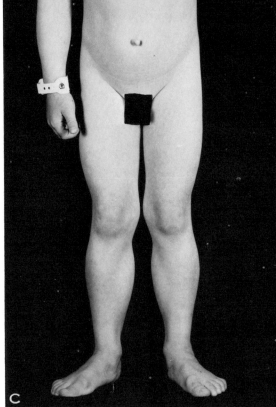

Figs. H-1A, B and C. *G.B.*, age 4 years. The enlarged calf muscles are pictured.

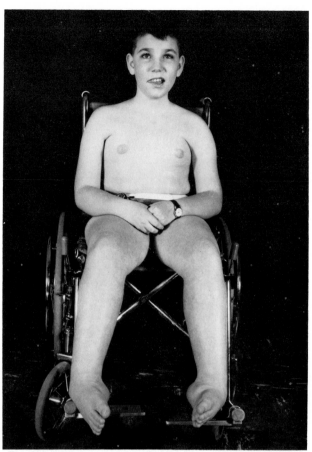

Fig. H-2. *G.B.*, age 11 years. Confined to a wheelchair. Dependent edema somewhat obscures the calf pseudohypertrophy.

next 8 years, but there had been no further progression since the age of 30 years. She was able to walk quite well on the level, but on climbing stairs needed to pull herself up by the rail, and could not rise from a kneeling position without using a chair for support. In order to get up out of a chair she had to flex her trunk and then push herself up by pressing on her thighs to aid the weak extensor muscles of her hips. She had no weakness of the upper limbs.

Examination in February 1969 showed that she had a somewhat waddling gait with some exaggeration of the normal lumbar lordosis. Pseudohypertrophy of both calves was present, the left being more apparent than the right (Figs. H-3A–C). The weakness of her legs was mainly confined to the pelvic girdle musculature. The straight leg raising test was very weak whereas movements of the knee and ankle were strong. Sensation was normal but the deep tendon reflexes were sluggish. The arms appeared normal.

Enzymes (in 1962): CPK 9.4 units (normal up to 4.0 units); LDH 600 units (normal up to 400 units); SGOT 42 units (upper limit of normal—50 units); SGPT 34 units (upper limit of normal —50 units).

Urine Creatinine 906 mg/24 hr (normal up to 1500 mg); urine creatine 576 mg/24 hr (normal 150–200 mg).

EKG: normal record.

Muscle biopsy: variation in muscle fiber size with a rounded rather than polygonal outline, focal necrosis of muscle fibers with phagocytosis of the necrotic tissue by histiocytes. Increase in connective tissue with some fatty infiltration.

(This family was reported by Emery, *Lancet* **1:** 1126, 1963.)

Bryan A. Walker

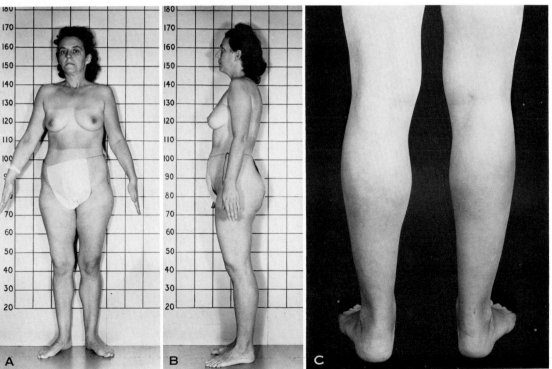

Fig. H-3A, B and C. *B.B.*, age 42 years. Pseudohypertrophy of the calves is shown

I—Duchenne Muscular Dystrophy, Preclinical Diagnosis

M.G. (JHH 1199049), a white boy born 3/4/66, was the 4th child of an unwed mother and was to be placed for adoption. He had been carefully followed since birth as there was a family history of Duchenne muscular dystrophy. His mother's affected older brother died at age 23 and she had 3 affected maternal cousins. The patient's 2 older brothers had been evaluated previously and were found to have normal creatine phosphokinase (CPK) levels (Fig. I-1). A CPK level drawn at birth on the patient was elevated to 40 milli-units but fell to 5 mu by 3 days of age (normal up to .72 mu). At 2 months CPK was again elevated to 60 mu and a needle muscle biopsy showed nonspecific changes with increased connective tissue and regenerating muscle cells. CPK levels drawn at 1 and 2 years of age were elevated to 100 times normal.

Developmental landmarks were normal and the adoptive parents, who knew of the risks of muscular dystrophy, could see no signs of muscular weakness in any of his activities. At 29 months of age his gait was slightly wide-based and his calves were a little firm. Otherwise the physical examination was unremarkable.

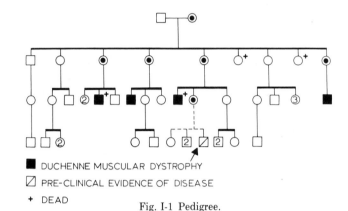

■ DUCHENNE MUSCULAR DYSTROPHY

▨ PRE-CLINICAL EVIDENCE OF DISEASE

+ DEAD

Fig. I-1 Pedigree.

Comments: Early diagnosis of muscular dystrophy of the Duchenne type can be established by appropriate studies prior to the onset of clinical signs and symptoms. Prenatal diagnosis using amniotic fluid CPK levels is not possible. (Personal communication from Dr. Alan Emery and Dr. Henry Nadler.)

J. Lamont Murdoch

J—Benign Muscular Dystrophy, Becker Type

Case 1. M.C. (JHH 1076654), a white male born in October 1956, was noted to have enlarged calves before he was 1 year old and was walking on his toes from the age of about 1 year. Gradual onset of clumsiness in legs occurred about 6 months after he began walking.

Family history: The patient was the 2nd of 4 children. His 2 brothers and 1 sister were living and well. Three maternal uncles had muscular dystrophy affecting mainly lower limbs, with pseudohypertrophy of the calves. All had onset in the late teens. They are now aged 51, 41 and 32 years old. The maternal grandmother had diabetes (Fig. J-1).

At $6\frac{8}{12}$ years the patient was for the first time seen at JHH (Moore Clinic) because of clumsiness in legs but no weakness.

Physical examination showed a friendly cooperative child. Speech was not very clear though the father denied any marked abnormality. He walked on his toes and no waddling gait was noted. The arches of the feet were high bilaterally. Both calves were markedly hypertrophic (Fig. J-2). Gower's sign was not present. He tended to hold onto things when climbing steps; he ran well, played with no apparent difficulty, and was able to walk distances with no complaints. Motor function showed good power in all four limbs, except perhaps for some slight weakness in straight leg raising. Sensory function was intact to coarse testing.

Cranial nerves were intact. No facial weakness was present. Reflexes were sluggish but equal. Respiratory system and abdomen were unremarkable.

Laboratory data: Creatine phosphokinase levels were: 304.5 units Ebashi, normal < 10; 156.5 units Aebi, (N < 1). Repeated after 1 month the values were: 265.5 Ebashi and 257.2 Aebi. Serum transaminases were: SGOT 280, SGPT 290. An EKG was normal. A biopsy of cell muscles showed focal groups of altered muscle fibers. All fibers within a given group were similar in appearance. The changes in various groups were blue fibers with vesicular nuclei, phagocytosis and hyaline necrosis with eosinophilic response. There may have been an increase in the number of muscle fibers within a fasciculus. On the basis of these data a diagnosis of muscular dystrophy of the Becker type was made.

Additional findings at age 8 years: Moderate lordosis which was more marked on ambulation. The gait appeared waddling with weight borne on distal end of the metatarsals. Some hypertrophy of masseter and deltoid muscles was noted. Gower's sign was now positive. Muscle measurements: Deltoid R 20 cm, L 20 cm; triceps R 18 cm, thigh R 32 cm, L 31.25 cm; calf R 26.6 cm, L 26.5 cm; serum transaminases were still high; SGOT 132; SGPT 230.

Mild weakness of dorsiflexion of the feet was noted at 9 years of

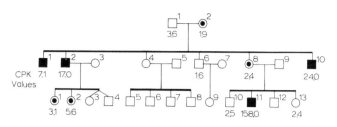

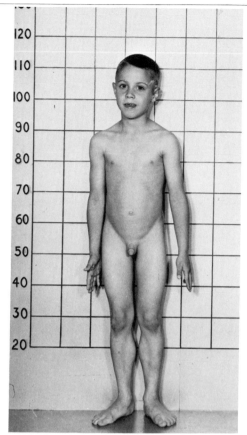

Fig. J-1. Pedigree. *Case 1, M.C.:* III-11; *Case 2, F.I.:* II-10.

age. CPK determination was 20 units (normal under 2 units). When the patient was examined at 12⁷/₁₂ years of age (Figs. J-3A-C) the following measurements were obtained: weight 68 lbs, height 58¾ inches, U/L 1.0, head circumference 51 cm.

	Right	Left
Arm	21 cm	20.5 cm
Thigh	35 cm	34.5 cm
Calf	33 cm	32.5 cm

Additional findings included: Marked lumbar lordosis, mild dorsal scoliosis, winging of the scapulas. Muscular weakness was not apparent. Knee jerks were very sluggish and the patient walked on tiptoes with a waddling gait. He was able to climb stairs by holding to the railing.

Fig. J-2. *M.C.* age 6⁸/₁₂ years. Enlargement of the calves is marked.

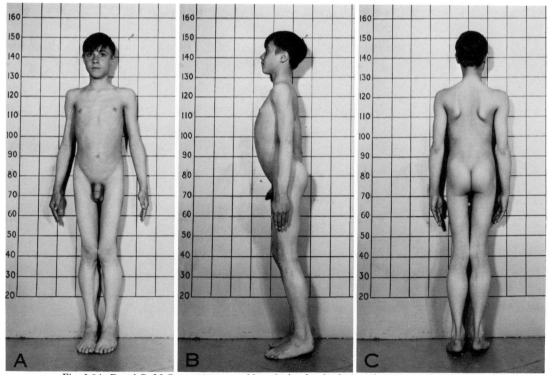

Fig. J-3A, B and C. *M.C.* age 12⁷/₁₂ years. Note the lumbar lordosis and winging of the scapulas

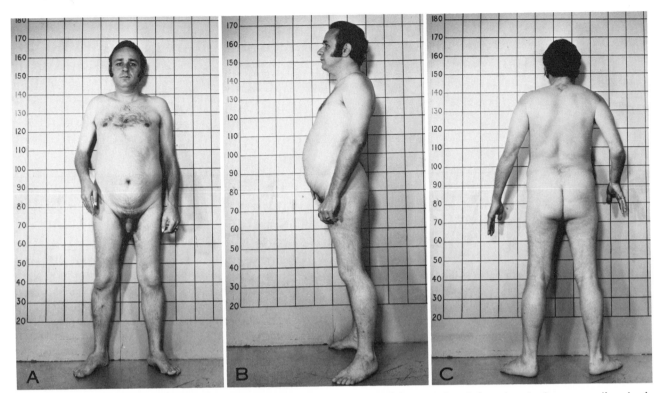

Fig. J-4A, B and C. *F.I.* age 32⁶/₁₂ years. Atrophy of the thighs and pseudohypertrophy of the calves is shown as well as lumbar lordosis and obesity.

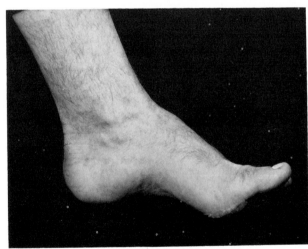

Fig. J-5. *F.I.* Left foot showing high longitudinal arch

Case 2. F.I. (JHH 514101), maternal uncle of *Case 1, M.C.* was born in 1936. At the time of his birth the patient's father and mother were age 40 and 34 years, respectively. Pregnancy and de-

livery were normal. At 14 years of age his mother noticed he had some difficulty in climbing stairs. Muscular weakness developed at a slow pace, mainly in the pelvic girdle and lower limbs.

Physical examination (at 32½ years) showed a well-nourished white male who walked with a waddling gait and could climb stairs only laboriously with the aid of a railing (Stage 3 of disease). He rose from the floor only by holding his hands on some support (Gower's sign). Measurements: weight 156 lbs, height 65½ inches, upper segment 35 inches, lower segment 30½ inches, U/L = 1.16, head circumference 22½ inches, chest circumference 35 inches.

	Right	Left
Arm	26 cm	26 cm
Thigh	40 cm	39 cm
Calf	37 cm	39½ cm

Marked lumbar lordosis was present. His calves showed considerable pseudohypertrophy and there was also marked atrophy of the thighs (Figs. J-4A–C). Deep tendon reflexes were very depressed. Pes cavus was present bilaterally (Fig. J-5). The review of other systems was unremarkable.

Laboratory data: EKG at 27 years and at 32½ years was normal. CPK level was 24 units. Other serum enzyme levels were: LDH 204 units, aldolase 43 units, SGOT 30 units and SGPT 45 units.

Comment: It is noteworthy that differentiation from Duchenne muscular dystrophy would be difficult without the family history.

Giorgio Filippi

K—X-Linked Muscular Dystrophy, Benign Form with Contractures

The following patients, uncle and two nephews, have a benign form of X-linked muscular dystrophy which has occurred in 5 other males in 3 generations of their kindred and is accompanied by contractures of the elbows and Achilles tendons.

Case 1. C.R. (JHH 1334565), a white male born in 1907, was first noted to have increased lordotic curvature of his back and flexion contracture of the elbows at about age 6. Weakness in the back and legs slowly progressed. Contractures of the Achilles tendons, first noted in his teens, were corrected by tendoplasty at age 19 years. In his 40s walking became increasingly difficult.

At the age of 58 years, the patient was forced by his disability to stop work as a schoolteacher. At the age of 52 years, surgical lengthening of the Achilles tendons was done bilaterally. By age 62 he was able to rise from a chair only with great difficulty, walked with a laborious, waddling gait and was unable to climb stairs. He experienced occasional episodes of palpitations, awakening him at night. He suffered for many years from a chronic cough, intermittently productive of purulent sputum, and bronchiectasis of the lower lobes was discovered at another hospital. Antibiotics had been administered in interrupted course.

Physical examination (1969) showed a man appearing somewhat younger than his 62 years (Figs. K-1A and B). The musculature of the shoulder and pelvic girdles and of the limbs was greatly wasted and the arms were held in a position of flexion contracture limiting extension to about 110°. He had a lordotic stance. He could not abduct the arms beyond 90°. Although weakness was generalized, the muscles of the face and distal portions of the limbs were less affected. Sensation was intact. None of the deep tendon reflexes could be elicited in the limbs.

Auscultation of the chest showed rales, which cleared incompletely with cough, at the left lung base posteriorly and over the right upper and lower chest anteriorly. The left border of cardiac dullness extended 2 cm beyond the left midclavicular line. Cardiac rhythm was regular. A high pitched grade III/VI systolic murmur was loudest at the apex.

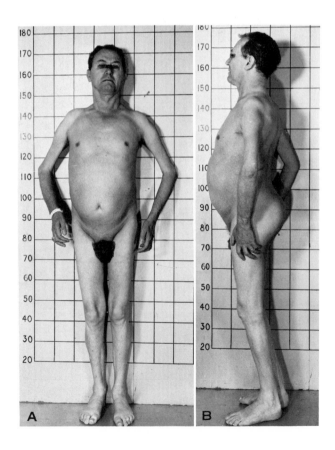

Fig. K-1. *Case 1*, age 62 years. A. Frontal and B. lateral views

113

Laboratory tests: Electrocardiogram showed atrial flutter with 3:1 atrioventricular block. (About 9 years previously ECG showed nodal rhythm with occasional supraventricular extrasystoles.) X-ray views of the elbows showed no boney or articular changes (Fig. K-2). Chest x rays showed increased markings indicative of bilateral basilar bronchiectasis. Cineroentgenograms of the pharynx and esophagus during swallowing showed incomplete relaxation of the cricopharyngeal sphincter and minimal pharyngeal retention but the changes were considered within the normal range. Serum enzymes were measured as follows: lactic dehydrogenase 131 units (normal < 155), aldolase 25 units (normal < 33), creatine phosphokinase 3.1 units (normal < 4.3), SGOT 47 units, SGPT 41 units.

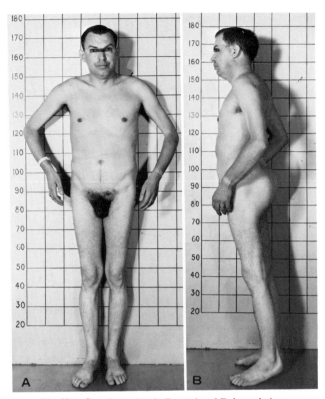

Fig. K-3. *Case 2*, age 35. A. Frontal and B. lateral views

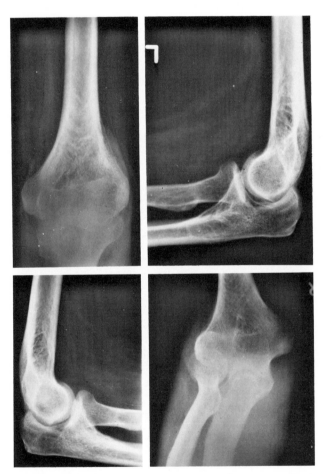

Fig. K-2. X-ray views of the elbows show no boney or articular abnormality (*Case 1*).

Case 2. K.L.Y. (JHH 1334567), a nephew of *C.R.*, born in 1934, was first thought to have muscular dystrophy at age 3 years because of waddling gait and flexion contracture of the elbows. He never considered himself disabled and worked as a schoolteacher. At age 35 years he admitted to being unable "to run up the mountain" as fast as he could in the past. He denied impairment of strength in the shoulder girdle.

Examination (1969) showed underdevelopment of the musculature of the shoulder and pelvic girdles and flexion contracture at the elbows preventing extension beyond 90° on the right and 100° on the left (Figs. K-3A and B). His stance and gait were lordotic and Achilles contracture prevented application of the heel to the

floor. Sensation was intact but deep tendon reflexes were not elicited. Blood pressure was 160/100 mm/Hg. The cardiac rhythm was totally irregular.

Laboratory tests: The heart was at the upper limit of normal for size by x ray. Serum enzyme levels were determined as follows: SGOT 37 U, SGPT 45 U, aldolase 10 U (normal < 33), lactic dehydrogenase 170 (normal < 155), creatine phosphokinase 13 (normal < 4.3). Electrocardiogram showed atrial fibrillation (known to have been present at least since 1960) with aberrant conduction of some beats.

Case 3. H.E.Y. (JHH 1334566), a brother of *K.L.Y.*, born in 1946, was first noted to have limitation of extension at the elbows when 2 or 3 years old. During childhood he developed a waddling gait. At age 23 the patient felt he had no significant weakness or disability. He was in the habit of walking with his heels slightly off the floor. He worked as a bookkeeper.

Examination (1969) showed atrophy of the musculature of the limb girdles and contractures of the elbows and Achilles tendons (Figs. K-4A and B). No deep tendon reflexes could be elicited (knee jerks had been present 7 years previously). Abdominal and cremasteric reflexes were intact.

Laboratory tests: The heart and lungs were normal by x-ray. Serum enzyme levels were as follows: SGOT 33 U, SGPT 47 U, creatine phosphokinase 8.8 U (normal < 4.3), lactic dehydrogenase 159 (normal < 155), aldolase 25 (normal < 33). Electrocardiogram was normal.

Family history: These patients are members of a kindred of English extraction in which 8 males have had the disorder under discussion. The relationship of the 8 is shown in the pedigree (Fig. K-5).

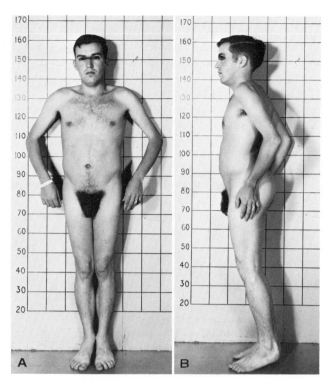

Fig. K-4. *Case 3*, age 23. A. Frontal and B. lateral views

Comment: The observations recorded above corroborate the existence of a distinct form of X-linked muscular dystrophy, as described on the basis of this same kindred by Dreifuss and Hogan (*Neurology* **11:** 734, 1961) and by Emery and Dreifuss (*J. Neurol. Neurosurg. Psychiat.* **29:**338, 1966). (The 3 patients are, respectively, III4, IV5 and IV9 in the latter report.) The clinical picture is remarkably consistent with weakness, as well as elbow and Achilles contractures, noted at the age of 3 or 4 years, and a slow progression thereafter. In younger patients mild elevation of serum enzymes, particularly creatine phosphokinase, was observed. The myocardium appears to be involved as an integral part of the syndrome, with arrhythmia as the principal manifestation. Bronchiectasis in *Case 1* may have been a result of aspiration from a defect in swallowing even though cineesophagogram failed to show any clear abnormality.

Victor A. McKusick

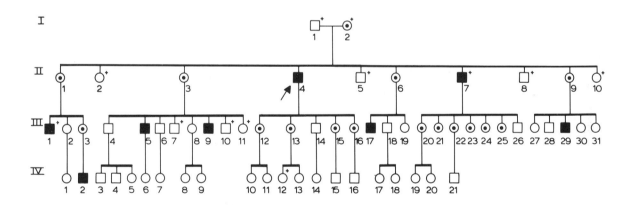

Fig. K-5. *Pedigree. Cases 1, 2 and 3* are individuals II-4, III-5 and III-9 respectively in the pedigree.

L—Facioscapulohumeral Muscular Dystrophy with Congenital Absence of Sternocleidomastoid Muscles

Case 1. R.L.B. (JHH 1092225), a white female, was born in 1916. Since early childhood she was noted to have "absence of muscles" in the neck. Her complaints at that time were impairment of neck flexion and inability of dorsiflexion of feet that produced a floppy gait. These symptoms were stationary until age 30 when she noticed marked weakness of her knees with increasing difficulty in running, climbing stairs and getting up from a sitting position. By the age of 40 she developed progressive weakness of the flexion of the distal phalanx of the right thumb and had to write with her thumb extended. Later on she developed increasing difficulty in abducting the right arm. She had always had a peculiar nasal voice and never could whistle or pucker her lips. She had never had dysphagia, diplopia, lid drooping or loss of cutaneous sensation.

The patient's mother was noted to have absent sternocleidomastoids with no other muscular disability. An elder brother, who is similarly affected (*J.F.G.*, JHH 1092224), has 5 offspring, 3 of whom are affected. The patient has had 2 normal children (Fig. L-1).

In 1963, at 47 years of age, examination showed bilateral facial weakness with inability to whistle and pucker the lips, absence of both sternocleidomastoids (Figs. L-2A and B) and the clavicular and lower costal portions of the pectoralis major bilaterally. There was wasting of the muscles of the shoulder girdle, especially the deltoids, the thenar regions and the lower part of quadriceps ("wine bottle" legs) (Figs. L-3A and B).

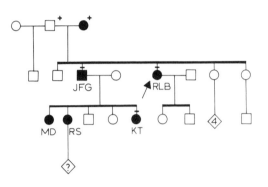

- EXAMINED

+ DECEASED

Fig. L-1. Pedigree

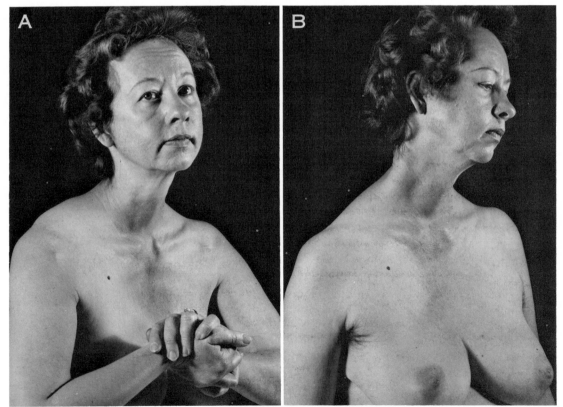

Figs. L-2A and B. *R.L.B.* Absence of the sternocleidomastoid muscles is evident

116

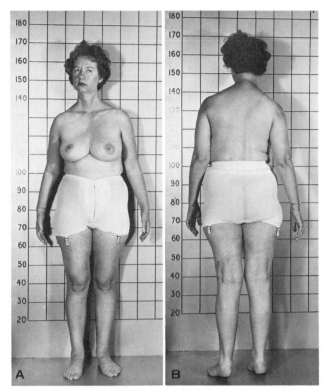

Figs. L-3A and B. *R.L.B.* Age 47 years. Note the wasting of the muscles about the shoulder girdle and lower quadriceps femoris.

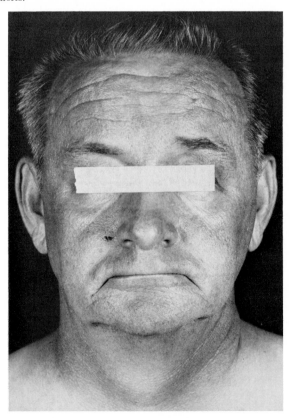

Fig. L-4. *J.F.G.* Age 51 years. Facial weakness and ptosis are demonstrated.

Pectus excavatum, winging of the scapula and pes cavus were evident. The patient could not flex the neck or the distal phalanx of the right thumb. Shoulder abduction and adduction were normal but she could not raise the right arm above 90°. Osteotendinous reflexes were present but sluggish, except the knee jerks which were absent bilaterally. Eye, palatine and tongue movements were normal. The voice was nasal and dysarthric but deglutition was not impaired. There were no myotonia, fasciculations or sensory abnormalities. Serum SGOT and SGPT were normal and the EKG showed frequent atrial ectopic beats with runs of bigeminy.

During the following years the muscle strength decreased in general with particular special increase in the weakness of the right upper limb and deterioration of speech. The gait became more waddling and she developed increasing difficulty in arising from a sitting position.

In 1969, at 53 years of age, examination confirmed a further loss in general muscle strength and wasting of shoulder, arm and hand musculature bilaterally, more striking on the right side. Weakness of anterior tibial and proximal leg muscles had also increased and osteotendinous reflexes were absent. The rest of the findings were essentially similar to those recorded 6 years before.

Case 2. J.F.G. (JHH 1092224), brother of *R.L.B.*, born in 1912, developed difficulty walking and weakness of the neck in youth. Upper and lower limb weakness progressed slowly but steadily, involving proximal as well as distal segments. He also developed facial weakness and partial bilateral ptosis (Fig. L-4), although no diplopia or dysphagia was ever present. An EKG in 1964 was normal. The EMG showed myopathic response without evidence of a neurogenic element. His physical examination was essentially similar to his sister's, in particular the absence of sternocleidomastoids (Figs. 5-A and B).

Case 3. K.T. (JHH 1233752), a daughter of *J.F.G.* was born 5/7/44 and developed similar symptoms in childhood. On physical examination, absence of sternocleidomastoids and weakness of facial muscles and slight dysarthria were evident. She had weakness and wasting of shoulder and pelvic girdle and upper and lower limbs, involving distal as well as proximal segments.

Victor Penchaszadeh

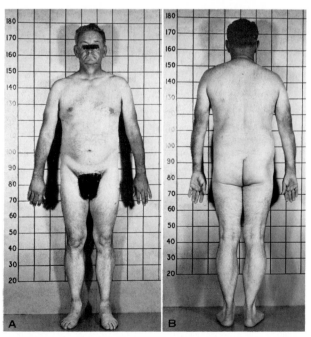

Figs. L-5A and B. *J.F.G.* Note the similarity of features to *Case 1*, *R.L.B.*, especially absence of the sternocleidomastoid muscles.

M—Oculopharyngeal Muscular Dystrophy

E.H. (JHH 246278), a white male born in 1916, started insidiously with lid drooping at the age of 16 years. The ptosis was more marked on the left side, and progressed steadily in the following years. Limitation of extraocular movements developed by the age of 26 and some years later he began to note swallowing difficulties and occasional nasal regurgitation of liquids. His speech had always been mumbling and of nasal tone. He never complained of difficulties with his lower limbs but proximal upper limb weakness developed in recent years.

There was no parental consanguinity and no other member of the family was affected. Both parents were 32 years old at his birth. The patient had one normal daughter.

He was followed up in the Ophthalmologic and Neurologic Clinics of JHH from 1941 to 1966 and very slow progression in the weakness of the affected muscles was noted. In 1963 an electromyogram of the orbicularis oris and the external anal sphincter showed a myopathic pattern. A deltoid muscle biopsy obtained in 1966 was also consistent with myopathy. These findings were reported by Teasdall *et al* in 1964 (*Arch. Neurol.* 10:446).

When seen in February 1969 he was found to be a well-developed, small statured 52-year-old, white male. The muscles of the face were all weak, giving an expressionless appearance (Figs. M-1A and B). He had bilateral ptosis, more marked on the left side where the pupil was almost completely covered by the lid. Lid closure was very weak on both sides and during sleep he had been noted to have incomplete closure of the lids. The pupils were round, regular and normally reactive to light. Extraocular movements were practically nil. The eyes were in a concordant position.

The masticatory muscles were weak and he was not able to whistle or pucker the lips. Palate movement was normal. The muscles of the neck, shoulder girdle and proximal arms were weak bilaterally, while the rest of the musculature was of normal strength. There were no fasciculations, myotonia or sensory abnormalities. The osteotendinous reflexes were depressed in upper limbs and normal in lower limbs. The rest of the physical examination was normal. Serum CPK levels were normal.

Victor Penchaszadeh
Robert D. Teasdall

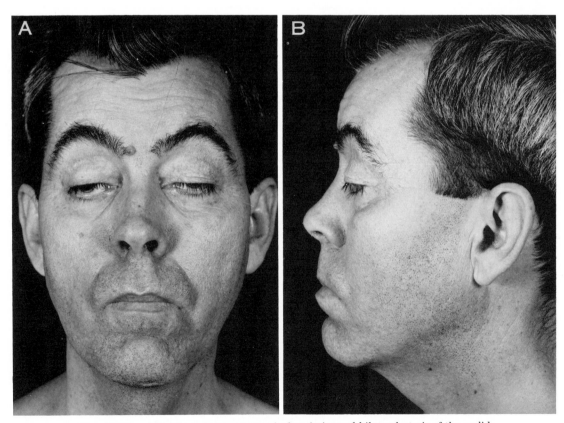

Figs. M-1A and B. Views showing expressionless facies and bilateral ptosis of the eyelids

N—Myotonic Dystrophy with Mental Retardation

Case 1. F.K. (JHH 673489), a white female born in 1922 noted weakness in legs and difficulty in relaxing her hand grip when she was 30 years of age. She first came to medical attention at age 38 after the diagnosis of myotonia had been made in an older sister. At that time the patient had frontal baldness, myotonic facies and myotonia in hands, but no cataracts were present. Muscle biopsy confirmed myotonic dystrophy. Her electrocardiogram showed left bundle branch block.

The patient has 1 affected and 1 normal daughter and 5 affected sibs (Fig. N-1). Her father was said to be normal and lived to an old age, but he had an affected son by his first marriage and 5 affected children by his second marriage. Nothing is known about the grandparents. All family members affected with myotonic dystrophy had mental retardation of varying severity.

Physical examination showed an obese white female with frontal baldness and myopathic facies (Fig. N-2). There was weakness of orbicularis oculi and sternocleidomastoid muscles. Neither ocular cataracts nor myotonia in the tongue were observed. Obvious myotonia in the hands, with slow relaxation of the hand grip, and myotonic reflexes was demonstrated. The deep tendon reflexes were markedly hyperactive, sensory examination was normal and no cardiac murmurs were heard. The electrocardiogram was unchanged.

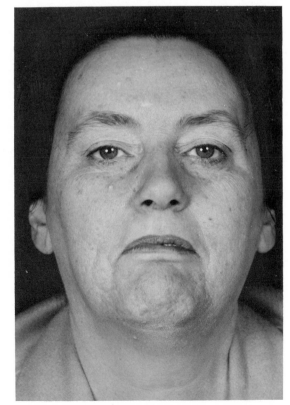

Fig. N-2. Myopathic facies of *F.K.*, age 47 years

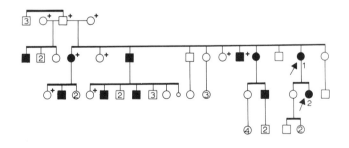

■ ● MYOTONIC DYSTROPHY & MENTAL RETARDATION

+   DECEASED

Fig. N-1. Pedigree

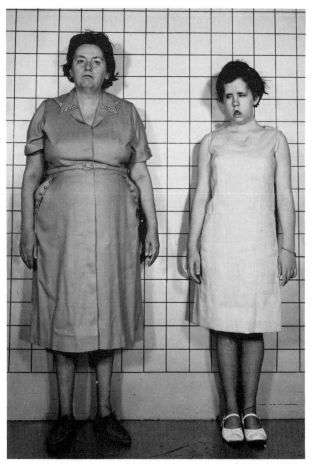

Fig. N-3. The patient *R.K.* at age 17 years with her mother

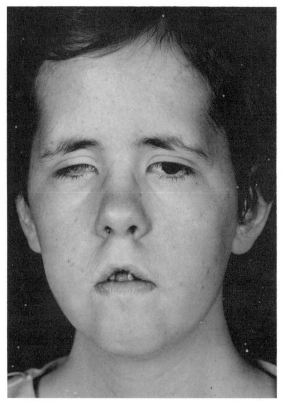

Fig. N-4. *R.K.* Note the expressionless face and corneal opacification of the right eye.

Case 2. R.K. (JHH 666588), the affected daughter of *F.K.* (*Case 1*), was born in 1952, the product of a normal pregnancy and term delivery. Her birthweight was 8 lbs. No abnormalities were noted at birth except right talipes equinovarus. She had frequent upper respiratory infections and tonsillectomy and adenoidectomy were performed at the age of 3. Her developmental landmarks were delayed. She sat up at 6 months, walked at 2 years, talked at 1 year but did not develop coherent speech until she was 4 years of age. Psychometric examination at the age of 5 showed an IQ of 59 and the social habits of a 2½-year-old child. Some atrophy of leg muscles was noted at 18 months but no diagnosis was made until age 8 when the condition was recognized in her mother. Gastrocnemius muscle biopsy confirmed the diagnosis. At that time physical examination showed the patient to be mentally slow, with expressionless facies and protruding lips and tongue. She was clumsy with a suggestion of myotonia in the hands. The sternocleidomastoid muscles and tongue were normal and no cataracts were present. The patient was in Rosewood State Hospital for the Mentally Retarded from the age of 9 to 12. Diabetes mellitus was diagnosed at the age of 12. At the age of 13 right cataract operation was complicated by endophthalmitis, with resultant blindness in the right eye. At the age of 14 successful left cataract extraction was performed. A recent electrocardiogram was of very low voltage, consistent with myocardiopathy.

Physical examination showed a slightly obese white girl with frontal baldness and myopathic facies (Fig. N-3). She was blind in the right eye and had dim vision in the left (Fig. N-4). The palate was highly arched and narrow and the patient was a constant mouth breather. Sternocleidomastoid muscles were almost completely atrophic. A grade II/VI systolic ejection murmur was heard at the base. The patient had normal pubertal sexual development. There was weakness in the hand grip and myopathic reflexes were present. The deep tendon reflexes were absent. The sensory examination was normal. The gait was broad-based and awkward. The heel cords were tight and there was bilateral equinus deformity of the feet.

Recent psychometric evaluation with the Stanford-Binet Intelligence Scale showed a mental age of 4⅔ and an IQ of 30, placing her in the mentally defective-low trainable category.

The patient has been reported by Calderon in the *Journal of Pediatrics*, Volume 68, p. 423f, 1966, in which he reviewed 55 cases of myotonic dystrophy (49 from the literature and 6 examined at JHH), among whom he found 43 with mental retardation.

Robert E. Tipton

O—Myotonic Dystrophy

Case 1. Ja.D. (JHH 997782), a white male born in 1919, diagnosed his own condition in 1966 after he had read about muscle disorders in a medical textbook. Cataracts were removed from both eyes when he was 10 years of age, but he remained generally well until he was 40, when muscle weakness commenced. This progressed so that when he was seen in 1969, he was able to walk only with the aid of crutches.

Examination at this time revealed generalized muscular weakness and wasting in the limbs and the limb girdles (Figs. O-1A and B). The sternomastoids were particularly wasted and the left brachioradialis muscle was absent. The presence of myotonia was demonstrated by the slow relaxation of his handshake. Apart from the scars of his cataract operations, and a mild degree of frontal baldness (Figs. O-2A and B), physical examination was unremarkable. His EKG was normal.

A son, born in 1960, was said to have no stigmata of the disorder. A brother (*Jo.D.*, vide infra) was also affected, and the mother, born in 1894, had frontal baldness and cataracts of six years' duration, but was otherwise apparently well. Three of her 9 sibs had the disorder, which had also appeared in some of their progeny (Fig. O-3).

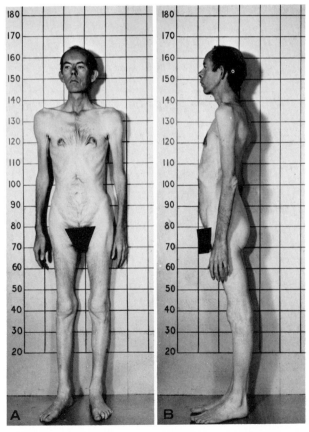

Figs. O-1A and B. *J.D.*, age 46. Note the generalized muscle atrophy and typical facies.

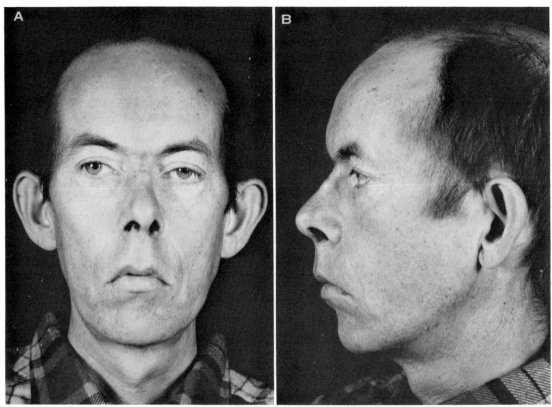

Figs. O-2A and B. Face in myotonic dystrophy. Temporal hair recession, downturned corners of the mouth and lack of facial expression are seen.

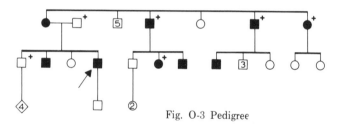

Fig. O-3 Pedigree

■ ● MALE, FEMALE, with MYOTONIC DYSTROPHY

  ✚ DECEASED

Case 2. Jo.D. (JHH 1071167), the elder brother of the proband, born in 1912, noticed visual disturbance in 1958, and in 1960 a cataract was removed from the left eye. In 1962 he gave up his job because of muscle weakness in the legs and hands. The weakness progressed, and when he was seen in 1969, he was able to rise from the sitting position only with great difficulty. Myotonia was pronounced.

He had a cataract on the right, frontal baldness and a moderate degree of bilateral ptosis. Generalized ichthyosis was present, but no abnormality was noted in any other system.

Peter H. Beighton

P—Limb-Girdle Muscular Dystrophy (?)

Two brothers are presented with a similar history of muscular weakness which began in early infancy, progressed very slowly, and affected mainly the limb-girdle musculature.

Case 1. E.D. (JHH 986958), a white male, was born in April 1946 after an 8-month pregnancy. He was noted to be hypotonic and hypoactive soon after birth and generally weak throughout infancy. He started to walk at 18 months of age but fell easily and always needed help to get up. Since childhood he had had difficulties in walking long distances, could not run, and needed to use the banisters to climb stairs. Weakness of the arms, especially the upper arms, started also in early childhood.

The muscular weakness progressed very slowly and remained localized in shoulder and pelvic girdles and proximal segments of the limbs. He never complained of trouble with vision or dysphagia.

His parents and 4 of his 5 sibs were normal (Fig. P-1). A younger brother (*Case 2, R.D.,* JHH 986959) was similarly affected. There was no parental consanguinity or increased parental age (the father was 23 years old and the mother 18 at the time of his birth). No other member of the family was affected.

Examination in April 1969 showed a 24-year-old man with poor muscular development and thin body (Figs. P-2A, B, and C). His gait was slightly wobbling and he had slight scoliosis, winging of the scapulas and somewhat increased lumbar lordosis. The facial muscles were diffusely weak and partial left ptosis was present. The extraocular movements were full. The voice was slightly dysarthric, but tongue, palatal movements and deglutition were normal.

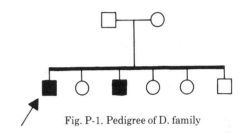

Fig. P-1. Pedigree of D. family

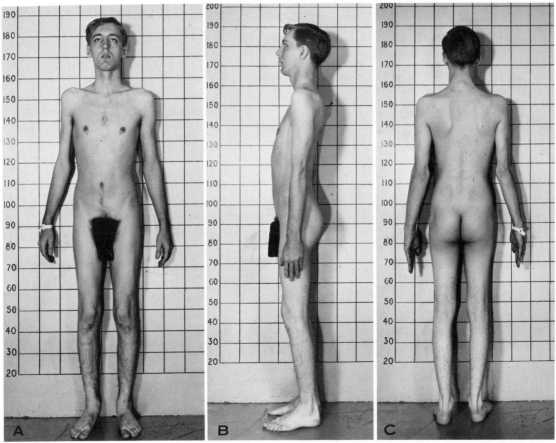

Fig. P-2A, B and C. *E.D.,* age 24 years, showing the thin body habitus and wasting of the girdle muscles, especially of the shoulder girdle.

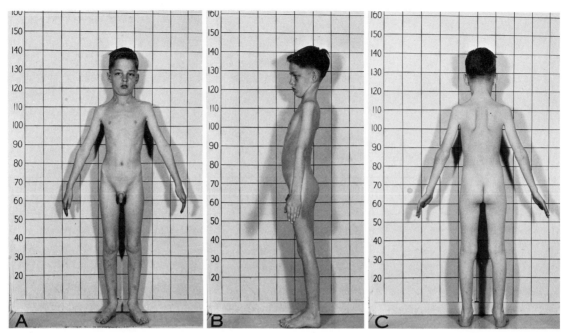

Fig. P-3A, B and C. *R.D.* at age 11 years. Note the similarity of the body habitus to that of his brother, *E.D.*

The neck muscles were remarkably spared except for the clavicular portions of the sternocleidomastoids, which were atrophic. The muscles of the shoulder girdle and upper arms were weak and wasted, especially the deltoid, pectoralis major, rhomboid, biceps and brachioradialis, and he was not able to raise his arms above the shoulders. The distal muscles, including the small interossei, were not affected, and he had a normal grasp.

The pelvic girdle muscles and both quadriceps were weak and slightly wasted, but less so than the arm and shoulder muscles. The muscles of the feet had normal strength. He was able to rise from a chair but could not get up from a squatting position without help and had to climb on himself to rise from the lying position.

The osteotendinous reflexes were all depressed except the ankle jerks, which were normal, and there was asymmetry in the responses. The patient had no myotonia, pseudohypertrophy, fasciculations or sensorial abnormalities.

The chest x ray and the electrocardiogram were normal. Serum creatine phosphokinase level was 1.8 units and aldolase was 8 units (both normal values). The electromyographic study showed normal nerve conduction times, no denervation potentials, and good interference patterns. Complex and polyphasic potentials were recorded from proximal muscles of upper and lower limbs, suggesting a primary myopathic process. No myositic potentials were noted. Biopsy specimens from deltoid and gluteus maximus muscles stained with H&E PTAH, Gomori trichrome and Masson stains failed to show any histologic abnormality, including the absence of rod-like inclusions in muscle fibers.

Case 2. R.D. (JHH 986959), the brother of *Case 1*, was born in May 1950 and developed since birth the same pattern of muscular weakness as his elder brother. Shoulder and pelvic girdles and proximal segments of the limbs were involved since early infancy and showed very slow progression. On examination in April 1969 his muscular symptoms and signs were remarkably similar to those of his brother (Fig. P-3A, B and C), with a more marked facial involvement and left ptosis. Serum creatine phosphokinase level was 1.5 units (normal).

Victor B. Penchaszadeh

Comment

I will use the first patient as the case for discussion. His weakness was from early infancy and probably from birth. He acquired motor skills at later times than normal. His disease seems to be slowly but minimally progressive because he has gradually lost some motor functions which he once had. (I estimate that this loss was more than could be attributed to increasing size and weight of the body and limbs to be moved by muscles which, if the disease were static, would have failed to grow but not actually deteriorated.)

Weakness, wasting, and reduced tendon reflexes indicate disease of the motor unit (the lower motor neuron and those muscle fibers innervated by it) ie a neuromuscular disease. The differential diagnosis of a neuromuscular disease which appears clinically from early infancy or birth and is minimally progressive includes: a) lower motor neuron diseases—chronic infantile spinal muscular atrophy,[1] infantile idiopathic peripheral motor neuropathy (with or without sensory involvement[2]; b) neuromuscular junction disorders—none, because typical infantile myasthenia gravis does not resemble this patient's disease; c) muscle diseases—congenital/infantile histologically nonspecific myopathy[3] which some might call "limb-girdle dystrophy"; rod (nemaline) myopathy[1, 4-6], possibly myotonic dystrophy[1] and possibly mild childhood acid maltase deficiency[7-9]; d) diseases of uncertain pathogenesis, which may be atypical neurogenic disorders[10]—central core disease,[10-12] and Type I fiber hypotrophy with central nuclei[13, 14] (and the similar condition of less pure fiber-type expression, "myotubular myopathy"[15-17]; e) new disease. None of these can be satisfactorily distinguished on clinical examination alone and therefore each must be considered in this patient. The proximal pattern of weakness is only against motor peripheral neuropathy and slightly against myotonic dystrophy, but is seen in the other disorders mentioned. All these diseases have normal levels of "muscle" enzymes in the serum at the age of the present patient. Benign congenital hypotonia is by definition a nonprogressive or improving disorder.[3]

In addition to the electromyogram (EMG) summarized by Doctor Penchaszadeh above, a later EMG by Dr. John R. Warmolts showed in the right deltoid and biceps decreased amplitude and duration of motor unit potentials, short polyphasic potentials, an increased number of motor units recruited with slight effort, no giant potentials, and no fibrillations.

The right quadriceps EMG was normal. Motor conduction times were normal in the right ulnar and peroneal nerves. This study reaffirmed apparently decreased size and effectiveness of individual motor units—what one sees in typical myopathies and theoretically can also be seen in special neuropathies in which motor units are smaller but not numerically reduced.[10, 18]

Thus, the EMG showed no evidence of typical neurogenic disease, thereby excluding chronic infantile spinal muscular atrophy and typical motor peripheral neuropathy. Myotonic dystrophy is not supported clinically or electrically. The EMG changes are compatible with the remaining diagnoses, which can only be distinguished by muscle biopsy.

The first muscle biopsy was reported to be normal in paraffin sections. I had the opportunity to study a second biopsy, of the left quadriceps, by histochemistry of fresh-frozen sections as well as in paraffin sections. It showed significant atrophy of muscle fibers, mainly Type II fiber atrophy, as the only abnormality. About 50% of the Type II muscle fibers (dark with myofibrillar or "myosin" ATPase and phosphorylase, light with succinate and DPNH dehydrogenases) were moderately to severely atrophic and were angular in cross-sectional contour; only about 5% of the Type I fibers (opposite histochemical characteristics) were atrophic and were round in cross-sectional contour. There was no necrosis, phagocytosis, or regeneration; no target fibers, rods, or central cores; no type grouping or type predominance; no endomysial connective tissue increase or fatty replacement; no excess glycogen and no abnormal collections of mitochondria or other architectural abnormalities within fibers. Needle biopsy of the left biceps showed the same changes.

Thus the biopsy did not disclose evidence of rod myopathy, central core disease, Type I fiber hypotrophy with central nuclei (nor myotubular disease), acid maltase deficiency, or morphologically nonspecific myopathy.

A minimally weak muscle was chosen for the biopsy to seek the early stage of involvement, and the changes were confirmed by needle biopsy of a weaker muscle. Since both disclosed only atrophy, mainly of the Type II fibers, the question is whether the cause is a neural abnormality (neuropathy) or a disease of the muscle fibers alone (myopathy). With the evidence available from this patient, both pathogeneses remain possible. My *hunch* is that this is a form of neural disease wherein the motor units have become smaller and less efficient by atrophy of their muscle fibers without any significant numerical loss of total motor units, giving rise to an EMG which by custom is usually erroneously called "myopathic" because it is like that seen in the typical muscular dystrophies and polymyositides. However, such an EMG is really not diagnostic of a myopathic pathogenesis but merely reflects the fact that the motor units are smaller and less effective than normal but are numerically preserved—theoretically this could also be caused by a neural disease, such as one affecting the trophic function of a motor neuron to all muscle fibers within its unit or one affecting some distal branches of a motor neuron.[10, 18, 19]

Preferential atrophy of Type II muscle fibers is seen in experimental total denervation.[20-23] I have seen it in occasional patients who have typical motor neuropathies (eg peroneal muscular atrophy), and often in myasthenia gravis[24, 25] which I think is a form of neuropathy,[10, 18] and in corticosteroid-induced atrophy,[10, 25, 26] which I think may be a mild pan-neuropathy. Cachetic atrophy and disuse atrophy also show Type II fiber atrophy, and these, too, may be thought of as possibly neurogenic phenomena.[10, 18, 25] The present patient is not cachetic and does not have disuse, furthermore those do not seem to be factors in the patients with the aforementioned diseases with Type II fiber atrophy.

There is no firm evidence of a myopathic disorder in this patient. Rather, in line with the ideas just mentioned, I propose that he and his brother may have a new form of familial congenital neurogenic disorder.

W. King Engel

REFERENCES

1. Hogenhuis, L. A. H. and Engel, W. K.: Early onset chronic motor neuropathies. Clinical and muscle histochemical studies in "Neuromuscular Disease," *Proc. of the VIII International Congress of Neurology* (Vienna) **I**:499, 1965.
2. Byers, R. K. and Taft, L. T.: Chronic multiple peripheral neuropathy in childhood. *Pediatrics* **20**:517, 1957.
3. Engel, W. K.: Muscle biopsies in neuromuscular diseases. *Pediat. Clin. N. Amer.* **14**:963, 1967.
4. Engel, W. K.: The essentiality of histo- and cytochemical studies of skeletal muscle in the investigation of neuromuscular disease. *Neurology* **12**:778, 1962.
5. Shy, G. M.; Engel, W. K.; Somers, J. E. and Wanko, T.: Nemaline myopathy—A new congenital myopathy. *Brain* **86**:793, 1963.
6. Conen, P. E.; Murphy, E. G. and Donohue, W. L.: Light and electron microscopic studies of myogranules in a child with hypotonia and muscle weakness. *Canad. med. Ass. J.* **89**:983, 1963.
7. Zellweger, H.; Brown, B. I.; McCormick, W. F. and Tu, J. B.: A mild form of muscular glycogenosis in two brothers with alpha-1,4-glucosidase deficiency. *Ann. paediat. (Basel)* **205**:413, 1965.
8. Swaiman, K. F.; Kennedy, W. R. and Sauls, H. S.: Late infantile acid maltase deficiency. *Arch. Neurol.* **18**:642, 1968.
9. Engel, A. G.; Seybold, M. E.; Lambert, E. H. and Gomez, M. R.: Acid maltase deficiency: Comparison of infantile, childhood, and adult types. *Neurology* **20**:382, 1970.
10. Engel, W. K.: Selective and non-selective susceptibility of muscle fiber types—A new approach to human neuromuscular disease. *Arch. Neurol.* **22**:97, 1970.
11. Shy, G. M. and Magee, K.: A new congenital non-progressive myopathy. *Brain* **79**:610, 1956.
12. Engel, W. K.; Foster, J. B.; Hughes, B. P.; Huxley, H. E. and Mahler, R.: Central core disease—an investigation of a rare muscle cell abnormality. *Brain* **84**:167, 1961.
13. Engel, W. K.; Gold, G. N. and Karpati, G.: Type I fiber hypotrophy and central nuclei—A rare congenital muscle abnormality with a possible experimental mode. *Arch. Neurol.* **18**:435, 1968.
14. Engel, W. K. and Karpati, G.: Impaired skeletal muscle maturation following neonatal neurectomy. *Develop. Biol.* **17**:713, 1968.
15. Spiro, A. J.; Shy, G. M. and Gonatas, N. K.: Myotubular myopathy. Persistence of fetal muscle in an adolescent boy. *Arch. Neurol.* **14**:1, 1966.
16. Bethlem, J.; Van Wijngaarden, G. K.; Meijer, A. E. F. H. and Hülsmann, W. C.: Neuromuscular disease with type I fiber atrophy, central nuclei, and myotube-like structures. *Neurology* **19**:705, 1969.
17. Munsat, T. L.; Thompson, L. R. and Colman, R. F.: Centronuclear ("myotubular") myopathy. *Arch. Neurol.* **20**:120, 1969.
18. Engel, W. K.: Classification of neuromuscular disorders, this publication.
19. Warmolts, J. R. and Engel, W. K.: A critique of the "myopathic" electromyogram. *Trans. Amer. neurol. Ass.* In press.
20. Hogenhuis, L. A. H. and Engel, W. K.: Histochemistry and cytochemistry of experimentally denervated guinea pig muscle. I. *Acta anat.* **60**:39, 1965.
21. Karpati, G. and Engel, W. K.: Histochemical investigation of fiber type ratios with the myofibrillar ATPase reaction in normal and denervated skeletal muscles in guinea pig. *Amer. J. Anat.* **122**:145, 1968.
22. Engel, W. K.; Brooke, M. H. and Nelson, P. G.: Histochemical studies of denervated or tenotomized cat muscle. Illustrating difficulties in relating experimental animal conditions to human neuromuscular disease. *Ann. N.Y. Acad. Sci.* **138**:160, 1966.
23. Bajusz, E.: "Red" skeletal muscle fibers: relative independence of neural control. *Science* **145**:938, 1964.
24. Engel, W. K. and McFarlin, D. E.: Skeletal muscle pathology in myasthenia gravis—histochemical findings. *Ann. N.Y. Acad. Sci.* **135**:68, 1966.
25. Engel, W. K.: Diseases of the neuromuscular junction and muscle. In *Neurohistochemistry*, ed, C. Adams. Elsevier Publishing Co., Amsterdam, 622, 1965.
26. Pleasure, D. E.; Walsh, G. O. and Engel, W. K.: Atrophy of skeletal muscle in patients with Cushing's syndrome. *Arch. Neurol.* **22**:118, 1970.

Q—Arthrogryposis Multiplex Congenita in Sibs

In December 1964, a female infant with the arthrogryposis syndrome was born to *J.H.E.* (JHH 768062), a 24-year-old married Caucasian primigravida with myasthenia gravis of eight years' duration. Her family history was positive for cleft lip in a first cousin but was otherwise noncontributory. The infant's father had unremarkable past medical and family histories and there was no known consanguinity. *J.H.E.* was carried on Mestinon 90 mgm daily for control of her myasthenia until the 29th week of gestation when the medication was discontinued without exacerbation of her symptoms. The pregnancy was essentially unremarkable until the 30th week when premature labor, unresponsive to progestational agents, ensued, culminating in the delivery of a 985 gm stillborn female infant with multiple deformities of the limbs. Initial examination revealed bilateral flexion of the upper limbs at the elbow with moderate rigidity, and flexion of both lower limbs at the hip, knee and ankle with marked rigidity throughout. At autopsy, pericerebellar subarachnoid hemorrhage was noted, but there were no other gross abnormalities beyond those noted in the limbs. Fixed specimens of the spinal cord and skeletal muscles were inadvertently discarded and thus are unavailable for microscopic examination. There were no abnormalities noted in the microscopic sections of the other organ systems.

Within five months of her first delivery, *J.H.E.* became pregnant for the second time. Mestinon had not been resumed after the first pregnancy. Her only medications were iron and prenatal vitamins which because of nausea were not administered prior to the 12th week of gestation. The pregnancy was uneventful until late November 1965 when, at 29 weeks' gestation, premature labor

again ensued. The patient was delivered of an 875 gm stillborn female infant (Figs. Q-1A and B) described as having the stigmata of arthrogryposis. The upper limbs were fixed in a position of flexion at the wrists and elbows and were bent against the anterior chest. There was bilateral hyperextension of the lower limbs with external rotation below the knees and plantar flexion of the feet. Scattered areas of subcutaneous hemorrhage were present throughout the trunk and limbs, as well as generalized subcutaneous edema. No other abnormalities were noted. Microscopic sections of all tissues except skeletal muscle and including the brain and the spinal cord were unremarkable. Sections were taken of both flexor and extensor muscle groups in the upper and lower limbs. All sections showed atrophy of the striated muscle and in some areas replacement of whole muscle groups by fat. In the upper limbs, there were scattered areas of focal hemorrhage within muscle. In the lower limbs, some areas of fibrosis were noted. Careful examination of the spinal cord revealed no abnormalities of the anterior horn cells. Since the delivery of the second affected infant, *J.H.E.* has not attempted further pregnancies.

Comment: The occurrence of arthrogryposis in sibs is an unusual finding. Of additional note is the presence of myasthenia gravis in the mother. The therapy with Mestinon cannot be considered a factor in the arthrogryposis inasmuch as it was not continued during the second pregnancy.

Marguerite K. Shepard

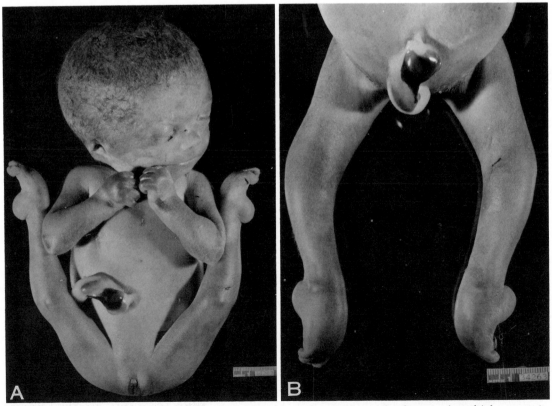

Figs. Q-1A and B. Second stillborn showing typical deformities and contractures of arthrogryposis multiplex congenita

R—Nemaline Myopathy: Second Autopsied Case in a Previously Reported Family

In Ford's textbook of pediatric neurology,[1] a mother and daughter were described as examples of congenital universal muscular hypoplasia of Krabbe. Autopsy studies in the mother showed the true diagnosis to be nemaline myopathy.[2, 3] The purpose of this report is to provide further clinical details and a description of autopsy findings in the daughter.

Summary of Previous Reports on the Mother and Daughter[2, 3]

The mother and daughter had strikingly similar clinical features and autopsy findings. No other members of the family are known to have been affected. The mother was one of 6 children. One of her brothers and her mother, now dead, were said to have been stoop-shouldered but were otherwise considered normal. The affected daughter was an only child.

The mother *E.D.* (JHH 333513) was described at age 31 years as "very tall and very slender...practically every bony prominence of the skeletal framework stands out in bold relief." The diagnoses of "severe emaciation and constitutional inferiority" were made, and it was noted that the daughter then aged 6 years, had apparently inherited the same disorder, being "an exact duplicate of her mother." At age 45 years the mother first noted difficulty walking up steps. At age 53 she was fitted with a surgical corset because of trunk weakness and increasing lordosis. During her last decade of life the weakness became more severe and was particularly associated with difficulty in holding her head up. Four years before death she fell from a chair, sharply flexing her neck. Head control became even worse thereafter and she complained of neck pain. X rays showed marked anterior subluxation of the 5th cervical vertebra. She died in the hospital at age 63 years, having been admitted because of fever and increasing breathing difficulties. Cardiac arrest followed by ventricular fibrillation occurred soon after admission. Although cardiac resuscitation was achieved, she developed acute renal failure and remained in coma until she died in cardiac arrest 12 days later.

Autopsy (JHH 33004) revealed pneumonia, acute renal tubular necrosis, cerebral anoxic degeneration, and other findings associated with her terminal illness. The skeletal muscle mass was grossly reduced and many skeletal muscle fibers showed rod-like bodies and myofibrillar fragments histologically (Fig. R-1). These lesions were not found in either cardiac or smooth muscle.

The daughter *J.D.* (JHH 349573) breathed poorly, sucked feebly, and cried weakly in the neonatal period. She did not hold up her head until the age of 1 year and did not walk until 3 years. The muscles were flabby during infancy and the diagnosis of amyotonia congenita was made by several pediatricians. There was increased range of passive movement of the joints, so that as a 10-year-old child she could, for example, easily place her feet

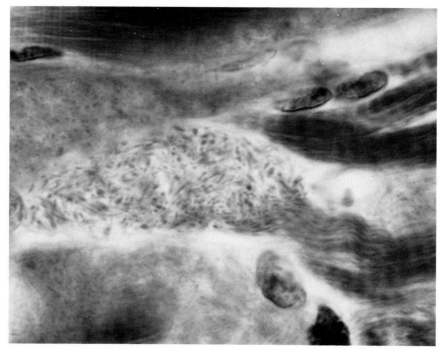

Fig. R-1. Quadriceps femoris muscle from the mother, showing a group of rod-like bodies intermixed with myofibrillar fragments. (1800×)

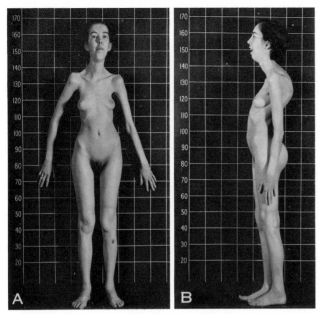

Fig. R-2 A and B. Appearance of the daughter, *J.D.* at age 31 years.

behind her head. Because of the "loose jointedness," the gangly, asthenic physique (Fig. R-2 A and B) and the remarkably high-arched palate, the possibility of the Marfan syndrome was considered at one point. Psychometric evaluation showed an IQ of 129 (Simon-Binet). The daughter was always considered to be clinically more severely affected than her mother at the same age. At age 40 years the daughter underwent a gastrocnemius muscle biopsy which confirmed the diagnosis of nemaline myopathy but showed her to have a much smaller proportion of affected fibers than her mother. The affected fibers in the daughter contained predominantly myofibrillar fragments with only rare rod-like bodies.

Follow-up Report on the Daughter

After her muscle biopsy the daughter's condition remained unchanged for a period of 2 years, during which time she was periodically seen in the Medical Genetics Clinic of the Johns Hopkins Hospital. In December 1967, at age 42 years she was admitted to the hospital for extraction of carious teeth under general anesthesia. Anesthesia was induced with multiple doses of intravenous Surital (total 150 mg) and succinylcholine. Following multiple unsuccessful attempts at intubation, 2 teeth were extracted, the operation requiring 2 hours and 40 minutes. Postoperatively, she failed to breathe adequately, requiring tracheostomy and mechan-

ical assistance to respiration. X rays showed signs of pulmonary aspiration which presumably occurred during operation. She was treated with ampicillin, Solu-Cortef, and digoxin. About 6 hours postoperatively, cardiorespiratory arrest occurred but resuscitation was achieved. During the next 6 days her course was characterized by hypotension, respiratory difficulty, fever, and later by oliguria and decreasing responsiveness. About 12 hours before death she developed marked hypotension which became refractory to pressor agents. She also complained of chest pain and was found to have electrocardiographic changes consistent with severe myocardial ischemia. On the 6th postoperative day she died in cardiorespiratory arrest. Postmortem review of her records revealed that she had significant respiratory difficulty following sodium pentothal anesthesia for a dilatation and curettage in 1945 and for extraction of carious teeth in 1947.

Autopsy (JHH 35737) showed extensive pneumonia and other findings typical of aspiration, prolonged respirator therapy, and shock. The skeletal muscles were grossly atrophic and histologically showed the lesions of nemaline myopathy identical to those previously described in the biopsy. The number of abnormal skeletal muscle fibers was rather small, even in the clinically more affected gastrocnemius, quadriceps femoris, and pectoralis major muscles. As in the mother, cardiac and smooth muscle was uninvolved.

Comment: Of note is the history of respiratory distress with previous anesthesia. This and the terminal episode should alert physicians to the possibility of similar difficulties on the part of other patients with nemaline myopathy. Of note also is the fact that the histologic changes considered specific for nemaline myopathy were much less striking in the daughter, even though the clinical picture in her was more striking than in the mother. Indeed, the histologic diagnosis could easily have been missed in this case.

James. R. Nickel
Victor A. McKusick

REFERENCES

1. Ford, F. R.: *Diseases of the Nervous System in Infancy, Childhood and Adolescence.* 4th ed Charles C Thomas, Springfield, Illinois, p. 1258, 1960.
2. Hopkins, I. J.; Lindsey, J. R. and Ford, F. R.: Nemaline myopathy. A long-term clinico pathologic study of affected mother and daughter. *Brain* **89**:299, 1966.
3. Lindsey, J. R.; Hopkins, I. J. and Clark, D. B.: Pathology of nemaline myopathy. Studies of two adult cases including an autopsy. *Bull. Johns Hopk. Hosp.* **119**:378, 1966.

Author Index

Subject Index